JERUSALEM PRAYER TEAM
"Pray for the Peace of Jerusalem..."

www.jerusalemprayerteam.org

DR. MICHAEL D. EVANS

MIKE EVANS

CURSED

THE CONSPIRACY TO DIVIDE JERUSALEM

TIMEWORTHY BOOKS

P.O. BOX 30000, PHOENIX, AZ 85046

"Yet regard the prayer of Your servant and his suppli-cation, O Lord my God, and listen to the cry and the prayer which Your servant is praying before You: that Your eyes may be open toward this temple day and night, toward the place where You said You would put Your name, that You may hear the prayer which Your servant makes toward this place. And may You hear the supplications of Your servant and of Your people Israel, when they pray toward this place. Hear from heaven Your dwelling place, and when You hear, for-give.... Now, my God, I pray, let Your eyes be open and let Your ears be attentive to the prayer made in this place." —II CHRONICLES 6:19-21,40

CURSED

"Behold, I will make Jerusalem a cup of drunkenness to all the surrounding peoples, when they lay siege against Judah and Jerusalem. And it shall happen in that day that I will make Jerusalem a very heavy stone for all peoples; all who would heave it away will surely be cut in pieces, though all nations of the earth are gathered against it. In that day," says the Lord, "I will strike every horse with confusion, and its rider with madness; I will open My eyes on the house of Judah, and will strike every horse of the peoples with blindness. And the governors of Judah shall say in their heart, 'The inhabitants of Jerusalem are my strength in the Lord of hosts, their God.' In that day I will make the governors of Judah like a firepan in the woodpile, and like a fiery torch in the sheaves; they shall devour all the surrounding peoples on the right hand and on the left, but Jerusalem shall be inhabited again in her own place—Jerusalem.

"The Lord will save the tents of Judah first, so that the glory of the house of David and the glory of the inhabitants of Jerusalem shall not become greater than that of Judah. In that day the Lord will defend the inhabitants of Jerusalem; the one who is feeble among them in that day shall be like David, and the house of David shall be like God, like the Angel of the Lord before them. It shall be in that day that I will seek to destroy all the nations that come against Jerusalem. —ZECHARIAH 12:2-9

In January 2001 President Bill Clinton almost accomplished the feat of giving half of Jerusalem to the Palestine Liberation Organization. Arab sources show that Clinton's far-reaching offer to the PLO involved an extraordinary new development: It gave the PLO almost everything it wanted, including 98 percent of the territory of Judea, Samaria, and Gaza, all of East Jerusalem except for the Jewish and Armenian quarters, Palestinian sovereignty over the Temple Mount, conceding only the right of Jews to pray there, and a compensation fund of $30 billion.

PLO chairman Yasser Arafat landed at Andrews Air Force Base then met with the ambassadors of Saudi Arabia and Egypt at the Ritz-Carlton Hotel. They promised to back him if he agreed to the Clinton plan and warned him that he would receive no backing if he reverted to war. Following his summit with the two Arab leaders, Arafat left the hotel for his meeting with Clinton at the White House. It was clear there were only two possible answers he could give: yes or no. Arafat was late returning to the meeting and things were not going as Clinton had planned. The president cautioned Arafat: "It's five minutes to midnight, Mr. Chairman, and you are about to lose the only opportunity that your people will ever get to solve their problem on satisfactory ground by not being able to make a decision. . . . The Israelis accepted."[1] Arafat had a check on the table and a pen at hand to sign the agreement. He walked out of the meeting clearly rejecting Clinton's offer. Why? Arafat was not satisfied with a portion; he wanted the whole pie—all of Jerusalem, all of Israel.

This was the only U.S. foreign policy decision made regarding the Middle East in the year 2001. Was it merely coincidence that eight months later, on September 11, 2001, America faced the worst attack on the mainland in its history? Was it an indication that God had lifted his hand of protection from America—a curse for trying to barter away Jerusalem?

In 2009 two men entered into a clandestine agreement to deliver the West Bank and most of Jerusalem into the hands of the Palestinians by 2012. Unnamed sources have identified the two men as President Barack Obama and Saudi Arabia's King Abdullah. Why would the president of the United States abandon America's most reliable ally in the Middle East? The answer:

Obama relayed a pledge to Saudi King Abdullah that he would take any measure to ensure an Israeli withdrawal from the West Bank and Jerusalem over the next 18 months. They said Obama relayed the pledge to Abdullah during the president's trip to Riyadh in June 2009, about four months after he assumed office, in exchange for Abdullah's help to arrange for the end of the Taliban war in Afghanistan.[2]

A high-level military source in Jerusalem told me that after Israel destroys Iran's nuclear program, the Arab world would demand Israel's land as an appeasement offering. He said that President Obama would accommodate them with the support of the Quartet (the U.S., UN, EU, and Russia.)

It seems that Obama's policy toward the Saudis and Israel was established in January 2009, on the heels of his inauguration. The president sent Richard Holbrook, a special envoy, to Saudi Arabia to urge the king to assist with the effort to secure a withdrawal from Afghanistan and to insure Israel's flyover rights. In other words, Obama is willing to sell Israel down the river in exchange for King Abdullah reducing the funds given to the Taliban in Afghanistan. The Saudis would deny this, of course, (plausible deniability) should Israel bomb Iran's nuclear sites.

Abdullah, smelling an opportunity to wrest control of Jerusalem and the West Bank from the Israelis, tied his assistance directly to Washington's adoption of the Saudi plan for an Arab-Israeli settlement. The proposal calls for Israel's withdrawal to 1967 borders, a Palestinian state with East Jerusalem as its capital, and the right of return for Palestinian refugees to Israel.

The president's Cairo speech followed his visit to Saudi Arabia for an audience with King Abdullah. During his initial meeting with the monarch in April 2009, the president bowed to the Saudi king, an unprecedented move by a U.S. head of state. While in Saudi Arabia in June 2009, the king presented Obama with a weighty gold chain representative of the highest honor bestowed.

How has Obama's pledge to King Abdullah affected the U.S. relationship with Israel? Detrimentally! Since cuddling up to the king, the Obama administration has denied almost every Israeli plea for weapons assistance. Decisions by the George H. Bush administration to supply attack helicopters, air transports, bunker-buster air bombs, and Hellfire air-to-ground missiles have been delayed. Perhaps this also explains Obama's treatment of Prime Minister Benjamin Netanyahu during his visit to the White House in March 2010.

The Obama administration seems to be treating Israel as a property to be bartered—or perhaps more accurately—to be betrayed for the sake of expediency. Our president claims to be a Christian but obviously has not read his Bible. Israel is God's possession, and in the words of the prophet Malachi: "Will a man rob God? Yet you have robbed Me!" (Malachi 3:8). In the next verse he defines what happens to those who persist in robbing God: "You are cursed with a curse, for you have robbed Me, *Even* this whole nation" (Malachi 3:9).

About 1465 B.C. two other men—one a king the other a prophet— stood on an outcropping of rock looking out over the valley below. The smell of blood and burned animals from their sacrifices to Baal permeated the air around them. On the plain below, stretching as far as the eye could see, were the children of Israel, miraculously delivered from Egypt.

Frightened to death of them, King Balak had hired his best diviner, Balaam, to curse Israel. Amazingly, the only words that would come from Balaam's mouth were words of blessing. No matter how hard the false prophet tried, he could not curse Israel.

For forty years God had seasoned the younger generation of the children of Israel in the desert of adversity. Now all the older, unbelieving generation that He had rescued from the hands of Pharaoh had died—except for Joshua, Caleb, and Moses. God took Moses to the top of Mount Pisgah and showed him all the land He was giving the Israelites. It was a land flowing with milk and honey, the land of blessing. He assured Moses that His people were now in the hands of a capable leader, Joshua, who would lead the fight against the inhabitants of Canaan and possess all He had given them.

When Balak, the king of Moab, heard the stories of how the Amorites and King Bashan had fallen before the onslaught of the children of Israel, he determined that it must have been by magic. Balak concluded that if he were to defeat this ragtag army, he would need a magic spell stronger than the one the Israelites had used for their victories. He immediately sent an envoy to recruit the greatest magician in his realm, Balaam. Balak's battle strategy was to have Balaam curse the armies of Israel. Now the two men stood, heads together, trying to determine how best to curse God's chosen people.

When Balak had sent for Balaam, something interesting happened. God warned Balaam not to proceed with the plan to curse the Israelites, so Balaam refused to go to Balak. When Balak sent princes to plead with Balaam to come, God told Balaam he could go, but he should only speak what He told him to speak. However, when Balaam got up the next morning and went with the princes, God was angry with him because his motivation was not to obey God but to gain wealth. Balaam thought he could act like he was obeying God, and when he got to Balak he could curse Israel and become a rich man. God saw the wickedness in Balaam's heart and sent an angel to stop him.

As Balaam set out with the princes, his donkey saw the Angel of the Lord, sword drawn, in the path. Frightened, she veered off into the field. Balaam struck the donkey and she returned to the path, where she saw the Angel again and lurched into a boulder. Balaam's foot was crushed, and he struck the donkey again. At that point she collapsed in the road at the feet of the Angel, and spoke to Balaam, "Am I not your donkey on which you have ridden, ever since I became yours, to this day? Was I ever disposed to do this to you?" (Numbers 22:30).

When Balaam answered no, the Angel of the Lord revealed himself to Balaam and said, "Go with the men: but only the word that I speak to you, that you shall speak" (Numbers 22:35).

Once in the presence of Balak, Balaam joined him in making a sacrifice to Baal. Obviously, his heart was not after God! He then went aside to a solitary place hoping to hear the curse that he was to pronounce upon the Israelites. God met him and put a word in his mouth, but it was not the word King Balak wanted to hear:

> *"How shall I curse whom God has not cursed?*
> *And how shall I denounce whom the Lord has not*
> *denounced?*

For from the top of the rocks I see him,
And from the hills I behold him;
There! A people dwelling alone,
Not reckoning itself among the nations.

"Who can count the dust of Jacob,
Or number one-fourth of Israel?
Let me die the death of the righteous,
And let my end be like his!"

NUMBERS 23:8-10

Balak was livid. How dare this mere mortal praise Israel rather than curse them as he had ordered? Balaam replied: "Must I not take heed to speak what the Lord has put in my mouth?" (Numbers 23:12). Balak offered a second round of sacrifices to Baal while Balaam waited for the word of the Lord to curse Israel. Again, only blessing poured from his mouth:

"God is not a man, that He should lie,
Nor a son of man, that He should repent.
Has He said, and will He not do?
Or has He spoken, and will He not make it good?"

"Look, a people rises like a lioness,
And lifts itself up like a lion;
It shall not lie down until it devours the prey,
And drinks the blood of the slain."

NUMBERS 23:19,24

Before heading home from his failed attempt to curse the children of Israel, Balaam took his last look at the camp of the Israelites. He proclaimed:

"How lovely are your tents, O Jacob!
Your dwellings, O Israel!

Like valleys that stretch out,

Like gardens by the riverside,
Like aloes planted by the Lord,
Like cedars beside the waters.

He shall pour water from his buckets,
And his seed shall be in many waters.

"His king shall be higher than Agag,
And his kingdom shall be exalted.

"God brings him out of Egypt;
He has strength like a wild ox;
He shall consume the nations, his enemies;
He shall break their bones.
And pierce them with his arrows.

'He bows down, he lies down as a lion;
And as a lion, who shall rouse him?'

"Blessed is he who blesses you,
And cursed is he who curses you."

NUMBERS 24:5-9

Balaam could very well have ended his association with Balak by saying, "I should have listened to the donkey!"

Cursed is an overview of how nations have come against Israel and attempted to curse her from the beginning of her existence. Yet, like the Phoenix, she has risen from the ashes each time. Not one ruler who ordered the destruction of Jerusalem survived. Nebuchadnezzar conquered Jerusalem in 586 B.C. and was doomed to live as a beast of the field for seven, terrifying years. He was restored to sanity when he recognized the God of the Israelites (Daniel 4:34,37). His kingdom of Babylon was conquered by Cyrus the Great, a friend to the Jews, who allowed them to rebuild their Temple.

In 332 B.C. Alexander the Great captured Jerusalem. His empire fragmented after his death, and the Ptolemy's of Egypt and then the Seleucids of Syria ruled over Jerusalem. The Jews, horrified by the desecration of the

Temple under the Seleucid ruler, Antiochus IV, staged a revolt and regained independence under the Hasmonean dynasty. It lasted for one hundred years, until Pompey established Roman rule in the city.

The nations who ransacked, burned, leveled, and tried to obliterate the Jewish people are rife with devastation. We have only to examine history to ascertain that the remnants of those once great empires are now dust and ashes. The Holy Roman Empire collapsed after destroying the Temple and leveling Jerusalem.

The British, who ruled over Palestine and Jerusalem following World War I, bragged that the sun never set on the British Empire. Indeed, one-fifth of the world's population was under its rule. However, after turning away Jews from both Britain and Palestine when they fled Hitler's gas chambers, and after arming Arabs to fight against them in Palestine, it quickly began to disintegrate. Great Britain today is comprised of just fourteen territories, consisting of a number of islands. Gone are the days when the empire stretched from India to Canada and from Australia to Africa.

Today Jerusalem continues to stand as a testimony to the determination and courage of the Jewish people. Our question is: Does America stand with or against Jerusalem and the nation of Israel?

During the decades since President Harry Truman's recognition of the rebirth of the State of Israel, America has been a sound ally. When that alliance was threatened during President Ronald Reagan's term in office, I challenged U.S. National Security Advisor Robert C. McFarlane at the White House regarding the status of Jerusalem. His response was: "Jerusalem must remain undivided but its final status should be determined through negotiations." I countered Mr. McFarland. "God doesn't negotiate; the status of Jerusalem has already been determined by the Bible, and it's not negotiable." Thankfully, President Reagan later changed his attitude toward Israel and Jerusalem.

The Persian Gulf War was the chink in the armor of American support. I was in Iraq, Saudi Arabia, and Israel during the conflict and saw firsthand that Israel would be called upon to pay the appeasement price for the support of the Arab League during the war against Saddam Hussein.

Israel was denied the right to defend herself during the conflict, yet she stood her ground during the war with Hussein. There was no retribution for the SCUDS that rained down on her. No reprisal for the threats of chemical warfare.

According to estimates, Israel paid highly for the privilege of not being permitted to defend her citizens:

> The damage caused by the 39 Iraqi Scud missiles that landed in Tel Aviv and Haifa was extensive. Approximately 3,300 apartments and other buildings were affected in the greater Tel Aviv area. Some 1,150 people who were evacuated had to be housed at a dozen hotels at a cost of $20,000 per night.
>
> Beyond the direct costs of military preparedness and damage to property, the Israeli economy was also hurt by the inability of many Israelis to work under the emergency conditions. The economy functioned at no more than 75 percent of normal capacity during the war, resulting in a net loss to the country of $3.2 billion.
>
> The biggest cost was in human lives. A total of 74 people died as a consequence of Scud attacks. Two died in direct hits, four from suffocation in gas masks and the rest from heart attacks.[3]

Following the conflict, Israeli leaders were ordered to Madrid and pressured to give up yet more land for peace. Attending every session at the Royal Palace, I saw the agony and pressure Israel endured—the pressure that ultimately collapsed the government of my friend, Prime Minister Yitzhak Shamir.

Today, we face the threat of a nuclear Iran. Although the vast majority of world leaders are horrified by this, they all know Israel is the only nation with the courage to stand up to the likes of Ayatollah Ali Khamenei and President Mahmoud Ahmadinejad. Israeli leaders recognize that a nuclear terror state of Iran would not only threaten their very survival as a nation, but also it would provide an umbrella under which Iran's terror regime could undermine all the sacrifices made by American troops in Iraq and Afghanistan. It would destabilize the entire Persian Gulf region, as well as the rest of the world.

The Jews, however, would suffer unspeakable hell if they ventured to attack Iran's nuclear reactors. Iran would surely retaliate through its proxies Hamas and Hezbollah. Outwardly, the world would unite in a hypocritical rage against Israel, while saluting her behind closed doors for the courage to stand against the modern day Goliath of terrorist nations.

Any peace summit that followed Israel's "impertinent strike" against Iran would doubtless be orchestrated by President Barack Obama. His agenda would be to divide Jerusalem and turn most of Judea and Samaria over to the Arabs and radical Islam. This president has, in fact, barred the words jihadist, Islamist, and Islamic terrorism from his lexicon of official terms. The enemy is now defined as "a loose network of violent extremists."

Columnist Charles Krauthammer explained why this is so detrimental:

> The administration's cowardice about identifying those trying to kill us cannot be allowed to pass. It is demoralizing. It trivializes the war between jihadi barbarism and Western decency, and diminishes the memory of those (including thousands of brave Muslims—Iraqi, Pakistani, Afghan and Western) who have died fighting it.[4]

President Obama's actions and his seemingly ambivalent attitude toward Israel could bring an apocalyptic curse upon America.

On September 2, 2010 President Obama and Secretary of State Hillary Clinton summoned Prime Minister Netanyahu to Washington for a peace summit. He and his team arrived for negotiations with Palestinian President Mahmoud Abbas. It was the first meeting between the two men in twenty months.

The day before the talks were to begin, Hamas claimed responsibility for the murders of four West Bank settlers, one a pregnant mother of six children. The teacher killed was the mother of an eight-year-old daughter. According to the terrorists responsible, it was but the first of many attempts to halt the peace negotiations. World leaders had little to say about this horrendous attack. It seems the general consensus in the more liberal circles is that if Israelis are murdered it is because they brought it upon themselves.

Conversely, there was a great hue and cry when a security guard whose vehicle was surrounded feared for his life and opened fire with his personal weapon. A Palestinian man was killed. Riots broke out in East Jerusalem and spread to the Temple Mount where Palestinian youths stood on the parapets above the Western Wall and tossed large rocks onto the Jews gathered below for prayer. According to the *Jerusalem Post*:

> Ten people were injured, including a 35-year-old Israeli in moderate condition who was stabbed in the back near the Mount of Olives. Police reported that attendees threw stones at officers, vehicles and buses causing injuries and damage, and that a police vehicle and several other vehicles were set alight near Jerusalem's Old City.
>
> Three Egged buses were destroyed by stoning near the Western Wall, injuring one of the bus drivers. The buses were missing all of their windows and one had blood splattered on the driver's seat.[5]

Given the disparity in world opinion regarding terror attacks and self-defense, Netanyahu still approached the peace talks uttering words and phrases not heard from him before. He said to Abbas: "I see in you a partner for peace. Together we can lead our people to a historic future that can put an end to claims and to conflict. Now this will not be easy. A true peace, a lasting peace would be achieved only with mutual and painful concessions from both sides."[6]

It seems President Obama is eager to win another unearned Nobel Peace Prize by somehow coercing Israel to kowtow to his peace plan. Israel is being badgered to acknowledge a sovereign Palestinian state on its border with Jerusalem as its capital—a state with an army, air space, and one that can form treaties with Israel's enemies. But what really is the goal of the Obama administration?

This summit was a nod to Obama's supposed pledge to Saudi's King Abdullah to hand the Palestinians East Jerusalem and the West Bank by 2012. After having approved a $60 billion weapons sale to Israel's Arab neighbors in the region—Saudi Arabia, Kuwait, Oman, the UAE, and Qatar, the president offered Israel a quid pro quo of sorts. The deal to the Arab states would include 84 of the latest F-15 jets and dozens of Black Hawk helicopters.

Israel has sought to purchase twenty of the fifth generation stealth F-35I Lightning II fighter jets from Lockheed Martin—a $2.75 billion outlay. To help fund the purchase by Israel, the acquisition agreement also includes a framework for purchasing parts from Israeli industry worth $4 billion.

The Arab world wants a twenty-second Islamic state with its capital in Jerusalem for one simple reason: Muslims believe Israel is Arab land occupied by foreigners.

Iran, the bully on the block, is well-positioned to attack Israel with its proxies in Gaza and Lebanon and its close friend, Bashar al-Assad in Syria.

On Friday, September 3, 2010, I participated in a conference call with Israeli Ambassador to the U.S., Michael Oren. The ambassador addressed Israel's concerns about Syria and Lebanon:

> The Syrian and Iranian backed Hezbollah poses a very serious threat to the State of Israel. Hezbollah now has four times as many rockets as it did during the 2006 Lebanon War. These rockets are longer range. Every city in Israel is within range right now, including Eilat. They have bigger payloads; they are far more accurate. And we also know that Hezbollah has internalized the lessons of the Goldstone report. In 2006, many of their missiles were basically out in

the open in silos and the Israeli Air Force was able to neutralize a great number of them. Today, those same missiles have been placed under hospitals, homes and schools because Hezbollah knows full well that if we try to defend ourselves against those missiles we will be branded as war criminals. So, Hezbollah and the situation in Southern Lebanon is of great concern to us and we're watching very vigilantly. We know that Hezbollah—in violation of U.N. resolutions—has once again penetrated southern Lebanon and transformed entire villages into armed camps and put in about 15,000 rockets along the Israeli border.[7]

For Obama to think Israel's support for his plan would pacify Iran is completely naïve. It will do just the opposite. Iran—the center of gravity for world terrorism—has made the lives of Jews a living hell on Israel's northern and southern borders through Iran's Hezbollah and Hamas proxies. To allow these terrorists to be a stone's throw from Israel's population center in a Palestinian state would just embolden Iran.

The questions that arose following the summit were myriad:

Was Mr. Netanyahu simply trying to appease President Obama before it becomes necessary to attack Iran?

Would he relinquish the West Bank in order to acquire approval from the Obama administration for a direct strike on Iran's nuclear facilities?

Perhaps for the first time in his political career Netanyahu was walking in the footsteps of those prime ministers before him willing to offer up Jerusalem.

Netanyahu's nemesis, Secretary of State Hillary Clinton, was tapped to head the second round of peace talks between Israel and the Palestinians in Sharm-el-Sheikh—an Egyptian resort town on the Red Sea. There Netanyahu and Abbas were expected to work out the framework for the implementation of an interim agreement. The demand was that all core issues were to be resolved within the one-year timeline laid out by President Obama.

Israeli Defense Minister Ehud Barak jumped into the fray. He first set tongues wagging in March of 2008, when he told *Al-Jazeera* that some Jerusalem neighborhoods might become part of a Palestinian capital. "We can find a formula under which certain neighborhoods, heavily populated Arab neighborhoods, could become, in a peace agreement, part of the Palestinian capital that, of course, will include also the neighboring villages around Jerusalem," Barak said.[8]

This assertion was not surprising given Barak's track record. As prime minister he pulled the Israel Defense Forces out of Lebanon, proposed giving the Golan Heights back to Syria, and even offered the late and unlamented Yasser Arafat the Temple Mount. Barak's "solution" for Jerusalem, as stated again on September 1:

> West Jerusalem and 12 Jewish neighborhoods that are home to 200,000 residents will be ours. The Arab neighborhoods in which close to a quarter million Palestinians live will be theirs. There will be a special regime in place along with agreed upon arrangements in the Old City, the Mount of Olives, and the City of David.[9]

According to Barak, a special regime would be put in place along with agreed-upon arrangements in the Old City, the Mount of Olives and the City of David. In the negotiations between Netanyahu and Abbas (or Abu Mazen as he was known when he helped orchestrate the Munich Massacre), the Palestinian leader would be paid handsomely for his participation, and in turn will furtively fill the pockets of his Palestinian cabinet and legislators with U.S. tax-payer dollars.

Having experienced Arab rule in part of Jerusalem prior to 1967, why would Ehud Barak again want to subject the Jewish people and Christians worldwide to such indignity? Obama's plan would place East Jerusalem, the home of Christianity and of the Holy Sites sacred to two billion Christians, under Palestinian control. Like Bethlehem, the Christians who live there would be driven out and *Shariah* law would be imposed.

Israeli prime ministers have allowed themselves to be dragged from one bargaining table to another and have been forced to give up land for a peace that has never materialized. The only thing the Jewish people received from the Palestinians has been two *intifadas*, terrorist attacks too numerous to recount, civilians maimed and slaughtered, and the disdain of the world at large.

The view within Liberal Left Washington that all Americans agree on the resolution of the Israeli-Palestinian conflict is totally erroneous. The idea that the U.S. will counter radical Islam and extremism in the Islamic world by resolving the Palestinian issue is ludicrous. There is immense anger in the Arab world because of perceived U.S. favoritism toward Israel and that will not be resolved by a signature on a piece of paper.

Mr. Obama seemingly thinks that the way to demonstrate his resolve is for the U.S. to drag or push Israel towards the creation of a Palestinian state—either by bribing the nation or blackmailing it. The president clearly has his work cut out for him, and not with Mr. Netanyahu.

On September 7, just days after the meeting in Washington, Abbas revealed his true feelings in an interview with Al-Quds when he rejected Netanyahu's demand that Israel be recognized as a Jewish state by the Palestinians:

> We're not talking about a Jewish state and we won't talk about one. For us, there is the state of Israel and we won't recognize Israel as a Jewish state.[10]

On that same day, Hamas fired a rocket into Israel. Fortunately, no one was injured. A Hamas spokesman told Arab language newspaper *Al-Hayat* that the group intends to continue its attacks on settlers because they are "legitimate targets".[11]

Jerusalem has been a bone in the throat of the world for centuries. Many have tried to wrest it from the hands of the Jewish people. International leaders think they can play a tune and Israel will respond like a cobra in the basket of a snake charmer. There is no fear of being bitten. Let them beware the venom of the cobra. It is deadly. If America touches prophecy—Jerusalem—a curse will come upon America and upon President Obama as decreed in Genesis 12:3:

> I will bless those who bless you, And I will curse him who curses you; And in you all the families of the earth shall be blessed.

The ancient prophet Zachariah cried out, "I will make Jerusalem a cup that will send all the surrounding people reeling ... an immovable rock for all nations. All who try to move it will injure themselves." It might be wise for those determined to divide the City of David, the Zion of old, to carefully consider the cost.

CHAPTER ONE

JERUSALEM:
ENDANGERED CITY

"But you shall seek the place where the Lord your God chooses,
out of all your tribes, to put His name for His dwelling place;
and there you shall go."—DEUTERONOMY 12:5

Outside the White House on March 26, 2010, the weather was cloudy and drizzly; the temperature inside was downright frigid. Prime Minister Benjamin Netanyahu and the Israeli entourage accompanying him could almost see the frost gathering on President Barack Obama's upper lip. The U.S. leader was glacial in his response to the prime minister's refusal to kowtow to Obama's demands that construction on 1,600 housing units in East Jerusalem be halted. It was apparently more important to appease the Palestinians and assuage world opinion than to stand firm with Israel. It was reported that as Mr. Obama left the conference room to have a private dinner with his wife and daughters, he coolly called out, "Let me know if there is anything new."

Global warming may be taking place in other parts of the world, but the atmosphere was decidedly chilly in Washington, D.C., and by proxy, in Jerusalem. It is difficult to determine just how wide the rift is in U.S./ Israeli relations. It isn't at all problematic to see where President Obama's arrogant treatment of Mr. Netanyahu is leading—directly to renewed efforts to divide Jerusalem to appease Palestinian leaders and the Arab world. Only the Israelis know for how long they will allow themselves to be pushed and prodded to give up more and more.

The unfortunate truth is that should the plan to divide Jerusalem succeed, the Arabs surrounding the tiny nation of Israel will have won without firing another shot. Jerusalem as we know it—prosperous, culturally rich, religiously significant, and economically stable—will wither and die. It will become a center of strife and bloodshed the likes of which we have not seen in any of Yasser Arafat's infamous intifadas. It will be Belfast on steroids—Hell on Earth not only for the Jewish people but also for the prosperous Palestinians who thrive under Israeli rule.

It is unclear who would eventually rule East Jerusalem. It will become a hotbed of terrorist activity for new groups such as the progressively more extreme and ferocious Israeli Arab movement, whose main target is the Temple Mount. It will be the incubator for heinous attacks against the Jewish people, the kindergarten for training younger and younger suicide bombers, the high school for Hamas and Hezbollah, and the university for graduating al-Qaeda operatives.

Would the Saudis, the self-appointed caretakers of designated Islamic holy places, be persuaded to undertake a leadership role in East Jerusalem? Perhaps Jordan might step into the fray, but does King Abdullah really have the stomach, not to say the backbone, to stand up to the likes of radical Islamists? He would place his own country at risk of attack. Would it be the Moroccans, members of the Arab League and overseers of the Supreme Jerusalem Committee?

Having a terrorist base just over the avenue from Jewish residents, government offices, commerce and holy sites would be like dangling Chivas Regal before an alcoholic—impossible to resist. Without the restraints of Israeli security, murder and mayhem would be the order of the day. Marksmen would be able to pick off shoppers, home-goers, office workers, and school children at will. The streets of Jewish Jerusalem would flow red with the blood of its citizens.

Jews would no longer risk praying at the Western Wall. Families would forgo outings together for fear that one or all might end up in the morgue. The Stations of the Cross that spans the Christian and Muslim Quarters would no longer be the destination for church tour groups from any country.

Women who did not adhere to the Muslim ideology of proper dress and behavior would be targeted.

The picture assumes nightmare proportions when one considers changes that would decimate Jerusalem if it were divided. Would a new business want to invest in a city where one stray rocket fired from East Jerusalem could wipe out its presence in Israel? It is only the security afforded by the IDF that spares Jerusalem from being a flashpoint of friction with skirmishes in every alley and side street. No other organization or entity would patrol and protect Jerusalem with the same care and concern as Jews who love their city.

The connection between the Jews and Jerusalem is deeply rooted and compelling. The tie is over three thousand years old. When Arabs pray they face Mecca; when Jews pray they face Jerusalem. For three centuries, Jews have ended each Passover meal with the pensive, "Next year in Jerusalem." In the words of Ehud Olmert, mayor of Jerusalem from 1993 to 2003, Jerusalem embodies "the purest expression of all that Jews prayed for, dreamed of, cried for, and died for in the two thousand years since the destruction of the Second Temple."[12]

The Arabs, on the other hand, have no real connection to Jerusalem other than that Muhammad visited it in a dream. The Muslims can point to no holy place except the Dome of the Rock, which they built on the site of the Temple Mount, knowing it was sacred to Jews. Statisticians have determined that Jerusalem and/or Zion are mentioned 823 times in the Old Testament and 161 times in the New Testament. Columnist Moshe Kohn wrote that the two proper nouns can be found in the Koran as often "as they do in the Hindu Bhagavad-Gita, the Taoist Tao-Te Ching, the Buddhist Dhamapada, and the Zoroastrian Zend Avesta—not even once."

It is politics not historical claims that make Jerusalem such an important issue for the Arabs. One has only to look at history books to discover that King David established Jerusalem as the capital of a united Israel in 1010 B.C.; Caliph Omer, a Muslim, first entered Jerusalem in 638 A.D. Anyone who can add and subtract should be able to figure out who has the most prolonged claim to Israel—and it isn't the Palestinian Arabs.

A divided Jerusalem would mean Israel would be bereft of a peacekeeping force capable of maintaining a terrorist-free Jerusalem. The U.S. president that accomplishes this feat would be signing a death warrant for the Jewish people in Israel. He or she will have to stand before God and give account of why the admonition to "touch not mine anointed" (Psalm 105:15) fell on deaf ears and a callous heart.

Now known as the city of three religions, under Arab rule Jerusalem would become inhospitable to Christians and Jews. How can this be determined beforehand? No Muslim country in the world welcomes other religions to openly practice their beliefs. As David Weinberg wrote,

> Under Palestinian Authority and Hamas rule, Christians in the West Bank and Gaza have been hounded, terrorized, and driven out. Christian Bethlehem is, effectively, no more. The Church of the Nativity was defiled by Palestinian Muslim terrorists who turned it into an armed refuge in 2002. Who will protect the churches of Jerusalem from the same fate under Islamic rule?[13]

It will go the way of Bethlehem, and yes, any territory under Muslim rule. Christians will be *persona non grata*—driven from the country or made to suffer intense persecution, perhaps even death, because of their rejection of Islam. Desecration of holy sites and Jewish graves will follow the pattern set under Jordanian rule, and no one will be able to stop it.

Just as much of the civilized (?) world turned its back while some six million Jews were barbarically murdered during the Holocaust, it will once again keep its distance from a Jerusalem overrun by fanatical Islamic terrorists. Nothing will be sacred. The Arabs care nothing about Jerusalem; it has never really been the issue. That has been proven time and again as suicide bombers targeted the city and its inhabitants, indiscriminately killing Jews and Israeli Arabs alike. Jerusalem is coveted only because it is the most sacred city to the Jews and is under Jewish control.

Jerusalem is a beautiful, cosmopolitan city—the jewel in the crown of modern-day Israel. It will be neglected and targeted for ruin simply because it is loved by the Jews. If it were possible, every Jew in Israel would be driven into the Mediterranean while the Arabs on shore celebrated the demise of their enemies. Jerusalem would be laid waste. It could become just another dirty, neglected, poverty-stricken Arab village with its streets piled with garbage and its gutters flowing with human excrement.

Jerusalem must not be divided. It is impossible to imagine any part of the regal city under Arab rule. Hillary Clinton seemed unduly condescending as she admonished the attendees of the AIPAC convention in 2010, insisting they must "tell the truth when it is needed." Unfortunately she, like so many others, does not recognize the truth when it is staring her in the face.

> **TRUTH:** Jerusalem was built stone-by-stone from a dusty desert town in the hills of Judea to become a thriving metropolis—sophisticated and multinational. It is a home for the Jews, a symbol of survival through the centuries.

> **TRUTH:** Jerusalem is a magnet for scholars, clergy, artists, archaeologists, and tourists—Jews, Christians, and Muslims alike.

> **TRUTH:** All that Jerusalem has become under Jewish governance would vanish under Arab rule.

When polled privately, the Arabs who live in Israeli-controlled Jerusalem agree wholeheartedly. Many Palestinians who reside under the safety and security of the IDF prefer that to the misrule of Hamas or the toothless Palestinian Authority. Few Arabs who reside in Jerusalem ever become involved in terror tactics. They don't want to chance being banished to the other side of the security fence, and those who live on the other side avail themselves of every opportunity to cross into Israeli-controlled Jerusalem.

Homes in Jewish neighborhoods such as Talpiot, French Hill, and others are being purchased at an incredible rate by wealthy Arabs.

Forcing Israel to divide Jerusalem would deprive the world of one of the most urbane, stylish, erudite, cultured, historical cities in the Middle East. Jerusalem would once again be reduced to rubble by the rabble surrounding it. Christians and Jews who truly treasure David's City would be left to shake their heads in horrified sadness. Yet American presidents continue to push for a divided Jerusalem.

Barack Obama is not the first president to stake his legacy on trying to force Israel to the bargaining table. Jimmy Carter, Bill Clinton, and even George W. Bush are among the number. Who in their administrations took time to sit down and actually count the cost of dividing Jerusalem? Will anyone in succeeding administrations consider the price of a divided Jerusalem to be much too costly?

CHAPTER TWO

WHO OWNS JERUSALEM?

The Lord had said to David and to Solomon his son, "In this house and in Jerusalem, which I have chosen out of all the tribes of Israel, I will put My name forever."—II KINGS 21:7

E ach year the people of Israel celebrate the anniversary of the reunification of Jerusalem. On June 5, 1967, after months of saber rattling by Egypt, Syria, and Jordan, Israel unfolded a brilliant defense plan. Early that day almost the entire Israeli Air Force took off for Cairo. Less than two hours later, its planes returned to home base having destroyed three hundred of Egypt's jets on the ground. After refueling and rearming, Israeli planes took to the air again and attacked airfields in Syria, Jordan, and Iraq. At the end of the day, the air forces of Egypt and Jordan had been all but destroyed, and Syria had lost half its planes.

In three days of ground fighting, the IDF overcame Jordanian and Egyptian forces, and the battle moved northward to the Golan Heights. On June 7 the IDF moved into Jerusalem and recaptured the Old City, including the Western Wall. On June 9, Israeli forces broke through Syrian lines and secured that area. Since then the question of who owns Jerusalem—biblically, historically, and legally—has been asked repeatedly. Biblically, the city has belonged to the Jewish people since the time of King David. In 1053 B.C. King David defeated the Jebusites and reigned for thirty-three years in Jerusalem. After David's death, Solomon ascended the throne. When he died the land was divided into two kingdoms—Israel to the north and Judah in the south. Jerusalem became the capital of Judah. Solomon's death was the beginning of a succession of Jewish rulers, until the day Nebuchadnezzar destroyed Jerusalem, leaving only a remnant of Jewish people.

In three thousand years, twenty-six empires have conquered and occupied Jerusalem. The city has been leveled numerous times, and the Jews banished and forced to flee to other nations. Yet, in the midst of the destruction and despite ongoing terror attacks, Jews have continued to cry, "Next year in Jerusalem!"

Historically, Jerusalem is the capital of the Jewish homeland. Perhaps this was best summed up by Moshe Dayan at the 34th UN General Assembly in September 1979:

> Jerusalem has known many foreign rulers during the course of its long history, but none of them regarded it as their capital. Only the Jewish people have always maintained it as the sole center of its national and spiritual life. For thousands of years Jews have prayed daily for their return to Jerusalem, and for the past century and a half, Jerusalem has had a continuous and uninterrupted Jewish majority.

When the Ottoman Empire collapsed following World War I, the British Mandate for Palestine set aside an area of 45,000 square miles for the Jews' national homeland. From the designated area, the British took 35,000 square miles of the land in 1921 to create the Trans-Jordan (later Jordan). Jews were not allowed to live or own property in the area east of the Jordan River. Later, Britain ceded 454 square miles of the Golan Heights to Syria. About 10,000 square miles of the original grant were left to the Jews. This included part of the Negev.

Adolf Hitler's determination to destroy the Jewish people during World War II resulted in the murder of six million Jews. European Jews pled with many nations to grant them asylum, but their pleas fell on deaf ears.

Many more longed to return to their homeland. In the midst of incredible persecution and suffering, Ezekiel's words beckoned to all:

> For I will take you from among the nations, gather you out
> of all countries, and bring you into your own land.
>
> **EZEKIEL 36:24**

Between 1948 and 1967, conditions in Jerusalem were deplorable, even by medieval standards. Jews were barred from worshiping at the Western Wall, the Jewish quarter in the Old City was destroyed, and synagogues were demolished. Three-fourths of the tombstones in the Mount of Olives Cemetery were ripped out and used to build a hotel and to pave a path leading to army latrines.

During the late 1970s and early 1980s, I was privileged to form a wonderful relationship with Prime Minister Menachem Begin. Our talks often centered on Jerusalem. To him it seemed unfair that, while every country in the world was free to choose its own capital, Israel could not.

He reflected on how Israel had fought to reunite Jerusalem and make it a city whose holy sites were available to everyone. He related to me an exasperating discussion he had had with President Jimmy Carter. According to Carter, his "government did not recognize Jerusalem as the capital of Israel." Begin said, "Here in Jerusalem is the [government]. Whoever says we don't recognize Jerusalem as the capital of Israel, my reply is always, 'Excuse me, sir, but we don't recognize your non-recognition.'"

Over the years I have debated national security advisors, secretaries of state, and even Yasser Arafat on this issue. On December 11, 1988, at the UN General Assembly, I was surrounded by members of the PLO. Yasser Arafat had just concluded his address to the group. Holding my Bible up, I made the case of why Jerusalem was Israel's capital. Arafat screamed at me, demanding that I shut up. In 1991, I made the same case to Secretary of State James Baker at the Madrid Peace Conference. His response: "The status of Jerusalem has to be determined by negotiations." I countered with: "God doesn't negotiate."

Maps in Muslim countries show Israel as simply unnamed or as "Palestine." She is surrounded by hostile Muslim countries with a land mass 640 times her size, yet some thirteen million Jews worldwide are constantly charged with being accountable for the frustrations of the three hundred million Arabs in the region.

It seems the Jews are even responsible for the dissatisfaction of President Barack Obama. It seems he is obsessed with dividing Jerusalem and forcing the Jews to give away even more land. In a much-touted speech broadcast from Cairo, Egypt, on June 4, 2009, Obama outlined what he saw as the first and second greatest sources of tension between the Muslim world and the United States. Al-Qaeda topped his list, but the Israeli/Palestinian conflict came in second. The president intimated that Israel had been depriving the Palestinians of their homeland for sixty years. It did not go unnoticed that no mention was made of centuries-old Jewish claims to the land.

CHAPTER THREE

JERUSALEM,
CITY BESIEGED

Now the Lord had said to Abram:
"Get out of your country,
From your family
And from your father's house,
To a land that I will show you.
I will make you a great nation;
I will bless you
And make your name great;
And you shall be a blessing.
I will bless those who bless you,
And I will curse him who curses you;
And in you all the families of the earth shall be blessed."

GENESIS 12:1-3

Over the past ninety years Jerusalem and its ownership has been the subject of treatise after treatise, resolution upon resolution, and verbose thesis upon erudite essay. Treaties abound which bestow the rightful ownership of Jerusalem upon the Jewish people—from the early San Remo Resolution to the predecessor of the United Nations, the League of Nations, to the UN itself.

The San Remo Resolution was established following World War I. Italy, France, Japan, and Great Britain established a national homeland for the Jewish people—the Land of Israel. The resolution states that the above parties agreed "to entrust...the administration of Palestine, within such boundaries as may be determined by the Principal Allied Powers, to a Mandatory [authority that] will be responsible for putting into effect the [Balfour] declaration...in favour of the establishment in Palestine of a national home for the Jewish people."[14]

The treaty specifically states, "Nothing shall be done which may prejudice the civil and religious rights of existing non-Jewish communities in Palestine."[15] Nowhere does it address the political aspect of governance.

The League of Nations declaration regarding Palestine included: "whereas recognition has thereby been given to the historical connection of the Jewish people with Palestine and to the grounds for reconstituting their national home in that country."[16] No mention is made of Palestinian Arabs. The directive established by the League contained a proviso that had never been set before or after: Palestine was to belong to the Jewish people.

When the UN assumed the duties of the League of Nations in 1945, it adopted Article 80: "Nothing in this Chapter shall be construed...to alter in any manner the rights whatsoever of any states or any peoples in terms of existing international instruments which Members of the United Nations may respectively be parties."[17]

In 1947 the UN General Assembly enacted Resolution 181, a partition plan that outlined borders for a Jewish Palestine. It dictated a special government for Jerusalem and established political rights for the Palestinian Arabs. As has often been the case with treaties and resolutions, the Arabs took exception to the plan and obstructed its passage. The Jews, on the other hand, welcomed it. The resolution never became operative. The war was launched on May 15, 1948, to drive the Jewish people into the Mediterranean Sea, ending with Jordan in control of East Jerusalem. Jordan failed to follow the mandates of Resolution 181.

Another aspect of Resolution 181 was to call for a referendum within ten years of its adoption in order for the people of Jerusalem to express their wishes as to what kind of regime should oversee the city. David Ben-Gurion, Israel's first prime minister, was confident the Jews would be a majority in Jerusalem and would vote to return the city to Jewish oversight. Sixty-three years later, the citizens of Jerusalem have yet to vote on whom should govern the city.

On July 30, 1980, the Israeli Knesset voted to affirm a united Jerusalem as the capital of the State of Israel. Shortly afterward, I spoke with Prime Minister Menachem Begin. My questions to him centered on how inconceivable it was that Arab countries, 650 times the size of Israel, were calling for that tiny nation to cede land for peace. Israel is the size of New Jersey; the Arab countries are the size of the United States, Mexico, and Central America combined.

✧ Arab dictators control 13,486,861 square kilometers in the Middle East, and Israel controls 20,770 (Palestinefacts.org)

✧ The population of Israel is roughly six million, compared to the population of three hundred million living in the surrounding Arab countries

✧ The Arab nations are represented by twenty-one separate countries.[18]

In discussions about the above issues and statistics, I asked Mr. Begin, "How can this be possible when so many people in America and the world believe the Bible?" Mr. Begin just smiled that enigmatic smile of his. As we talked, I told him about a publication from the Egyptian state information service, "Jerusalem, an Arab City." It was printed by *al-Ahram Press* in Cairo. The booklet stated on page eight: "Jerusalem was invaded by Christian Arabs in the year 90 B.C. and remained under their domination until it was occupied by the Romans in the first century A.D."[19]

Of course, we were well aware that the Arab world's claim to Jerusalem was based on misinformation. How could a state publication declare a right to Jerusalem based on the presumption that Christian Arabs had invaded Jerusalem ninety years *before* the birth of Christ? It is this type of propaganda that floods the Arab world and feeds and fuels the hatred for the Jewish people.

The prime minister answered my unasked question. "Being a student of the Bible, you know that almost three thousand years ago King David united the kingdoms of Judea and Israel. He transferred the seat of power from Hebron to Jerusalem, where he ruled for thirty-three years. He wanted to build the Temple on Mount Moriah, where Abraham was to offer his son, Isaac, as a sacrifice."

David petitioned God to be allowed to build a home for Him in Jerusalem. God answered, "You have shed much blood and have made great wars; you shall not build a house for My name, because you have shed much blood on the earth in My sight" (I Chronicles 22:8). God promised David a son who would follow after him as king and would build the Temple. "Since then," said Mr. Begin, "Jerusalem has been the capital of the Jewish state… one of the oldest capital cities in the world." He continued:

> We have had to face a wrong done to a nation, which is absolutely unprecedented. Every nation has its capital, which is recognized by other nations. The United States declared the city of Washington, D.C., to be her capital. The Russians said their capital city would be called Moscow… Does anyone say to Luxembourg where its capital should be? The only capital in the world not yet recognized as a capital is Jerusalem.[20]

The prime minister was aware there are detractors who refuse to recognize Israel, much less Jerusalem, as its capital city. Begin went on to say,

> We went to Camp David [in 1978] to make peace with Egypt, and one of your statesmen told me that the government of the United States did not recognize Jerusalem as the capital of Israel. I answered, "Whether you recognize or don't recognize, Jerusalem is the capital of the State of Israel."
> After the Six Day War, we liberated the eastern part of Jerusalem from Jordanian occupation. For nineteen years we

couldn't go to the Western Wall to pray. That was the only time since the [second] Temple had been destroyed by the Romans. Under all other regimes we were free to go to the Western Wall to pray; but the Jordanians didn't allow us to go, in breach of the arms agreement.

The Olive Mountain Cemetery, in which our greatest sages are buried for centuries, was completely desecrated. Monuments were destroyed and turned into floors of places, which are unmentionable. I will not even use the names [latrines]. All of our synagogues were destroyed...the Jewish Quarter, which was centuries old, was leveled.

Under our jurisdiction, we again consecrated the Olive Mountain Cemetery and everyone has access to the Holy Shrines—the Holy Sepulcher, the Church of the Nativity. A Muslim goes to the mosque to pray in absolute safety.

Here in Jerusalem is the government, the Parliament, the president, the Supreme Court. Whoever says, either on behalf of a great power or of a small country, "We can't recognize Jerusalem as the capital of Israel," my reply is always the same: "Excuse me sir, but we don't recognize your non-recognition."

The prime minister's comments brought to mind something Moshe Dayan said during his address to the Thirty-Fourth General Assembly of the United Nations in September 1979:

Jerusalem has known many foreign rulers during the course of its long history, but none of them regarded it as their capital. Only the Jewish people have always maintained it as the sole center of its national and spiritual life. For thousands of years Jews have prayed daily for their return to Jerusalem, and for the past century and a half, Jerusalem has had a continuous and uninterrupted Jewish majority. [21]

Jerusalem is the symbol of all for which Israel stands in our world. Teddy Kollek, Jerusalem's first mayor, wrote, "Jerusalem, this beautiful, golden city, is the heart and soul of the Jewish people. One cannot live without a heart and soul. If you want one single word to symbolize all of Jewish history, that word is Jerusalem."[22]

Out of the long negotiations to establish a Jewish homeland, a friendship grew between Dr. Chaim Weizmann, a Jewish statesman, and Lord Balfour, then-British foreign secretary. Balfour was unable to understand why the Jews were insisting they would only accept Palestine as their permanent homeland. One day Lord Balfour asked Dr. Weizmann for an explanation: "Mr. Balfour, let's suppose I propose that you replace London with Paris, would you accept?"

A surprised Balfour responded, "But London is ours!"

Replied Weizmann, "Jerusalem was ours when London was still a swampland."[23]

The very name evokes a stirring in the heart and soul. It has been called by many names: City of God, City of David, Zion, the City of the Great King, Ariel (Lion of God), and Moriah (chosen of the Lord); but only one name resonates down through the centuries—Jerusalem!

A world map drawn in 1581 has Jerusalem at its very center with the then-known continents of the world surrounding it. It resembles a ship's propeller with the shaft in the center being Jerusalem. Another analogy is of Jerusalem as the navel of the Earth. Yet, the history of Jerusalem can be summed up in one word—troubled! Lying as it does between the rival empires of Egypt to the south and Syria to the north, both striving for dominance in the region, Israel was constantly trampled by the opposing armies. It has been conquered at various times by the Canaanites, Jebusites, Babylonians, Assyrians, Persians, Romans, Byzantines, Arabs, Crusaders, Ottomans, and the British.

While its origins are lost in the hazy mists of antiquity, archaeological evidence of human habitation goes back some four thousand years. Jerusalem is first mentioned in Joshua 10:1. We read there that Adoni-Zedek was the king of Jerusalem and fought unsuccessfully against Joshua. The Israelites first occupied Jerusalem during the days of the Judges (1:21), but did not completely inhabit the city until 1049 B.C., when David wrested it from the Jebusites and declared it the capital city of the Jewish people.

In *Jerusalem, Sacred City of Mankind*, Teddy Kollek and Moshe Pearlman wrote:

> The spiritual attachment of the Jews to Jerusalem has remained unbroken; it is a unique attachment. Should one doubt that statement, he would have to look long and hard to find another relationship in history where a people, even in captivity, remained so passionately attached to a city for three thousand years.[24]

When the Jews were driven from their land at various times, wherever they found themselves in exile, they faced toward Jerusalem when praying. After Nebuchadnezzar signed a decree making it illegal to pray to anyone except him, Daniel 6:10 says, "Now when Daniel knew that the writing was signed, he went home. And in his upper room, with his windows open toward Jerusalem, he knelt down on his knees three times that day, and prayed and gave thanks before his God, as was his custom since early days."

Jewish synagogues faced Jerusalem. When an exiled Jew built a house, part of a wall was left unfinished to symbolize that it was only a temporary dwelling—until he could return to his permanent home, Jerusalem. Even the traditional smashing of a glass during a wedding ceremony has its roots in the Temple in Jerusalem. This act of remembering the loss of the center of Jewish festivities during the marriage feast extols the eternal truth: "Jerusalem my highest joy" (Psalm 137:6 NIV).

When compared with the great cities of the world, Jerusalem is small. It stands alongside no great river as do London, Paris, and Rome. It boasts no port, no major industries, no mineral wealth, nor even an adequate water supply. The city doesn't stand on a major thoroughfare connected to the rest of the world. Why, then, is Jerusalem the navel of the Earth, the shaft that propels the world ever forward?

. The answer can be found in its spiritual significance. Jerusalem is the home of two of the world's monotheistic faiths—Judaism and Christianity—and is claimed by a third, Islam. Biblical prophets proclaimed that from Jerusalem the Word of the Lord would go out to the world—a Word that would change the moral standards of all mankind.

The spiritual stature of Jerusalem is echoed by its physical situation. It stands upon the Judean hills, high above the surrounding countryside. Traveling to Jerusalem is always referred to as "going up to Jerusalem." Those who leave the City of God are said to "go down"—in perhaps more than just the physical sense.

When examining the history of Jerusalem as a whole, no other city has suffered as David's City has suffered. At times the city has been overrun by violent assault. It is recorded in Jeremiah 19 that the city would surrender after suffering the horrors of starvation—and be reduced to cannibalism.

While Christian and Muslim claims to Jerusalem came much later, the story of the Jews in Jerusalem began three millennia ago and has never ceased. The link of the Jewish people has been historical, religious, cultural, physical, and fundamental; it has never been voluntarily broken. Any absence of the Jews from their beloved city has been the result of foreign persecution and expulsion. To the Jews alone belongs David's City, the City of God.

For the Jewish people, whose cry for centuries has been, "Next year Jerusalem," it is more than a location on a map. It is not just a tourist Mecca where one can visit various holy sites. Jerusalem is holy. It is the essence of all for which they have hoped and prayed and cried and died. It is their God-given land.

> *The Lord had said to David and to Solomon his son, "In this house and in Jerusalem, which I have chosen out of all the tribes of Israel, I will put My name forever."*
>
> **II KINGS 21:7**

Israel is *God's* dream. The title deed belongs to Him. It is His to bestow on whomever He will—and He has given that right of occupation to the

Jewish people. When God made His eternal promises to Israel, there was no United Nations, no United States, no Russia, no European Union, and no Arab League. There were only pagan nations to challenge this dream, to challenge God and His Word. Today, those same pagan voices are challenging the right of the Jews to occupy a unified Jerusalem.

When you and I as Christians are apathetic toward God's divine plan or His eternal purpose, it means we are rejecting our Lord's divine assignment to the Church. God's prophetic time clock has been set on Jerusalem time throughout history, and the spotlight of Heaven is still on the Jews as His chosen people. It began with them, and it will end with them.

We must embrace the name of Christ and serve the God of Abraham, Isaac and Jacob. We must heed the warnings of the prophets Isaiah, Jeremiah, Ezekiel, Daniel, Hosea, and Joel. We must sing the Psalms of King David and find hope. The mention of Jerusalem should quicken our hearts, for it is our spiritual city. We must support our Jewish brothers and sisters in their fight against anti-Semitism and the threat of terrorism.

God's plan is an eternal one! As Christians, we cannot afford to neglect our responsibility to stand with the House of Israel. It is as important as it is to believe the promises of God. As Christians, we are the engrafted vine. We bow before a Jewish Messiah, and what we do matters in the light of eternity.

Jerusalem is the only city for which God commands us to pray. He also commands a blessing on those who pray for Jerusalem! When you pray for Jerusalem, Psalm 122:6, you are not praying for stones or dirt, you are praying for revival (II Chronicles 7:14) and for the Lord's return. Also, you are joining our Lord, the Good Samaritan, in His ministry of love and comfort to the suffering. "Inasmuch as you did it to one of the least of these My brethren, you did it to Me" (Matthew 25:40).

This is our divine commission.

To simply say there is no need to pray and support the Jewish people is anti-Semitic nonsense. It is to say to Nehemiah, Esther, Paul the apostle, and even our Lord that they were wrong to pray and reach out in love to the House of Israel. There are hundreds of examples of prophets, priests, and kings who chose to light a candle rather than curse the darkness. Jesus is our perfect example. He fed the hungry, He gave water to the thirsty, and He healed the sick.

The Bible says the same thing about the entire world in II Timothy 3:1: "But know this, that in the last days perilous times shall come." In Matthew 24:6-8 NIV, Jesus says, "You will hear of wars and rumors of wars, but see to it that you are not alarmed. Such things must happen, but the end is still to come. Nation will rise against nation, and kingdom against kingdom."

If we are to do nothing, then why do we do everything in our power to help hurting people in our own country? One may say, "I don't need to reach out to the Jewish people. The Bible says there will be wars until the Messiah returns." Another may say, "I cannot support an ungodly nation." Let me ask you, then, why do you sing "God Bless America?" America is rampant with drugs, alcohol, pornography, divorce, abortion, child abuse, homosexuality, and murder. You pray for God to bless America because your heart is filled with love and compassion. The heart of God is filled with the same love and compassion for the Jewish people in Jerusalem and throughout Israel.

Proverbs 6:16-19 records seven things God hates:

> *These six things the Lord hates,*
> > *Yes, seven are an abomination to Him:*
> > *A proud look,*
> > *A lying tongue,*
> > *Hands that shed innocent blood,*
> > *A heart that devises wicked plans,*
> > *Feet that are swift in running to evil,*
> > *A false witness who speaks lies,*
> > *And one who sows discord among brethren.*

Perhaps anti-Semitism should be added to that list, but then, perhaps those seven things *are* the definition of Jew-hatred: The proud, who think themselves better than the Jewish family who lives down the street; who tell lies to incite the neighbors against them; who attack with stones or sticks, knives or guns; who plan wickedness against the Jewish neighbor; and who spread lies in order to foster antagonism.

CHAPTER FOUR

JERUSALEM, DAVID'S CAPITAL

Give the Lord no rest until he completes his work, until he makes
Jerusalem the pride of the earth. —ISAIAH 62:7 NLT

In order to look forward, we must first walk back through the pages of Jerusalem's history. Jerusalem seems always to have been exceptional—almost an oddity. Back in Joshua's time, when the Israelites were fighting to take the land of Canaan from its previous inhabitants and conquered Jerusalem, its name was omitted from the review of Joshua's conquests. We see later in Joshua 15:63 that the tribe of Judah was unable to rid the village of the Jebusites who controlled it. It remained that way until roughly four hundred years later.

When David became king something important happened. After King Saul's death on Mount Gilboa, David ceased to be a fugitive running for his life. God told him to establish his headquarters in Hebron in the midst of his own tribe. This is where the people of Judah anointed David king. Abner ruled over the northern tribes after Saul's death, but after his murder, the elders of Israel made a pact with David and anointed him their king. The prophet Samuel's words had come to pass, and the nation of Israel was reunited.

Now David needed a city from where he could rule a united Israel. Jerusalem was ideally located. It stood on the border between the northern tribes and Judah, and more importantly, it had never been associated with any specific tribe of Israel. It would be the capital of all tribes and a center for the worship of *Yahweh*, to whom David was deeply devoted.

David and his men marched to Jerusalem. The Jebusites refused to take David's challenge seriously. They had successfully held the Israelites at bay from their high perch before; why should things be different this time? David, however, succeeded where others had failed. He used a water channel to get inside the Jebusite fortifications surrounding Jerusalem. In short order, he took the city and began to consolidate his people from the new capital.

Hiram, King of Tyre, sent men and material to assist David in building a palace. David saw it all as God's favor and understood that God was making his reign glorious for the sake of His people Israel. David's success would not go unchallenged. Enter the Philistines. They viewed David as just a renegade shepherd, who had been lucky in killing the giant Goliath, and set out to punish this upstart! David soundly defeated them in two separate battles and sent them back to their fortresses along the south coast.

Afterward, David mustered his troops to escort the Ark of the Covenant to the new capital. This was of vital importance to him. It was *Yahweh*, the God of Abraham, Isaac, and Jacob, who had brought him through his years of shepherding, Samuel's anointing and prophecy, battling Goliath, Saul's attempts to kill him, and his years of exile. Never had God forsaken him.

The false gods of Astarte and Baal held no allure for King David. *Yahweh* was his only God. He was so devoted that he was unashamed to let everyone know of his dedication. His wife Michal, Saul's daughter, ridiculed and scorned her husband for making a fool of himself. David was unperturbed and informed Michal that he would gladly do that and much more. No display of heartfelt exuberance was inappropriate to the worship of this great and wonderful God who had blessed him so abundantly.

Once David had settled in Jerusalem, it became the center for worship of the God of the Hebrews. King David wanted to build a Temple for the Lord he loved, but the prophet Nathan told him his warlike ways had made it inappropriate for him to carry out such a task. He was encouraged by the news that his son, Solomon, would be the one to erect the Temple to honor *Yahweh*.

During David's reign, although the Ark of the Covenant continued to dwell in a tent, it in no way hampered David's enthusiasm in promoting the worship of *Yahweh*. Animals were sacrificed morning and evening, and the Sabbath was rigorously observed. Even today, David's intimate relationship with his God and the worship that relationship evoked is preserved in the book of Psalms. Both Christians and Jews are deeply affected by its beauty and sense of awe of Almighty God.

Jerusalem is what it is—a center of worship. No river flows through it; no harbor sits beside it. No other reason can be offered for its importance. It is a mystery to be pondered at length. It sits astride a range of unremarkable hills at a narrow neck of land that joins the two largest continents on Earth: Asia and Africa. From ancient times great and prosperous societies flourished either north of Jerusalem in Mesopotamia, that fertile region around the Tigris and Euphrates, or south of Jerusalem around the Nile River valley. Alternatively those great societies sought to impose their rule over each other. To do so, they had to pass through Israel—everybody's doormat.

For one shining moment, all that changed when God found in David a man after His own heart. During David's reign the great tides of history that generally governed events around Jerusalem were interrupted. Neither Mesopotamia nor Egypt was active; both great centers of civilization were stagnant. During this temporary lull, David's star rose to heights unimaginable in the little backwater province he ruled. To this day, it is difficult to imagine a kingdom centered in Jerusalem that would extend almost from the Nile to the Euphrates. But that is the land David and his son Solomon ruled in peace and prosperity.

It was a golden age unforgotten by the Jews. In the dark days during Solomon's reign, when his heart began to go after the false gods of some of his many wives and concubines, the prophets of Israel comforted those who remained faithful to *Yahweh*. They announced that God would one day bring another like David, an anointed one, a messiah who would reestablish Zion (Jerusalem.) He would exalt it in the eyes of all men so that the nations, the *goyim*, would come from the four corners of the Earth to acknowledge the God of Israel as the one true God of all creation—the King of Glory, *Yahweh*

Sabaoth. It was to this promise alone that God's people clung in succeeding centuries.

After Solomon's death, the kingdom split. Samaria became the kingdom of the northern tribes of Israel. All that was left to Jerusalem was the tribe of Judah. By then Jerusalem with its Temple had become fixed in the hearts and minds of all true worshippers of *Yahweh* as the place to bring one's sacrifices, fulfill one's vows, and offer loud songs of praise.

This posed a problem for the northern rulers who didn't want their subjects to make pilgrimages down to Jerusalem—capital of a rival kingdom. They sought to offer the people substitute places of worship with substitute gods. The worship of *Yahweh* barely survived in the north. It did, thanks to prophets like Elijah and Elisha, who never let the fire go out. It was essentially a time of decline. In the south where the worship of *Yahweh* was still the official religion, decline happened more slowly. It was occasionally interrupted by the fires of revival, but most kings who ruled in Jerusalem were little better than the kings who sat in Samaria. The worship of *Yahweh* was fading, almost irretrievably.

In 722 B.C., Samaria fell to the Assyrians, and in 568 B. C. Jerusalem fell to the Babylonians—just as Jeremiah had warned. On each occasion inhabitants of the cities were carried into exile by their captors. The sharp rebuke of exile had a cleansing effect on those who suffered it. In losing Jerusalem, they began to value it as never before. Perhaps they sang:

> *Beside the rivers of Babylon, we sat and wept as we thought of Jerusalem.*
>
> *We put away our harps, hanging them on the branches of poplar trees.*
>
> *For our captors demanded a song from us. Our tormentors insisted on a joyful hymn: "Sing us one of those songs of Jerusalem!"*
>
> *But how can we sing the songs of the Lord while in a pagan land?*

If I forget you, O Jerusalem, let my right hand forget how to play the harp.

May my tongue stick to the roof of my mouth if I fail to remember you, if I don't make Jerusalem my greatest joy.

PSALM 137:1-6 NLT

Jerusalem had become much more than David's capital. Because of the Temple Solomon had built there, it had become God's special dwelling place on Earth. It was not that He was contained there, but in that building and its environs He had covenanted to receive the worship of His people and to hear their prayers. It was there that *Yahweh* met His people in a very special way. Although He could be praised and thanked anywhere in all the Earth, Jerusalem became the only place appointed for the sacrifice of burnt offerings for the sins of the people.

When Nebuchadnezzar sacked Jerusalem in 586 B.C., he looted and burned the Temple and knocked down the walls. That's the way the city remained for seventy years, while the land enjoyed a rest. Israel had repeatedly violated God's Law by not resting the land every seven years (Leviticus 25:1-7), so God removed His hand of protection. They were taken captive by Babylon, the walls of Jerusalem were razed, and their Temple was destroyed.

Babylon fell to the Persians in 539 B.C., and a year later the Persian Emperor Cyrus issued a decree authorizing the rebuilding of *Yahweh's* Temple in Jerusalem. A remnant of God's people returned to the hills of Jerusalem. Their arrival was not greeted with rejoicing by those who had made the area their home during the previous fifty years. Questions of ownership and authority gave immediate cause for conflict.

It didn't help the cause when locals—some of them half-breed Samaritans who had adopted the worship of *Yahweh*—were offended when their offers of help to rebuild the Temple were rebuffed. They actively opposed the work of the Jews by trying to frighten or discourage them. They sometimes bribed the Persian officials to do what they could to hinder progress.

The Jews did manage to quickly erect an altar and the other items needed for sacrifices and offerings that were at the heart of *Yahweh's* worship.

Rebuilding the Temple—a more modest structure than the one erected by Solomon—took much longer, for poverty and shortages persisted in and around Jerusalem.

The new Temple was dedicated around 515 B.C., under the direction of Zerubbabel the prince and Joshua the priest. Later Ezra, a priest thoroughly versed in God's Law, arrived with authorization from the Persian emperor, Artaxerxes. Ezra was chosen to take the offerings to Jerusalem and do everything he could to strengthen Temple worship and devotion to *Yahweh* there.

Then God sent Nehemiah to rebuild the walls of Jerusalem. Nehemiah worked hard and courageously in the face of violent resistance. He arranged for more people to live inside the city, recognizing that its puny population was insufficient to defend the city.

Between Ezra and Nehemiah, the worship of *Yahweh* and the life of His people underwent change. Some would even argue that it was in this time of revival that the essential groundwork for modern Judaism was laid. These men loved and endeavored to serve the God of David. They cared greatly about His laws and sought to observe them strictly. Intermarriage with Gentiles was banned, the weekly Sabbath was honored, land reforms limited the extent to which the rich could exploit the poor, tithing was observed, and priests and Levites were properly certified and ordained for the service of the Temple.

The fire was still burning—perhaps less intensely than in the days of David—but still burning after it nearly had been extinguished by waves of adversity and judgment. Jerusalem was and remains the symbol of the persistence and perseverance of the Jews—led by David—to inhabit his city with the praise and worship of *Yahweh*. David is known for his worship of the Lord, and so is his city, Jerusalem.

CHAPTER FIVE

JERUSALEM:
CITY OF GOD

If I forget you, O Jerusalem, Let my right hand
forget its skill. —PSALM 137:5

In the past three thousand years, Jerusalem has experienced more sorrow than any city in the world. Twenty-six empires have conquered and occupied her. The city has been leveled numerous times by various violent invaders. And yet, each time the walls have been rebuilt and the city reoccupied by the Jews. In the midst of destruction and despite ongoing pogroms and holocausts, they have never ceased to cry out, "Next year in Jerusalem!" They utter the words at the Seder on the eve of Passover. In the Amidah, the silent part of the prayer, they pray, "May our eyes behold thy return to Zion in mercy." Traditional Jews face the east and fast and pray for the return of the Jews to the Holy City.

In saying grace after meals, traditional Jews plead that "the Almighty might rebuild Jerusalem speedily in our days." In 1991, when "Operation Solomon" took place, many Ethiopian Jews were brought back to the land of the Bible. They only knew two words in Hebrew, *Yerushalayim* and *shalom*— "Jerusalem" and the word of greeting which means "peace." Everything in the life of a Jew, the very scarlet thread of Judaism and the Jewish people, has run through the heart of Jerusalem, the holiest of cities for both Christians and Jews for two thousand years.

Jerusalem has been broken and abused, but one day she will be completely renewed. In the New Testament, John the Revelator declares in his mighty vision of the end times,

> Then I, John, saw the holy city, New Jerusalem, coming
> down out of heaven from God, prepared as a bride adorned for
> her husband.
>
> REVELATION 21:2

For all of the stress and strain of the last sixty-plus years, a new day is coming, when Jerusalem will experience true and everlasting peace!

As the center of Israel's worship, Jerusalem was preceded by Shiloh, where Joshua placed the tabernacle and the Ark of the Covenant, around the thirteenth century B.C. Some three thousand years later, King David made Jerusalem his capital. After David's son Solomon built the magnificent Temple there, every aspect of Jewish life became focused around Jerusalem. It was the center of commerce and religion. Jews came to Jerusalem for the feasts of Passover, Pentecost, and Tabernacles. They thronged Jerusalem to bring their sacrifices, to study the Torah, and to rejoice.

Even Jesus of Nazareth went to Jerusalem each year, as Luke declares: "His parents went to Jerusalem every year at the Feast of the Passover" (Luke 2:41). Jesus foresaw the sorrows and tragedies that would come upon Jerusalem, and He wept over the city. Indeed, for Him it was a city of tears. He prophesied its destruction by the Emperor Titus, and the Romans destroyed the city in 70 A.D. They left "not one stone on top of another," just as Jesus had forewarned in Matthew 24:2.

Down through the centuries even greater indignities have been heaped upon the ancient capital, and all too often America has led the international pack with ruthless and unnatural demands in contemporary times. How terrible that so much of the world's injustice has been focused here, on this city and on these people.

Contrary to what you may hear, when the Old City was under Jordanian sovereignty between 1948 and 1967, Muslims the world over did not bother to make pilgrimages to the Al-Aqsa Mosque in Jerusalem. Today the power-brokers say the site of the Muslim mosque is of great importance to Arabs, yet after the Six-Day War in 1967, the traffic was one-way. Israeli Arabs flocked to Egypt by the thousands, while not even a trickle of Egyptians trekked to Jerusalem. The fifteen million Egyptian Muslims felt no urge to make the pilgrimage to Jerusalem to pray at the Al-Aqsa Mosque. They did not long to see the Dome of the Rock, as some have said, in spite of the fact that the bus fare was a mere forty dollars and the Israeli army assured their safety.

The prophetic history of Jerusalem has been ignored or conveniently forgotten by those determined to rape her once again. The ancient city is treated with supreme disrespect. For example, American embassies are never located in any city except the accredited capital of the nation. Jerusalem is the heart and soul of Israel and its true capital, but America has only con-sular offices there, a second-level presence. For politically correct reasons, our embassy has been located at Tel Aviv. Despite the Jerusalem Embassy Relocation Act (U.S. Senate Bill S. 1332, Public Law 104-45 of the 104th Congress) legislation to force the White House to move the embassy, the answer is still a resounding no.

America's foreign-affairs specialists have an overriding desire to placate the Arab world, assuring that the status of Jerusalem remains open to nego-tiation. But it is diplomacy more appropriate for the theater of the absurd; in fact, it is sheer hypocrisy. I was in Dhahran when America spent billions of dollars to defend Saudi Arabia, a dictatorship, and American blood was being shed to restore another dictatorship in Kuwait. We gave Kuwait back to the Kuwaitis and paid billions to the Arab world for their show of force. Our secretary of state paid homage to one of the most notorious aggressor-nations on Earth, Syria, and its late president, Hafez al Assad. I was shocked to see America's leaders groveling before these terrorists.

I stood near the Kuwait-Saudi border with General Khalid bin Sultan as he reviewed the Syrian high command, never thinking even in my wildest imagination that the money we were paying them would be used to buy mis-siles from North Korea for one purpose only: to mobilize for war against Israel. Syria continues to threaten the safety and security of Israel at this writing.

More blood has been shed over the stones of Jerusalem than any spot on Earth for thousands of years. The attempts throughout history to desecrate this holy place are not coincidental; they are not mere chance events. I am convinced they are demonic acts, birthed from the bowels of Hell itself. They are events that will one day be consummated by the wrath of God Almighty against those who dare to lift their hand against Jerusalem and God's chosen people, the Jews. The Bible assures us that the worst battle in all of history, the Battle of Armageddon, will be waged for control of this city; but He who holds title deed to the land will have the final word.

If claims are true that Muslim countries have treated the Jews in their midst fairly and in democratic fashion, then why have the Jews in those Arab nations been forced to flee for safety to Israel? Why have Jews been driven to return to the land of Palestine throughout the centuries? Quite simply, it is because of the unspeakable persecutions they have endured. Under Islamic law, Jews and Christians are granted slight protection because of a policy called "Dhimmi." Discriminatory practices against Christians and Jews are listed in the covenant "Shurut," attributed to the Caliph Omar 634-644 A.D. Consider the implications of just these historic restrictions listed in the *Encyclopedia Judaica*:

> The Islamic courts would not admit the sworn testimony of Jews and Christians.
>
> Their graves had to be level with the ground so that anyone could walk over them.
>
> Their houses and tombs were not allowed to be higher than those of Muslims.
>
> They were not to employ Muslims in their service.
>
> They were not to raise their voices in churches or be seen in public with a Cross.
>
> Jews were to wear yellow cloth sashes, and for Christians the color blue.
>
> The color of their shoes had to be different from that of Muslim's shoes.

They were to accommodate Muslim travelers for three days free of charge.

Subjects were to honor Muslims and stand in their presence.

If struck, they must not hit back.

The Qur'an was not to be taught to Christians and Jews.

The building of new churches and synagogues was prohibited.

Jews and Christians were not to ride horses or camels, but only donkeys.

Christians were forbidden to ring their church bells, a ban that remained in force for one thousand years until the mid-nineteenth century. The Muezzin, on the other hand, is called loudly five times a day from every minaret, "Allah is one God, and Mohammed is his prophet."[25]

So much for tolerance. Are these just archaic Islamic policies from centuries past? Hardly. A Christian who has that illusion should try making his residence in any one of the twenty Arab dictatorships in the Middle East. What happens to a Christian who practices his faith with enthusiasm in one of these Muslim countries? His life will be short on this Earth, for he will be imprisoned and most likely beheaded. Islam is not just a religion; it is a way of life. It impacts every aspect of society in a Muslim nation, and it is making inroads and having an impact in other nations worldwide, including America.

In 1514 Jerusalem's Golden Gate was sealed by Muslim authorities. It remains sealed to this day. The reason behind that act is believed to have been inspired by the prophecy that the Messiah would enter Jerusalem through the Golden Gate, and also because Christians had used this gate for their Palm Sunday processions. Today, a Muslim cemetery stands just outside the gate for that reason. A Muslim cemetery was also built on top of Mount Calvary for a similar reason.

Many have witnessed the desecration of the holy city, including some who admit no love for God or his commands. Karl Marx, father of communism, admitted in an article in the *New York Daily Tribune* published on April 15, 1854, "The sedentary population of Jerusalem numbers about 15,500 souls, of whom four thousand are Moslem and eight thousand are Jews. Nothing equals the misery and suffering of the Jews who are the constant object of Moslem oppression and intolerance." Even Marx could see the truth.

The oppression and intolerance has never stopped. Neglect and abuse of Jewish holy places has continued for decades. Between 1948 and 1967, conditions were considered deplorable, even by medieval standards. Jewish residents were expelled from the Jordanian-controlled area, and Jordan transformed part of its territory into an armed camp, with guns, land mines, and snipers.

Under Jordanian oversight, Jews were not permitted to live in Jordan. The country's Civil Law # 6 was very specific: "Any man will be a Jordanian subject if he is not Jewish."[26] Jews were barred from worshiping at the Western Wall. The Jewish Quarter in the old city was destroyed, and fifty-eight synagogues were demolished. Zion's Karaite Synagogue was destroyed, the Kurdish Synagogue was destroyed, and the Warsaw Synagogue was destroyed. These are just a few of the places of worship destroyed and then used as cowsheds, stables, or public lavatories. Others were razed. Still, the world cries to the Jews in Israel, "Let the peace process continue! Give up your land for peace!" Until 1967 the Jews did not have the land, and they certainly did not have peace. They won back the land God had given them by wresting it from those whose aim was to decimate them, and today the land provides a buffer by which Israel can defend herself. How, then, can we or anyone ask the Jews to relinquish what they have suffered so long and paid so great a price to win back from their enemies?

In Exodus 23:25 the Lord God declared, "And I will take sickness away from the midst of you." Many believe the time will come when the misery will depart, but there seems to be a sinister force that works to destroy the ancient city and its people. Some call it a death angel, and others say it is a demon; but they feel some sinister force hovering over the city of Jerusalem, a demonic entity that holds the wounded soul of Israel in distress. It is a brutal form of terrorism that never ends, with moments of joy and days of deep heartache and despair.

When will it end? What strange mysteries are yet to be uncovered on this soil? How can anyone explain the injustices that take place on a daily basis? Columnist Richard Cohen defined the consummate problem: "How the Arab world will ever come to terms with Israel when Israelis are portrayed as the devil incarnate is hard to figure out."[27] It will never end until Arab schoolchildren are not subjected to anti-Semitic tirades disguised as education.

Kindergarteners are taught to hate the Jews. King Ibn Saud of Saudi Arabia was quoted as saying, "For a Muslim to kill a Jew, or for him to be killed by a Jew, ensures him an immediate entry into Heaven and into the august presence of God Almighty."[28] According to Syrian Minister of Education (1968) Suleyman Al-Khash, "The hatred which we indoctrinate into the minds of our children from their birth is sacred."[29]

In 1977 the Hashemite Kingdom of Jordan provided a guide for instructors of children in the first grade. It was used to educate West Bank teachers. It reads in part: "Implant in the soul of the pupil the rule of Islam that if the enemies occupy even one inch of the Islamic lands, jihad (holy war) becomes imperative for every Muslim."[30]

Standing in the warm sun at the White House on September 13, 1993, I watched a brave Israeli prime minister grit his teeth with a crooked smile as the president of the United States shoved his thumb into his backbone and forced him to shake hands with Yasser Arafat for the sake of a politically expedient "photo op."

Yitzhak Rabin was a gentleman, however, and took the fateful step with eyes open. I will never forget the words he spoke at the White House ceremony: "We have come to you from Jerusalem, ancient and eternal capital of the Jewish people." Chairman Arafat never mentioned Jerusalem during his visit at the White House, but in his speech that same evening, he beamed via satellite to the Arab world, "By God's will, we shall raise our flag over the walls of Jerusalem, capital of the Palestinian State, over all minarets and churches in the city." We should not be ignorant of what Arafat had planned for the churches and synagogues in Jerusalem. Thousands of jubilant Arabs draped Palestinian flags over the city walls upon hearing the chairman's words.

When Prime Minister Yitzhak Rabin invited me to his office, he shared his hopes for the restoration of his people, an end to hostilities, and the beginning of peace in the land. He dreamed of his grandchildren not having to go through what he and his generation had experienced. He was a great general and a fine prime minister, but he was keenly aware of the enormous economic pressure on his nation—and perhaps a little too willing to compromise because of it. I considered him a friend, and I know his motives were not small or naïve. He loved Jerusalem with all his heart, and he was willing to give his life for her if it came to that. In the end, he did.

This pinpoints another significant reason why Christians should rejoice in Israel's physical restoration and strongly support her continued existence in the Middle East: Jerusalem is the prophesied capital of our Messiah Jesus when He returns. Holy Scripture reveals that Zion is to be the seat of the Messiah's earthly reign. The nations on Earth will come to worship King Jesus in Jerusalem. From there He will rule as King of kings and Lord of lords! This is revealed in several scriptures:

> Many people shall come and say,
>   "Come, and let us go up to the mountain of the Lord,
>   To the house of the God of Jacob;
>   He will teach us His ways,
>   And we shall walk in His paths."
>   For out of Zion shall go forth the law,
>   And the word of the Lord from Jerusalem.
>
> ISAIAH 2:3

> "Look upon Zion, the city of our appointed feasts;
>   Your eyes will see Jerusalem, a quiet home,
>   A tabernacle that will not be taken down;

Not one of its stakes will ever be removed,
Nor will any of its cords be broken."

ISAIAH 33:20

"Thus says the Lord:
 'I will return to Zion,
 And dwell in the midst of Jerusalem.
 Jerusalem shall be called the City of Truth,
 The Mountain of the Lord of hosts,
 The Holy Mountain.'"

ZECHARIAH 8:3

"I will not give sleep to my eyes
 Or slumber to my eyelids,
Until I find a place for the Lord,
 A dwelling place for the Mighty One of Jacob."

For Your servant David's sake,
 Do not turn away the face of Your Anointed.

For the Lord has chosen Zion;
 He has desired [it] for His dwelling place:
"This [is] My resting place forever;
 Here I will dwell, for I have desired it."

PSALM 132:4-5,10,13-14

*"Moreover I will appoint a place for my people Israel, and will plant them, that they may dwell in a place of their own, and **move no more**; neither shall the children of wickedness afflict them any more, as previously."*

II SAMUEL 7:10 (emphasis mine)

It is evident from Scripture that the Sovereign Lord of Creation chose Jerusalem as His earthly capital. This decision was made by the very same God who promised to restore His covenant, and the Jewish people to the sacred city and surrounding land in the last days before the Second Coming of the Messiah. How can Christians look for and welcome Jesus' prophesied return and not rejoice in and actively support the Jewish return to their homeland?

God described the details and boundaries of the land in Genesis 15:18: "On the same day the Lord made a covenant with Abram, saying, 'To your descendants I have given this land, from the river of Egypt to the great river, the River Euphrates." This was a royal land grant, perpetual and unconditional.

> *"Also I give to you and your descendants after you the land in which you are a stranger, all the land of Canaan, as an everlasting possession; and I will be their God."*
>
> GENESIS 17:8

> *"I am the Lord God of Abraham your father and the God of Isaac; the land on which you lie I will give to you and your descendants."*
>
> GENESIS 28:13

God has never revoked Abraham's title deed to the land, nor has He given it to anyone else.

The spot where God confirmed His covenant is an area north of Jerusalem between Bethel and Ai. It is in the heart of what is called the West Bank, or Judea and Samaria. (The United Nations refers to this as "occupied territory" and demands that Israel relinquish it.) An inalienable right is one that cannot be given away. The Bible declares this to be so in Leviticus 25:23. The people were forbidden to sell the land because, "The land shall not be sold permanently, for the land is Mine; for you are strangers and sojourners with Me."

Jerusalem is the only city God claims as His own, and it is called the City of God and the Holy City in Scripture. He declared to Solomon in II Chronicles 33:7, "In this house and in Jerusalem, which I have chosen out of all the tribes of Israel, I will put My name forever."

God sent me to be a witness at the 1991 international peace conference at the Royal Palace in Madrid, Spain. I challenged Secretary of State James Baker to recognize Jerusalem as Israel's capital. I asked, "Why can't America recognize Jerusalem as Israel's capital? Secondly, we are moving a military presence into the Arab world for security. Why can't we have a military presence in Israel to help its security? It has suffered so greatly and has especially paid a dear price during the Persian Gulf War." Baker was incensed by my remarks. He said he refused to be entangled in a fruitless debate, and that the status of Jerusalem should be determined by negotiations. I have made much the same challenge to every political leader I have met over the last nineteen years at conferences and summits around the world.

To this day America has refused to recognize Jerusalem as Israel's capital. This is a grave mistake. By declaring East Jerusalem as "occupied territory," the U.S. is effectively calling for the redivision of Jerusalem. I have shouted Begin's words to world leaders from the White House in Washington to the Royal Palace in Madrid with the words, "God does not recognize America's non-recognition of Jerusalem!"

The late Dr. Jerry Falwell observed,

> God deals with nations in accord with how those nations deal with Israel…Down through the centuries, those nations, those potentates, those emperors, who dared to malign the apple of God's eye, the Jewish people, paid severely…I think I can take pride in saying that outside the Jewish community itself, the best friends the Jews and the State of Israel have in the world are among Bible-believing Christians here in America. We believe that God honors His Word. God blesses His people, and God honors those who honor His Word.[31]

For sixty-two years Israel has been America's one true friend and strategic ally in the Middle East, yet today Dr. Falwell's words continue to fall on deaf ears. The actions of President Obama and his administration have clouded the relationship between the two nations. Israel's Prime Minister Benjamin Netanyahu was stiff-armed during his March visit to Washington, D.C. In the words of one reporter, Obama "treated [Netanyahu] like some third-world, tin-pot dictator" and even denied him the customary state dinner.

Obama's arrogant and cavalier treatment of the prime minister of Israel has endangered the longstanding alliance between Israel and the United States—one that dates back to the presidency of Harry S. Truman. It was Truman who courageously led the world in being the first country to recognize Israel on May 14, 1948. A year or so after the Jewish state came into being, its Chief Rabbi paid an official call on Truman. The Israeli dignitary blessed the president with the words: "God put you in your mother's womb so you would be the instrument to bring about Israel's rebirth after two thousand years."[32] Tears flowed down Harry Truman's face.

Since Harry Truman, all U.S. presidents have considered the support of Israel a moral imperative, believing that a secure and strong Israel is in America's self-interest. Now it appears America has a president who is not going to celebrate the birthday of the nation and even further disputes the birth certificate.

Are the battle lines about to be drawn before the cataclysmic event that will usher in the return of the Messiah to Jerusalem? The Scriptures give evidence that a "man of sin" will step forth with a plan for world peace. In light of some of the strange things happening today, it is imperative that the Church be alert to developments that could signal further fulfillment of prophecy. In Luke 12:40, Jesus warned, "Therefore you also be ready, for the Son of Man is coming at an hour you do not expect."

There are certain events that are to serve as a sign or forewarning that the last days are upon us. The prophets outlined three specific conditions that would have to be met for the end of time to come—all of which center on Israel:

✧ The Jewish nation would be reborn. This was fulfilled in 1948.

✧ The Jews would repossess Jerusalem and the sacred sites. This was fulfilled in 1967.

✧ The Temple would be rebuilt upon its historic site. This condition has not yet been fulfilled.

I believe Israel is the key to America's survival, and the future is certain. Although no person knows God's timetable or when the prophetic clock will chime the midnight hour, we can be sure of one thing: Jerusalem is God's city, and one day soon Jesus will reign from there.

CHAPTER SIX

JESUS & JERUSALEM

Now when the days of her purification according
to the Law of Moses were completed, they brought Him to
Jerusalem to present Him to the Lord. —LUKE 2:22

J
esus was the literal Son of God, and God was His Father. However, as Mary's child He was also a natural descendant of King David. Jesus, therefore, is called both the Son of God and the Son of Man in the Bible. It is also no accident that He was born in Bethlehem of Judah, David's hometown, which was prophesied in Micah 5:2:

> *"But you, Bethlehem Ephrathah,*
> *Though you are little among the thousands of Judah,*
> *Yet out of you shall come forth to Me*
> *The One to be Ruler in Israel,*
> *Whose goings forth are from of old,*
> *From everlasting."*

Just after His birth, Mary and Joseph took Jesus to Jerusalem to comply with God's commandments for the purification of the mother after childbirth and for the redemption of a first-born child (Luke 2:22-24). While the young family was in the Temple, they encountered a stranger—Simeon—just as they were presenting the baby to the Lord. The old man walked up and took the baby right from Mary's arms. Neither Mary nor Joseph was alarmed; after all, they had very recently entertained angels and shepherds in a stable. It was a fitting introduction for the child who would turn the world upside down.

The old man cradled the child gently in his arms, and with tears in his eyes, turned his face heavenward. Quietly he prayed,

> *"Lord, now You are letting Your servant depart in peace,*
> *According to Your word;*
> *For my eyes have seen Your salvation*
> *Which You have prepared before the face of all peoples,*
> *A light to bring revelation to the Gentiles,*
> *And the glory of Your people Israel."*
>
> LUKE 2:29-32

Perhaps Simeon explained to the awed mother that God had promised him he would see the Messiah before he died. As the years passed and he grew old, maybe he had begun to wonder if God would keep His promise— the promise he now held in his arms. However, there was more to Simeon's message. Along with the Good News of the arrival of the Messiah, he gave Mary an admonition:

> *Then Simeon blessed them, and he said to Mary, the baby's mother, "This child is destined to cause many in Israel to fall, but he will be a joy to many others. He has been sent as a sign from God, but many will oppose him. As a result, the deepest thoughts of many hearts will be revealed. And a sword will pierce your very soul."*
>
> LUKE 2:34-35 NLT

As Simeon paused, an old woman ran up to the group:

> *She gave thanks to the Lord, and spoke of Him to all those who looked for redemption in Jerusalem.*
>
> LUKE 2:38

From His birth, Jesus was recognized as the promised Messiah by many in Jerusalem.

After the purification rites, Joseph was warned in a dream that Herod was seeking the child to kill him. He took Mary and Jesus and departed for Egypt until another angel was sent to tell them it was safe to return to their homeland. The family settled in Nazareth in the Galilee region, but each year they returned to Jerusalem for the Passover celebration.

When Jesus was twelve, Mary and Joseph discovered that He was not with them as they returned to Nazareth after celebrating Passover in Jerusalem. They searched the caravan and then turned back to the city to look for their son. After three days of frantically seeking Him, He was found—not making mischief nor apologetic for having stayed behind—but in the Temple with a group of Bible scholars discussing the Scriptures. The men in the group were amazed at Jesus' understanding and knowledge of God's Word.

The years following the Temple incident give us little insight into Jesus' life. Apparently He worked with Joseph in the carpenter shop, studied with the local rabbis in the synagogue, and grew strong and robust as a young man. He began His ministry when He was baptized at the Jordan River by His cousin John. He performed His first miracle at a wedding He attended with His mother, where He turned water into wine. Then He chose twelve men to accompany Him on His travels.

Jesus moved about in the Galilee region preaching, teaching, healing, and performing other miracles—establishing His credentials as the Messiah to a people hungry for rescue. He made no attempt to ingratiate Himself to the religious Jewish leaders of the day, preferring instead to reach out to the common people and those "obvious" sinners—tax collectors and prostitutes among them. Thus, He was fulfilling Isaiah 9:2:

> *The people who walked in darkness*
> *Have seen a great light;*
> *Those who dwelt in the land of the shadow of death,*
> *Upon them a light has shined.*

It was after Peter's confession of faith in Matthew 16:16, "You are the Christ, the Son of the living God," that Jesus set his face toward Jerusalem to observe the Passover. However, first He would perform one of His most noted miracles in Bethany, just outside Jerusalem. This was the miraculous resurrection of Lazarus, who had been in the grave four days. After this great miracle, Jesus entered Jerusalem on a lowly donkey, the exuberant welcome of the crowds ringing in His ears. He did not go to win the city as He had the Galilee, however. He went to be rejected, to die a cruel death, and to rise from the dead three days after.

It was just before Passover began in Jerusalem, when the priests in the Temple would slit the throats of thousands of spotless lambs to cover the sins of Israel, while the Messiah hung on a Roman cross to pay the price for the sin of all mankind. Totally innocent and without sin, Jesus had been beaten and scourged beyond recognition, stripped of His clothes, and nailed in ignominy to the most brutal instrument of torture. Within hours He died and was buried. Then three days later—after conquering death, Hell, and the grave—He arose just as He had prophesied He would!

Jesus had to go to Jerusalem to accomplish the task the Father had given Him—that of becoming the Sacrificial Lamb which would take away the sins of the world—the Passover Lamb. Had He stayed in the Galilee, He would have simply been one of many itinerant preachers—unremarkable and unusual—but still only a preacher. God had a bigger plan for Him than most thought He would accomplish.

At the dawn of creation, God was faced with His creatures' rebellion. The first eleven chapters of Genesis relate the story of mankind's unrelenting mutiny—the fall of man, Cain murdering Abel, mankind's descent into depravity, and the Flood. Following the Tower of Babel episode, God turned his attention to one man—Abraham. From that one man, He fashioned the nation of Israel as His chosen people. This people would bear witness to the truth about God in the midst of all who had turned their backs on Him, the one true Creator.

Even as Israel's story was marked by cycles of intense worship that turned to backsliding, apostasy, and idolatry, a fresh shoot sprang forth from the rotting stump—Jesus was born. With His life, He purchased the forgiveness of sins and opened the door to the kingdom of God to the Gentiles—the other nations—as well as the nation of Israel.

In his humiliation, Jesus revealed the heart of God to a degree never known before:

> For God so loved the world that He gave His only begotten Son, that whoever believes in Him should not perish but have everlasting life.
>
> JOHN 3:16

He also sowed the seeds of the destruction of the kingdom of darkness; Satan's hold on the planet was broken. In Matthew 16:18 Jesus avowed that the very gates of Hell would not stand against His Church. Since then, the Church has had the glorious task of bombarding the gates of Hell to free its captives to become the men and women God designed them to be.

In Jerusalem, Jesus carried out the unlikely series of tasks by which He unlocked the mystery hidden from all previous generations. The writer of Philippians captured God's purpose and plan perfectly in chapter 2, verses 6-11:

> ...who, being in the form of God, did not consider it robbery to be equal with God, but made Himself of no reputation, taking the form of a bondservant, and coming in the likeness of men. And being found in appearance as a man, He humbled Himself and became obedient to the point of death, even the death of the cross. Therefore God also has highly exalted Him and given Him the name which is above every name, that at the name of Jesus every knee should bow, of those in heaven, and of those on earth, and of those under the earth, and that every tongue should confess that Jesus Christ is Lord, to the glory of God the Father.

Jerusalem became the focal point of God's determination not to lose mankind—despite our best efforts to squander our lives in sin and degradation.

It is God's city, and though the *salem* in its name refers to peace, there always has been and continues to be strife, contention, and conflict, Why? The answer is simple—Satan is determined to wrest God's creation from His hand.

There are only two instances in the New Testament of Jesus weeping publicly—just before He raised Lazarus from the dead (John 11:35), and when He rode into Jerusalem on a donkey (Luke 19:41). As Jesus entered the city, He warned the people of Israel that a time would soon come when their enemies would encircle them, hem them in on every side, and leave not one stone standing atop another. He said this would happen because they had rejected Him as their Messiah:

> *Your enemies will not leave a single stone in place, because*
> *you did not accept your opportunity for salvation.*
>
> **(L U K E   1 9 : 4 4   N L T) .**

When the disciples asked when these things would come to pass, Jesus used the opportunity to teach them about future events. He talked of tribulation, of armies surrounding Jerusalem, and of Gentile domination "until the times of the Gentiles are fulfilled" (Luke 21:24). Forty days after Jesus' resurrection, He ascended back to the Father from the Mount of Olives in Jerusalem. Upon Jesus' command, the disciples tarried in Jerusalem until the Day of Pentecost, when the Holy Spirit was poured out upon them in the Upper Room. The Church was gloriously born in Jerusalem.

CHAPTER SEVEN

JERUSALEM,
MESSIAH'S CAPITAL

For the Lord shall build up Zion, He shall
appear in his glory. —PSALM 102:16

When we pray for Jerusalem, we are saying "*Maranatha!* Come, Messiah!"

The Messiah is indeed coming back, and He is coming to Jerusalem. That is something on which both Jews and Christians agree. As Christians, we believe we know His identity; He is Jesus of Nazareth. The Jewish people say they do not know who He is. There is no question, however, that when Messiah comes, everyone will recognize Him.

In 1995, from the top of Megiddo, I looked out over the plain that was prophesied to be the site of the Battle of Armageddon. The Plain of Jezreel spreads from the Mediterranean to the Jordan River. Napoleon is said to have stood on the same hill and, awed by its grandeur, exclaimed, "All the armies of the world could maneuver their forces on this vast plain."[33]

Looking down on what the Old Testament prophet Joel called the "Valley of Jehoshaphat" (Joel 3:2), I found myself wondering how long it would be before this scenic, tranquil spot would be filled with the men and machines of death and war, ultimately bringing back the Messiah Jesus. It seems inevitable. When Israel was reborn on May 14, 1948, she was immediately embroiled in a controversy over ownership of the land. The Middle East conflict has become a sore that never heals—a pit of white-hot coals that can burst into roaring flames at any second. It is a black hole of strife and enmity, which could suck in all the nations of the world.

Since my first climb up that prophetic hill, little has changed. As it was then, so it is now. It appears that Israel can do anything or nothing and be castigated for every problem that springs up on planet Earth. In early 2010, a housing project was initiated in the Ramat Shlomo neighborhood, in *northwest* Jerusalem. It is a sign of the basic irrationality of the conflict that every point on the Jerusalem compass is referred to erroneously as "East Jerusalem." This loaded term is cynically used to designate anywhere Arabs live in the city, despite the reality that more Jews than Arabs live in Jerusalem's eastern neighborhoods.

Many U.S. politicians have often failed to take seriously Israel's repeated overtures to the Palestinians. Perhaps Mr. Obama should review the history of the rejection by Palestinian leaders of Israel's olive branches. Noises from the Obama administration sound suspiciously like the same old rhetoric I heard in 1995 from a Radio Amman broadcast: Israel was being boycotted by the Islamic world; Israel should be barred from the United Nations General Assembly meetings; the United States is condemned for supporting Israeli aggression in the Palestinian occupied land. A later item in the report quoted a Kuwaiti man as saying, "The main obstacles to a just and comprehensive Middle East peace is Israel's intransigence and refusal to withdraw from the occupied Arab territories, as well as its denial of the Palestinian people's legitimate rights."[34]

A few weeks later a prominent Israeli government official said to me, "In the 1930s the strength and the might of Nazi Germany was its steel and coal. Now we have the Arabs with their oil. Their thrust is anti-Semitic now, just as it was then; and the attitude of the Western democracies is one of appeasement now, as it was then."

How will this end? Many Israelis take comfort in the words of the ancient Hebrew prophets. We have already seen that virtually all of the significant historical events in the story of the Jewish people were foretold before they actually came to pass. If these prophecies proved to be accurate, can we not expect other prophetic passages to reveal the future of Israel and the world?

The Old Testament is accepted by the Jews as the Word of God. In addition to the Psalms, which deal with prophecy, there are sixteen other prophetic books. Christians accept both the Old and New Testament writings, which are rife with prophetic utterances. For hundreds of years, Jewish and Christian Bible scholars have studied these prophecies. Many agree there is one inescapable conclusion: The Middle East crisis will continue to escalate until it threatens world peace and eventually brings the nations to Armageddon.

The warnings of Bible scholars who research prophetic events have been echoed by secular academics. Before his death in 2008, Soviet exile Aleksandr Solzhenitsyn warned:

> There are meaningful warnings that history gives a threatened or perishing society. Such are, for instance, the decadence of art, or a lack of great statesmen. There are open and evident warnings, too. The center of your democracy and of your culture is left without electric power for a few hours only, and all of a sudden crowds…start looting and creating havoc. The smooth surface film must be very thin, then; the social system quite unstable and unhealthy.
>
> But the fight for our planet, physical and spiritual, a fight of cosmic proportions, is not a vague matter of the future; it has already started. The forces of Evil have begun their decisive offensive; you can feel their pressure.[35]

To better understand what is happening today, and when the Messiah will return, it is imperative then to examine the writings of the prophets. We can begin with the prophet Daniel and his first recorded prophecies, which were the result of King Nebuchadnezzar's dream. The late Dr. Harry A. Ironside called Daniel's prophecy "the most complete, and yet the most simple, prophetic picture that we have in all the Word of God."[36]

Nebuchadnezzar's dream was of an image of a man. His head was gold, his breast and arms were silver, his midsection and thighs were brass, his legs were iron, and his feet were part iron and part clay. As the king watched, a great stone crashed down upon the image, smashing it so completely that the wind blew away the pieces. The stone then became a great mountain that filled the whole Earth (Daniel 2:31-35).

When called upon to interpret the king's dream, Daniel's explanation was simple yet profound. The head of gold represented Nebuchadnezzar, whose power in the Babylonian Empire was absolute. Later scholars summarized the dream as follows: The silver portion of the statue represented the Medo-Persian Empire, which came after the fall of Babylon. The belly and thighs of brass represented the Grecian Empire of Alexander the Great. The legs of iron were emblematic of the Roman Empire, while the ten toes of iron and clay represented the revival of the Roman Empire in the last days, or ten leaders of a European federation.

The stone is symbolic of an all-powerful divine force, which will ultimately destroy all earthly kingdoms and be recognized as supreme. Many agree this refers to the coming kingdom of the Messiah, which will be established upon His return to Earth. Jesus quotes Psalm 118:22 when He refers to Himself as the "stone which the builders rejected" (First Coming) and says He will become the "chief cornerstone" (Second Coming) (Mark 9:10).

Daniel had another dream recorded in Daniel 7:1-7, which is thought to reinforce Nebuchadnezzar's earlier dream. Daniel saw a lion with eagle's wings, a bear with three ribs in its mouth, a leopard with four wings and four heads, and a strange, ten-horned beast that was "dreadful and terrible, and strong exceedingly." The lion represented the Babylonian Empire, the bear was the Medo-Persian Empire. the leopard was the Empire of Alexander the Great, and the beast with ten horns was figurative of the coming Roman Empire or European federation.

Near the end of his life, Daniel began praying about returning to Jerusalem. He confessed his own sins and the sins of his people, crying out to God for forgiveness. During his prayer, the angel Gabriel appeared to Daniel and revealed a timetable of coming events that would affect Israel. This angelic vision is often referred to as "the vision of seventy weeks." It may very well be the backbone of all prophecy. This mathematical revelation gave the Jews the exact time to expect the coming of their Messiah. It also foretold His death, the destruction of Jerusalem, the rise of the Antichrist, and the ultimate establishment of the Messiah's kingdom on Earth.

The prophecy declared that seventy weeks of trouble would come upon the Jewish people. The weeks were not actually units of days but rather years—490 years that would cover a series of events determining the eternal destiny of the Jewish people. Daniel prophesied that from the time the order was given to rebuild Jerusalem, 483 years would elapse before the coming of the Messiah and His rejection (Daniel 9:24-27).

It is interesting to note that the Bible gives the exact date when Artaxerxes, King of Persia, would grant the decree that Jerusalem and its Temple should be rebuilt: "And it came to pass in the month of Nisan, in the twentieth year of King Artaxerxes" (Nehemiah 2:1). The king had ascended the throne in 465 B.C., and his twentieth year would have been 445 B.C. When translating the date given on our calendar, the king's decree to rebuild Jerusalem would have been issued on March 14, 445 B.C.

Precisely 483 years after that decree, the Messiah rode into Jerusalem as had been prophesied in Zechariah 9:9:

> *"Rejoice greatly, O daughter of Zion!*
> *Shout, O daughter of Jerusalem!*
> *Behold, your King is coming to you;*
> *He is just and having salvation,*
> *Lowly and riding on a donkey,*
> *A colt, the foal of a donkey.*

Daniel's extraordinary prophecy further decreed that the Messiah would be "cut off," a euphemism for being killed. After that, an army would march into Jerusalem and destroy it and the rebuilt Temple.

We are left to wonder what happened to the last week, the last seven years covered by Daniel's vision. Those events are yet to take place. The end of the age will be highlighted by the return of the Messiah, the bodily res-urrection of the dead, and the Millennium—when Messiah reigns on Earth for one thousand years. Scripture tells us, however, that the last seven years before the Messiah returns to Earth will be the most horrific time since the world began. Matthew 24:21 describes it this way:

> *For then there will be great tribulation, such as has not been*
> *since the beginning of the world until this time, no, nor ever shall be.*

Daniel recorded in chapter 12, verse 1:

> *And there shall be a time of trouble,*
> *Such as never was since there was a nation,*
> *Even to that time.*

As this fearsome week begins, the ten-horned beast Daniel described will arrive on the scene in the form of the revived Roman Empire. Out of the European federation will emerge a powerful political leader whose magnetic charm and personal appeal will win the confidence and loyalty of the world. The Bible identifies this individual as the Antichrist. This individual will offer solutions to the perplexing problems and international crises, which threaten the very existence of the world. Immensely powerful, the Antichrist will sign a seven-year peace treaty with Israel (Daniel 9:27).

In the beginning everything will go well. The peace treaty imposed by the powerful Antichrist will relieve centuries of armed tension. Israel will be able to turn its full attention to the development of the country and its resources as never before. Some arrangement will even be made for the rebuilding of the Temple in Jerusalem. There, sacrifices and oblations will be resumed.

After three and one-half years, just when everything seems to be going well for the Jewish people, perhaps for the first time ever, the Antichrist will break the treaty with Israel. He will halt the sacrifices and oblations in the Temple and declare himself to be God. This is the desolation of abomination spoken of in Daniel 12:11.

Ezekiel picks up the prophetic narrative at this point. His credibility has already been established by his foretelling of the scattering and returning of Israel some twenty-centuries before the fact. His vision of the valley of dry bones (Ezekiel 37:1-10) is one of the most vivid and moving in the Bible.

The Lord showed Ezekiel that the bones represented Israel. Their dry and disconnected condition represented the dispersed Jews around the globe and their despair at ever becoming a nation united again. Ezekiel proclaimed the message God had given him, and his words infused a glimmer of hope into the hearts of the Jewish people across the centuries. In the midst of incredible persecution and suffering, the promise of God offered a lifeline:

> *For I will take you from among the nations, gather you out*
> *of all countries, and bring you into your own land.*
>
> EZEKIEL 36:24

The words of the prophet were like a brilliant light slicing through the gloom and darkness of the ghettos and death camps that housed the Jews over the centuries.

With the survival of the Jewish people and the rebirth of Israel as a nation, Ezekiel's prophetic track record is totally convincing. He speaks in specific detail about events that will bring the world to the precipice of Armageddon. In chapters 38 and 39, he gives a detailed account of a great military offensive, which will be launched against Israel by Russia (called Magog) and a confederation of Arab and European countries. Ezekiel identifies the other participants as Meshech and Tubal (Moscow and Tobolsk), Gomer (Germany and Slovakia), Togarmah (southern Russia and Turkey), Persia (modern-day Iran and possibly Iraq), and Ethiopia and Libya (the black descendants of Cush and the North Africa Arabs.)

Led by Russia, this force will arm itself and march against Israel. The assault will be totally unexpected because of Israel's treaty with the Antichrist, and the three-and-one-half years of peace. Russia's resolve to attack is clearly written in the pages of Holy Writ:

> *"You will say, 'I will go up against a land of unwalled vil-*
> *lages; I will go to a peaceful people, who dwell safely, all of them*
> *dwelling without walls, and having neither bars nor gates'—to*
> *take plunder and to take booty, to stretch out your hand against*
> *the waste places that are again inhabited, and against a peo-*
> *ple gathered from the nations, who have acquired livestock and*
> *goods, who dwell in the midst of the land."*
>
> EZEKIEL 38:11-12

The concerted attack on Israel will ultimately be one of Russia's most egregious military blunders. The battle will be brief and hideously destructive. Ezekiel's description of the "cloud to cover the land," a great shaking, earth-rending explosions, mountains toppling, and a deadly rain of hail and fire could signify nuclear warfare, but will more likely be the result of divine intervention. The Bible declares that God alone will destroy Israel's enemies in a supernatural way (Ezekiel 38:22). The defeat of its invaders will make Israel aware that God has protected them.

Only one-sixth of the Russian army will survive. So many will have died that it will take Israel seven months to bury the bodies and seven years to burn the weapons left on the battlefield. The devastation wrought by this battle will empower the Antichrist to make his move to establish his seat of government in Jerusalem under the pretext of protecting the holy city.

With only forty-two months remaining in the prophetic week, the Antichrist will, according to Daniel 11:44, assert his power, break his treaty with Israel, and face his first challenge—the massive Oriental army marching toward the Middle East. When the clash occurs, casualties will total one-third of the remaining world population, according to this passage in Revelation 9:16-18:

> *Now the number of the army of the horsemen was two hun-*
> *dred million; I heard the number of them. And thus I saw the*
> *horses in the vision: those who sat on them had breastplates of*
> *fiery red, hyacinth blue, and sulfur yellow; and the heads of the*

horses were like the heads of lions; and out of their mouths came
fire, smoke, and brimstone. By these three plagues a third of man-
kind was killed—by the fire and the smoke and the brimstone
which came out of their mouths.

Following this conflagration, the Antichrist will assume total economic control, forcing the population to take his mark on the hand or forehead in order to transact business. The penalty for opposing him will be death. The Antichrist will then implement his foolhardy plan to defeat the Messiah.

So here it is: the last great conflict. The battle lines will be drawn with the vortex in the Valley of Megiddo. Indescribable slaughter will be the result. It will be so terrible that Revelation 14:20 tells us blood will rise to the bridle of a horse for a distance of two hundred miles north and south of Jerusalem. As the battle reaches its climax, the Messiah will return. Jesus prophesied in Matthew 24:22,30:

"And unless those days were shortened, no flesh would be
saved; but for the elect's sake those days will be shortened.
    Then the sign of the Son of Man will appear in heaven, and
then all the tribes of the earth will mourn, and they will see the Son
of Man coming on the clouds of heaven with power and great glory."

CHAPTER EIGHT

ALL EYES ARE ON
JERUSALEM

"'... that David my servant may always have a lamp before
Me in Jerusalem, the city which I have chosen for Myself,
to put My name there.'" —I KINGS 11:36

Many Bible scholars say there is nothing to delay the return of the Messiah for those who serve Him. It could take place at any moment. Just the first four months of 2010 brought ten earthquakes that registered above 6.0 on the Richter Scale. The eruption of Eyjafjallajokull Volcano in Iceland brought European air travel to a complete standstill for nearly a week, stranding tens of thousands and costing airlines hundreds of millions of dollars.[37]

In Mark 13:7, Jesus told His disciples there would be "wars and rumors of wars"—which sounds too much like the daily newscasts worldwide. In verse 8, Jesus said,

> *For nation will rise against nation, and kingdom against kingdom. And there will be earthquakes in various places, and there will be famines and troubles. These are the beginnings of sorrows.*

Each subsequent generation takes a giant step closer to entering Daniel's seventieth week.

The perilous position of our planet has world leaders talking about a one-world government that will guarantee peace at any price. With a global economic crisis threatening more each day, the constant threat of terrorism from largely unidentifiable sources, and trillions being spent on arms and security measures, the desire for global peace might very well cause even those leaders who have knowledge of the warnings of the prophets of old to take a step back and consider implausible solutions.

This unbridled desire for global peace will ultimately lead to the rise of a governing force headed by a politician of singular appeal and power. The great historian Arnold Toynbee wrote:

> One of the most conspicuous marks of disintegration, as we have already noticed, is a phenomenon in the last stage but one of the decline and fall, when a disintegrating civilization purchases a reprieve by submitting to forcible political unification.[38]

Each succeeding president who takes up residence in the White House seems determined to divide Jerusalem in an attempt to pacify Russia, the European Union, and the Arab League—a move designed to gain favor worldwide. If or when this is successful, both Israel and America will suffer. Genesis 12:3 says,

> *I will bless those who bless you,*
> *And I will curse him who curses you;*
> *And in you all the families of the earth shall be blessed.*

We who believe the Bible must believe that it is in our nation's best interest to be a firm ally of Israel, and we must have a greater goal. Our greater goal is to see God's kingdom come on Earth—not through jihad or some kind of religious war—but through the propagation of the Good News about the Messiah Yeshua—Jesus.

Our Lord clearly gave His disciples a view of the future, beginning with the destruction of the Temple. In Matthew 24:2, Jesus prophesied that the Temple would be taken apart stone by stone forty years before it happened. In verses 32-36, Jesus laid out the key sign of His return to Earth and the end of the age, which was the sign of the fig tree. The fig tree has always been a symbol of Israel, and that fig tree bloomed on May 14,1948, in fulfillment of Isaiah 66:8:

> *Shall the earth be made to give birth in one day?*
> *Or shall a nation be born at once?*

The United Nations accepted the establishment of the nation of Israel on that day.

Jesus warned us not to set dates, for "of that day and hour no one knows" (Mark 13:32), but He said the generation that saw the blooming of the fig tree would not pass away until He came (Matthew 24:32-33).

A generation is most often defined as seventy to eighty years. If a person were ten years old in 1948, when this prophecy was fulfilled, that person would be in their seventies now. There is no question that we will not know the day or the hour, but Matthew 24 indicates we are very close to Messiah's return. The events in the Middle East are surely lining up with this prophecy!

Jesus is coming soon! We had better be certain that what we are living for is worthy of all Christ died for, and we must ask ourselves this simple question: How does what we do to Israel and particularly Jerusalem matter in the light of eternity?

> *For Zion's sake I will not hold My peace,*
> *And for Jerusalem's sake I will not rest,*
> *Until her righteousness goes forth as brightness,*
> *And her salvation as a lamp that burns.*
> *The Gentiles shall see your righteousness,*

And all kings your glory.
You shall be called by a new name,
Which the mouth of the Lord will name.
     You shall also be a crown of glory
In the hand of the Lord,
And a royal diadem
In the hand of your God.
     You shall no longer be termed Forsaken,
Nor shall your land any more be termed Desolate;
But you shall be called Hephzibah, and your land Beulah;
For the Lord delights in you,
And your land shall be married.
     For as a young man marries a virgin,
So shall your sons marry you;
And as the bridegroom rejoices over the bride,
So shall your God rejoice over you.
     I have set watchmen on your walls, O Jerusalem;
They shall never hold their peace day or night.
You who make mention of the Lord, do not keep silent,
     And give Him no rest till He establishes
And till He makes Jerusalem a praise in the earth.
                                        ISAIAH 62:1-7

Christians have a date with destiny! The Church cannot fulfill its eternal purpose if it is not salt and light to Israel and does not pray for the peace of Jerusalem (Acts 1:8). When we support Israel, we are supporting the only nation that was created by an act of God: The royal land grant that was given to Abraham and his seed through Isaac and Jacob, with an everlasting and unconditional covenant.

My mercy I will keep for him forever,
     And My covenant shall stand firm with him.
His seed also I will make to endure forever,

And his throne as the days of heaven.
"If his sons forsake My law
  And do not walk in My judgments,
If they break My statutes
  And do not keep My commandments,
Then I will punish their transgression with the rod,
  And their iniquity with stripes.
Nevertheless My loving-kindness I will not utterly take from him,
  Nor allow My faithfulness to fail.
My covenant I will not break,
  Nor alter the word that has gone out of My lips.
Once I have sworn by My holiness;
  I will not lie to David:
His seed shall endure forever,
  And his throne as the sun before Me;
It shall be established forever like the moon,
  Even like the faithful witness in the sky."

PSALM 89:28-37

On December 12, 1988, the United Nations invited Yasser Arafat to speak in Geneva. Its aim was to unify the world behind his plan for a PLO state in Israel. He was asked to simply say the words, "I denounce terrorism." He not only denounced terrorism there, but many times afterward, mostly after terrorist bombers had blown up Jews upon his orders and with his financial backing.

The following day in Geneva, I was comfortably seated in a hotel restaurant sipping coffee. I couldn't help but overhear the conversation in the booth behind me. I was stunned when I realized the import of the conversation. I grabbed my pen and began to take notes. A man, apparently from the White House, was meeting with a Saudi prince. He was saying: "Everything is under control in Washington. Someone is working on the project with the Japanese. There's a special meeting set up at the Tokyo Club. I've just heard from Rome—we have the support of our partners throughout Europe."

The next statement riveted my attention: "We should have Jerusalem in your hands by '96—at the very latest by 2000. We're certain we can get you a good piece of Israel by 1995." I felt as though I were in the midst of a very bad "B" movie. A few days later I was at the airport, waiting to catch my flight back to the States. There, standing before me, was the American from the restaurant. I turned to him and quietly repeated the conversation between him and the Saudi. As the color drained from his face he said, "You're scaring me. Who are you?" I looked him directly in the eye and warned, "Don't fear me; fear God! He that keeps Israel neither slumbers nor sleeps." With that, I turned and walked away.

On September 28, 1995, one of the most important meetings in the history of the rebirth of Jerusalem took place in Washington, D.C. President Bill Clinton presided over a ceremony which finalized the transfer of over 2,270 square miles of Bible lands to the PLO. The acreage included Hebron, Bethlehem, and 450 other Israeli towns and villages.

Ambassador Dennis Ross, Clinton's special coordinator for the Middle East peace process, credited the president and Secretary of State Warren Christopher with mobilizing the international support of self-rule. He applauded the fact that the landscape of the Middle East was changing. The only problem with that mindset is that the land itself and many of the affected towns are historically and biblically significant for the people of Israel. Bethlehem of Judea was the birthplace of Jesus, unless one believes political activist Dr. Hanan Ashrawi's assertion:

> I am a Palestinian Christian . . . and I am a descendant
> of the first Christians in the world. Jesus Christ was born in
> my country, in my town. Bethlehem was a Palestinian town.[39]

If Dr. Ashrawi is truly a Christian, then she has been grafted into Israel and her spiritual roots come form the Jews, not the Arabs or Palestinians. If she is a true believer, she would know the town of Bethlehem was established and inhabited by Jews when Jesus was born.

Hebron, located eighteen miles from Jerusalem, has a rich Jewish heritage:

❖ Abraham first pitched his tent in Hebron (Genesis 13:18).

❖ God gave Hebron to Caleb as his inheritance (Joshua 14:12-14).

❖ Sarah, Abraham's wife, died in Hebron (Genesis 23:2).

❖ Caleb fought for and won Hebron (Joshua 14:14).

❖ David was anointed king in Hebron (II Samuel 2:1,4).

❖ God recognized Hebron as the first capital of Israel (I Chronicles 29:27).

The 1995 machinations gave birth to Oslo 2, which filled over four hundred pages and called for, among other things, the release of thirteen hundred terrorists from Israeli prisons. One thing to remember is that the geographical area labeled "Palestine" includes the present-day State of Israel, the Hashemite Kingdom of Jordan, and the disputed territory in the middle. The "liberation of Palestine" espoused by so many Arab countries literally means the eradication of Israel—and eventually Jordan as well—as an independent state.

Following the signing of the Oslo 2 accords in 1995, *Jerusalem Post* editor David Bar-Ilan and I talked about Arafat's intentions toward peace with Israel. David explained the PLO leader's intentions:

> Until the state of Palestine rules from the River Jordan to the sea, which means until the State of Israel is eliminated, the armed struggle will not stop...He [Arafat] glorified martyrs...who have died in suicide bombings against Israel... [Arafat's plan is to] get as much territory as possible through peace or some kind of agreement, and then, when Israel is dwarfed and becomes very small and vulnerable, then—and only then—attack...If you listen closely to Arafat's speeches, he says always 'Jerusalem.' He never says we want only half

of Jerusalem, only the eastern part of Jerusalem. He says, "We want all of Jerusalem. We will not rest until the flag of the Palestinians flies over all the churches of Jerusalem or the mosques of Jerusalem." He is not just talking about part of the city.[40]

At Camp David in July 2000, President Bill Clinton almost succeeded in dividing Jerusalem. Arafat refused to accept the deal, and the president was in shock.

The Bible says that Jerusalem will be in the hands of the Jewish people when Messiah returns. America was challenging God Almighty and His prophetic plan. Not a wise thing to do!

Why did Arafat not sign the agreement? He wanted ALL of Jerusalem, and in fact, all of Israel. Why did he not succeed in his efforts to exert control over this site? The sons of Esau live in the desert and run their oppressive governments by the bullet not the ballot. Those who take a stand against Israel fight God himself. Arafat died without having won the battle against God Almighty. Why? For thousands of years Arabs have spoken curses over Jacob's seed, but when the wars of the Middle East have ended, Jacob's sons will rule. Who will win the conflict in the Middle East? Those who bless Israel will be triumphant. Who will lose the battle in the Middle East? Those who fight the State of Israel will go down in defeat. God created Israel. God defends Israel!

Consider the nation of Egypt. Joseph birthed a generation of wealth. After his death, there arose a Pharaoh that persecuted the Jewish people and enslaved them. He not only starved them but also drowned their children in the Nile River. Why? He was trying to control that nation, a nation that now cried out to God. Through Moses, God gave Pharaoh ten chances to let His people go, and ten times Pharaoh hardened his heart toward God and refused—until the tenth and most deadly plague. The first-born child in every Egyptian home was slain by the Death Angel, including Pharaoh's son. In some Egyptian homes, every family member died.

For every Hebrew baby that died in the Nile River, an Egyptian child died. For every Hebrew father who died at the oppressive hands of the Egyptian overseers, an Egyptian father died. For every Hebrew mother who died of starvation or of a broken heart, an Egyptian mother died. What you do to another, God will cause to come to you.

At first broken, Pharaoh released the children of Israel. But after they had gone, an angry, bitter Pharaoh gathered his terrified, demoralized troops and pursued the Hebrews as they departed Egypt. He led his army directly into the path of God's wrath, and all drowned in the Red Sea. Overnight, Egypt became a land of poverty and disease. It remains that way four thousand years later...because of the choice to curse the Jewish people rather than to bless them.

God's chosen people have survived through the years because of God's protective hand upon them. Just as He provided a cloud by day and fire by night to protect the Children of Israel in the desert, just as He has always protected a remnant of the Jewish people, so He has sheltered and preserved Jerusalem. It is Zion, the City of God. His name is there; His people are there; the eyes of the world are fixed on Jerusalem.

CHAPTER NINE

GOD'S WORD
IS TRUE

"For out of Zion shall go forth the law, And the word of the Lord from Jerusalem." —ISAIAH 2:3

The survival of the Jews is a fulfillment of biblical prophecy. If the Jews had not survived through the centuries, God's Word would not be true; His covenant with the Jewish people would have been broken. Satan attempted to force Jesus to pervert the Word of God, but Jesus rebuked him. We must do the same. Throughout the Bible God has made promises to the people of Israel, some of which are yet to be fulfilled.

Either you believe the entire Bible, or you believe none of it. The nation of Israel is a fulfillment of biblical prophecy; she is the apple of God's eye (Psalm 17:8). To purposefully close our eyes to the cries of His people is like willfully and disdainfully poking our finger in God's eye. That the Jewish people exist is a miracle. The rebirth of the nation of Israel, the restoration of the Hebrew language, and the reunification of Jerusalem are all miracles and fulfillment of God's Word.

If you believe the Bible is the Word of God, you must support Israel and pray for the peace of Jerusalem. It's just that simple. Why do we as Christians support Israel? Because God commands it in His Word. I have heard some Christians say with pride, "I will not support the Jews in Israel. They are sinners, and the nation is a sinful one." How easily we forget the mercy God has shown to a sinful America, to whom He made not one direct promise! How can we sing "God Bless America" and expect God's blessings when America has killed millions of unborn babies? How can we expect Him to protect us when we curse Israel by adopting a self-righteous attitude, remaining silent in the face of her plight, and pressuring her to give away her land?

I seem to remember a scripture about a Jew who had compassion on all people and died for them, even though they were sinners (Romans 5:8). If Jesus, a Jew, could love us, how can we look in the face of His physical brethren—those with whom He lived and over whom He wept—and say, "I who profess to be a follower of Christ cannot love you or help you"?

No, God's covenant is everlasting:

> He remembers His covenant forever,
>   The word which He commanded, for a thousand generations,
> The covenant which He made with Abraham,
>   And His oath to Isaac,
> And confirmed it to Jacob for a statute,
>   To Israel as an everlasting covenant,
> Saying, "To you I will give the land of Canaan
>   As the allotment of your inheritance."
>   **PSALM 105:8-11**

In his letter to the Romans, the apostle Paul penned:

> I say then, has God cast away His people? Certainly not! For I also am an Israelite, of the seed of Abraham, of the tribe of Benjamin. God has not cast away His people whom He foreknew.
>   **ROMANS 11:1-2**

To summarize the sixty-six books of the Bible, you only have to say the word "Israel." The Holy Scripture begins with Israel in Genesis and ends with Israel in Revelation. No word is used more; no promises are given to any people more than to Israel. Her very existence demonstrates the faithfulness of God, the inspiration and infallibility of His Word, and the sovereignty of God.

To believe that God broke His covenant with Israel is heresy. The God of Abraham, Isaac, and Jacob is not a covenant-breaker. The writer of Hebrews 6:13 averred:

> For when God made a promise to Abraham, because He could swear by no one greater, He swore by Himself.

Theologian Matthew Henry explained:

> He [God] has not only given His people His word, and His hand and seal, but His oath. And here, you will observe, He specifies the oath of God to Abraham, which, being sworn to him as the father of the faithful, remains in full force and virtue to all true believers.[41]

The promises God made to Israel include that its capital is Jerusalem. Jerusalem is His choice, so it does not require the approval of Washington, D.C., London, Paris, or any other world capital. Three thousand years ago, He declared that Jerusalem would be the capital of Israel, and that the Messiah would stand in the Holy City to rule and reign. This is an undeniable fact.

Jerusalem, however, is much more than the capital of Israel; it is the emblem of the one true God of the universe. This proclamation has, from the beginning of time, been challenged by Satan, the prince of darkness. Through deception, he has staked a claim on all the kingdoms of the Earth—a claim to which he clings tenaciously and desperately. Why? Despite his bravado, he must know beyond a doubt that his days are numbered.

Satan, the deceiver, hurled two darts at the city of Jerusalem in further attempts to hinder God's purpose and plan. Those two darts are Islam and humanism, and they both defy what the Bible says concerning Jerusalem. In this chapter, we will take a look at Islam.

Islam was founded on the presumption that an angel appeared to a man named Mohammad in a dream, while he was meditating in a cave on Mount Hira in Saudi Arabia. The prophet claimed he was visited by the angel Gabriel, the messenger of God. I believe he was visited by a lying spirit that gained entrance into Mohammed's life for the sole purpose of developing the tenets we know as Islam.

Mohammad declared that in his dream he was taken to Jerusalem on a horse named Lightning, whose face was like that of a woman and whose tail was like that of a peacock. He further asserted that meeting him on an outcropping of rock were Abraham, Moses, and Jesus. All joined Mohammed in prayer. He then climbed a ladder to Heaven, where Allah taught him about prayer. He descended the ladder and was taken back to Mecca before day dawned.

Mohammad tried to interest the Jews in his new religious theories but was rejected. At that, he became angry and instructed his followers to pray towards Mecca rather than Jerusalem. Mohammad was canny enough to include just a smidgen of truth in his false teachings. He embraced Abraham, but rather than Isaac being the son of promise as God had proclaimed, Mohammad declared Ishmael to be the son of promise.

During the last ten years of his life, Mohammad's Islam enjoyed phenomenal success. He built an empire that covered all of Arabia and trained competent men called caliphs to carry on his work after him. But it wasn't until 691 A.D. that Islamic adherents of the Umayyad dynasty began a campaign to "exalt and glorify"[42] the city of Jerusalem.

Umayyad Caliph Abd al-Malik built the Dome of the Rock over the Foundation Stone, the Holy of Holies. It was thought to have been erected in direct competition with Christianity. The edifice still stands today. Later, Islamic leaders, in an attempt to solidify their claim to the Temple Mount, attributed another event to the Foundation Stone: the binding of the son of Abraham the "Hanif," the first monotheist. The Qur'an does not explicitly mention the name Isaac; therefore, commentators on the book have identified the son bound by Abraham as Ishmael. Thus Islam teaches that the title deed to Jerusalem, the Temple Mount, and all of Israel belongs to the Arabs—not the Jews.

Mohammed never actually set foot in Jerusalem. In fact, he died before Palestine fell into Muslim hands. Neither is the city mentioned by name in the Qur'an. The prophet's only connection to Jerusalem is through his vision, where he found himself in a "temple that is most remote" (Qur'an, Sura). It was not until the seventh century that Muslim adherents identified the "temple most remote" as a mosque in Jerusalem (perhaps for political reasons). Some scholars feel that Mohammed's reference to the remote temple was a metaphorical reference, perhaps to Heaven.[43]

Dr. Mordechai Kedar, a Jewish professor of Arabic literature, refuted the Muslim claim to Jerusalem on Al-Jazeera television. Said Dr. Kedar: "This was our capital three thousand years ago, and we were here when your forefathers were drinking wine, burying girls alive, and worshipping pre-Muslim idols. This is our city and will be our city forever."

Host Jimal Rian was enraged. He replied animatedly, "If you want to talk about history, you cannot erase Jerusalem from the Qur'an, and don't attack the Muslim religion if we want to continue talking." Rian began to quote a verse where he thought Jerusalem was mentioned by name in the Qur'an, only to trail off when he realized it was not there. Dr. Kedar reiterated,

> Jerusalem is not mentioned in the Qur'an even once;
> you can't rewrite the Qur'an on air on Al-Jazeera.[44]

The Muslims claim the Temple Mount and deny access to the Jews based on their denial that the Temple existed. Like the penchant for Holocaust denial, it has no basis in fact. Dr. Gabriel Barkay, professor at Bar-Ilan University and biblical archaeologist, addressed the torrent of Temple denial coming from the Arabs:

> This denial of the historical, spiritual and archeological connections of the Jews to the Temple Mount is something new. There was always talk about the temple of Solomon in Jerusalem—called the "praise of Jerusalem" in Arabic literature, in Islamic literature. This new idea of Temple denial is due to the Arabic fear of Jewish aspirations connected to the Temple Mount. It is part of something I call the "cultural intifada."...Temple denial is a very tragic harnessing

of politics to change history. It is not a different interpretation of historical events or archeological evidence. This is something major. I think that Temple denial is more serious and more dangerous than Holocaust denial. Why? Because for the Holocaust there are still living witnesses. There are photographs; there are archives; there are the soldiers who released the prisoners; there are testimonies from the Nazis themselves. There were trials, a whole series of them, starting with Nuremberg. There are people who survived the Holocaust still among us. Concerning the Temple, there are no people among us who remember. Still, [to deny the Temples] you have to dismiss the evidence of Flavius Josephus; you have to dismiss the evidence of the Mishna and of the Talmud; and you have to dismiss the writings of Roman and Greek historians who mention the Temple of Jerusalem. And you have to dismiss the Bible. That is, I think, way too much.[45]

Christians know the Church of Jesus Christ was born in Zion—Jerusalem. The disciples were dispatched from Jerusalem to Judea, Samaria, and the uttermost parts of the Earth. Christians believe Heaven and Earth met in Jerusalem in the person of Jesus. It is the place to which He will return to rule and reign over the Earth.

God has prophesied in the Bible that the destiny of the world is linked inexorably to Jerusalem. It is the epicenter of spiritual warfare, which affects a world that exudes hopelessness, not knowing what to do or where to turn. It is no accident that the Great Commission of Jesus to all His disciples— "But you shall receive power when the Holy Spirit has come upon you; and you shall be witnesses to Me in Jerusalem, and in all Judea and Samaria, and to the end of the Earth" (Acts 1:8)—is first directed to Jerusalem, then to Judea, and Samaria. All three are battle zones; all three need the redemptive love of the Messiah.

By contrast, Islam arrived in Jerusalem late in the game, in 637 A.D. After besieging the city for four months, the patriarch of Jerusalem, Sophronius, sent a request to Caliph Omar that he would surrender only to the caliph. Omar agreed to his request. Omar and Sophronius met at the Muslim encampment on the Mount of Olives. Omar agreed to allow the Christians in Jerusalem to remain in charge. Sophronius, however, urged the Muslim leader to ban the Jews from the city. Omar agreed, but the law was never enforced, and Jews remained an integral part of the Holy City.

After assuming governance of Jerusalem, Omar chose Ramla—not Jerusalem—as the district capital. He then had the garbage that overran the Temple site cleaned off. It was Caliph Abd al-Malik who had the Dome of the Rock built to protect the sacred rock beneath. By any standards, it is magnificent. Al-Walid I, the son of Abd al-Malik, had the Al Aksa Mosque constructed in the grand manner in which it stands today. Its original splendor has been diminished by earthquakes and lack of repairs.

During the latter part of the eighth century, Christians and Jews became more repressed under Muslim rule. By the end of the tenth century, a very strange and cruel man, Hakim, became caliph. In 1009 he ordered the destruction of all churches and synagogues within his domain. In Jerusalem the Church of the Holy Sepulcher was destroyed for the second time since its construction. Thousands of Jews and Christians were forced to embrace Islam or die. By 1014 he banned all non-Muslims from his kingdom. In 1021 Hakim mysteriously died, and thereafter his successors returned to the tradition of religious tolerance long practiced in Jerusalem.

Today Islam boasts over 1.5 billion adherents, but tolerance toward Christians and Jews is waning among them. The description of Ishmael in Genesis 16:12, from whom the Arab legions are descended, is an apt description of today's fanatical Muslim jihadists:

> He shall be a wild man;
> His hand shall be against every man,
> And every man's hand against him.

In 1070 the Seljuks—Turkish mercenaries—took control of Jerusalem. When tales of their maliciousness reached Pope Gregory VII, he urged all Christendom to launch the Crusades to free Jerusalem from the Turks. By the time the Frankish knights of Godfrey de Bouillon gazed at last upon the walls of Jerusalem on June 7, 1099, they had already endured battles against the Saracens. It had taken them three long, hard-fought years to reach their true goal—Jerusalem, the great prize.

During the first four weeks of battle, the Muslims stoutly resisted the Crusaders, and it began to look as if they were in for another long and arduous siege. Peter the Hermit, a preacher in their midst, convinced the leaders that the ghost of a dead Crusader had come to him with a message: March around the city daily for nine days, chanting the praises of God, and as they did, the city would fall into their hands. For whatever reason, it worked. While some marched and sang, other Crusaders were able to successfully fight their way over the northern wall. On July 15, 1099, the Crusaders overwhelmed the forces inside Jerusalem.

Unfortunately, the Christian conquerors launched a rampage of carnage almost unparalleled in Jerusalem's history. Many of the city's defenders were beheaded, shot with arrows, or forced to jump from the parapets. Torture and burnings were common. Piles of heads, hands, and feet littered the streets. Corpses lay everywhere. Even infants were slaughtered. What Jews the Crusaders could find were herded into a synagogue and incinerated. Estimates of the total number of dead rose to forty thousand men, women, and children—most were civilians.

Godfrey de Bouillon became king of Jerusalem and reigned for one year before his death. The Crusader kings of Jerusalem built or rebuilt almost forty churches in the city, including the Church of the Holy Sepulcher. In 1118, the Knights Templar was established. Assuming that the Dome of the Rock was the Temple of Solomon, they regarded themselves as the protectors of the Temple. Their effect on European history would be profound. Even today the court district of London is located in Temple Bar, where, in the Middle Ages, the Templars were headquartered.

In 1171 a new Muslim leader arose—Saladin. He unified Syria and Egypt, and by 1184 he was ready to retake Jerusalem. He marshaled one hundred thousand troops and soundly defeated the forces of Guy of Lusignan, the king of Jerusalem. So bitterly did Saladin hate the Templars that he beheaded those whom he captured. In 1187 he reached Jerusalem. Saladin regarded the city as holy and offered the small Christian garrison time to retrench and resupply. They refused, and the siege began the next day. It lasted only a few weeks.

Saladin permitted no slaughter; however, fifteen thousand Christians were sold into slavery. Unarmed Christian pilgrims were allowed access to Jerusalem, and once again, Jews were allowed to enter Jerusalem. The Crusader period was the last time Jews would be allowed free access to the Holy City until 1947.

Saladin was challenged by Richard the Lionhearted in 1189. Although he took Acre on the Mediterranean coast, he was unable to wrest Jerusalem from the Muslims. After the death of Saladin, Jerusalem changed hands several times both by battle and by treaty. During that time, the Jews continued to multiply and recover from the losses suffered during the Crusades.

During one of my first trips to Israel nearly three decades ago, I spent an afternoon with a brilliant Jewish scholar. He was researching and writing a book on the Spanish Inquisition. We talked for hours about some of his investigative findings. For instance, have you ever wondered why Columbus sailed in search of a new land in 1492? Queen Isabella and King Ferdinand had issued an edict of ejection regarding the Jews. It stated that every person of Jewish descent had to leave Spain or be executed.

Several highly-placed and influential Jewish businessmen went to Christopher Columbus, an Italian, and pledged to help finance his efforts to discover a new land. Jewish scientist and cosmographer, Joseph Diego Mendes Vezinho, and mathematician, inventor, and expert on nautical matters, Avraham Zacuto, imparted navigational knowledge to Columbus which would enable him to cross the ocean to the shores of what would become America.

At the end of the fifteenth century, Ferdinand and Isabella succeeded in driving the Moors from Spain. In their zeal to procure a purely Catholic state, the highly educated and cultured Jewish community was expelled. It was a disastrous blow to the Jews, and many went to Jerusalem.

In 1516 the Ottomans captured Jerusalem. By 1683 their empire was one of the most vast in the history of man. It was Suleiman the Magnificent who reigned over the strongest and most robust period of the Ottoman Empire. He did much to restore the Islamic shrines in Jerusalem, and he provided the glazed Persian tile mosaic that bedecks the Dome of the Rock today. He rebuilt the walls, the results of which can be seen to this day. Furthermore, legend has it that it was he who had the Golden Gate sealed to prevent the entry of the Jewish Messiah into Jerusalem.

During the Ottoman reign, the Jewish population grew slowly but persistently. The Jews in Jerusalem were beginning to receive support from the Jews in Western Europe and elsewhere. In the seventeenth century, the Jews suffered an economic recession as a result of the anti-Semitic pogroms in Poland. The capacity of the Polish Jews to send charity to Jerusalem Jews was greatly diminished. So, through the seventeenth and eighteenth centuries, Jerusalem sat idly in the backwaters of the Ottoman Empire.

American ties to Jerusalem were not by battle or treaty but rather by missionary zeal. The very fact that the United States existed was due to well-timed aid by a Jewish businessman. In 1776, when the thirteen colonies were fighting the British during the American Revolution, the colonial soldiers were poorly armed, starving to death, and on the verge of defeat. A Jewish banker from Philadelphia, Hyman Solomon, went to Jews in America and Europe and gathered a gift of one million dollars. He gave the money to George Washington to buy clothes and arms to outfit the American troops. Life, liberty, and the pursuit of happiness were born on American soil as a result of that gift.

To show his appreciation, George Washington had the engravers of the U. S. one dollar bill include a memorial to the Jewish people over the head of the American eagle. Look closely, and you will find thirteen stars or the Magen David, the Star of Israel. Around that star is the cloudburst of the glory in the tabernacle. Our God-fearing President George Washington decreed that there must be a memorial to the Jewish people for the contributions they made to birth this nation.

The nineteenth century saw the influence of Napoleon in the Middle East. His adventures in the region served notice to the Ottoman rulers that the empire was no longer the impregnable bastion it had once been. It also made abundantly clear the strategic importance of the area in the quest for an empire that would dominate the politics of nineteenth century Europe. Napoleon launched a secret struggle among the Europeans for control of this vital area—a struggle that would last until the end of World War I in 1917.

Meanwhile, the missionary zeal of American evangelical Christians was more than adequate for the task of spreading the Gospel in the Middle East. The people of the region were not necessarily ripe for revival, but two young ministers, Levi Parsons and Pliny Fisk, were dispatched from New England to explore the possibilities of missionary activity in the Holy Land and to establish a station in Jerusalem. Parsons died after three years; Fisk endured for a time, but with disappointing results.

While missionaries and archaeologists were busily working, life was moving ahead in Jerusalem. The influx of Europeans and Americans and the flood of westernization seemed irresistible. New forces were at work in the city, and the Jewish population was increasing. By the middle of the century they constituted nearly half Jerusalem's population. Many of the new immigrants fell into the classification of scholars and sages. It would take time for the idea of reclaiming the desolate countryside to capture the Jewish imagination.

In 1905 the Jewish National Fund was established for the purchase of property in Palestine wherever it could be found for sale. Real estate prices suddenly mushroomed, but the Jews were not deterred. The Jewish population of Jerusalem was growing impressively. Now, they were no longer primarily Talmudic scholars. There were craftsmen, professionals, technicians, and merchants. Public libraries, an art school, and light industry began to find places along the streets of Jerusalem. The struggle for a homeland would culminate in 1948 when a portion of the British Mandate of Palestine would become the State of Israel.

Since President Harry S. Truman first recognized the State of Israel, America has been blessed (Genesis 12:1-3). But America is in danger of moving away from the place of blessing to the place of cursing. The same nation that has killed more than 43 million babies through legalized abortion has led the world into a false sense of peace that has cost the lives of thousands of Jews in Israel. The land-for-peace deals of recent years have placed Israel and the Jewish people in grave danger, all because the Muslims have decreed that Jerusalem belongs to them and not to the Jews.

Vladimir Lenin is credited with saying, "A lie told often enough becomes truth." In 1967 Yasser Arafat made the false claim that the Temple Mount—and all of Jerusalem—was the third most holy site of Islam. It is one thing to be able to convince the Palestinian people and other Muslims of this falsehood; it is absolutely ludicrous that Bill Clinton, George Bush, Barack Obama, and other political leaders of the world have been convinced of the lie that Jerusalem belongs to Islam.

The site on which the Dome of the Rock now stands is sacred to the Jews as the site of Solomon's Temple. It appears that the battle over Jerusalem is fueled by politics and not by religion. To the Muslims, Mecca is the city to which they pray five times daily—not Jerusalem. Mecca is forbidden to non-Muslims upon threat of death—not so Jerusalem, where Christians, Jews, and Muslims are welcome to worship at their various holy places. To the Jews, Jerusalem is the navel of the world; to the Muslims, Mecca is the center of their world and worship. Just as the Muslims rule their holy city—Mecca—so the Jews should have the right to rule Jerusalem.

CHAPTER TEN

THE CRADLE OF
ZIONISM

"Thus says the Lord:
  'I will return to Zion,
  And dwell in the midst of Jerusalem.
  Jerusalem shall be called the City of Truth,
  The Mountain of the Lord of hosts,
  The Holy Mountain.'" —ZECHARIAH 8:3

Between 1860 and 1880 the concept of Zionism began to take shape through a series of books about the subject. Orthodox Jews had long insisted that any return to the Holy Land would be carried out by the Messiah, and to take matters into their own hands would be blasphemous. The group that took its name from the portion of Jerusalem most associated with King David, the new Zionists, vigorously denied this and urged a serious program of immigration and settlement in what was then called Palestine.

Theodor Herzl, a Viennese playwright and journalist, became concerned when confronted by the intransigence of anti-Semitism growing in Europe. For several years he struggled with various solutions—including the idea of mass conversion of the Jews to Christianity. He was unable to resolve the issue to his satisfaction. Then, while working in Paris as a journalist during the Dreyfus Affair,[46] he heard the crowds taunt the unfortunate (and innocent) French Jewish army captain Dreyfus with shouts of "death to the Jews." This experience became Herzl's critical moment of recognition—nothing would do except a Jewish state, a sovereign nation. For the first time in his life, he began to attend Jewish religious services.

In 1886 he published *Der Judenstaat*—a classic testament of Zionism. The title is usually translated *The Jewish State* to be politically correct. It is much more correctly rendered *The Jew-State*. It was a title Herzl chose in order to fling his concept into the faces of anti-Semites and of Western Jews who preferred euphemisms such as "Israelite" or "Hebrew."

Shortly after the book's publication, Herzl was placed at the helm of the burgeoning World Zionist Organization. In 1897 its first Congress was held in Basel, Switzerland. The immediate goal was to gain the sponsorship and support of one of the great European powers. Finally, in 1903 the British offered the Jews territory in East Africa. Herzl died in 1904, before a decision could be made. In 1905 the Zionist Congress rejected the offer and resolved instead that the Jewish homeland had to be in Palestine.

While Herzl helped to birth an active Zionist movement, the secret struggle among European powers for control of the Holy Land had continued. The precarious status quo became more unstable as Britain, France, and Russia connived to wrest more territory from the Ottoman Empire. Only Germany held out a helping hand to Turkish sultan, Mehmed IV. During the 1880s Kaiser Wilhelm sent a number of German military and economic missions to Istanbul. In 1889 he traveled there in person.

On October 29, 1898, Kaiser Wilhelm II entered Jerusalem via the Jaffa Gate astride a white stallion escorted by Prussian and Turkish cavalry. His spiked helmet glistened in the sun. During the next two days he and the Kaiserin Augusta Victoria (a daughter of Queen Victoria), visited the city's shrines and sites. They dedicated an orphanage in Bethlehem, an impressive Protestant church near the Holy Sepulcher, and presented the city's German Catholics with a plot of ground on Mount Zion for the erection of a new church.

In one of his speeches, Wilhelm declared, "From Jerusalem a light has arisen upon the world—the blessed light in whose splendor our German people have become great and glorious."[47] After their visit, the Augusta

Victoria Hospice was erected on Mount Scopus. The Kaiser had staked his claim as firmly as he could. A year later, the German-Turkish alliance began to take formal shape. The die was cast. The Englishmen knew that if they were going to have Palestine, they would have to fight both the Germans and the Turks to get it.

It was now 1913, and everyone felt war was inevitable. T. E. Lawrence, who later became known as Lawrence of Arabia, traveled to the Negev (Wilderness of Zin) to engage in archaeological research. He and his traveling companion, Leonard Woolley, had been employed by The Palestine Exploration Fund, a church-sponsored organization in London. It had been active since the mid-nineteenth century.

The two men stood atop the lofty site of the ancient Nabatean city, Nizzana, roughly thirty-five miles southwest of Beersheba. It was their job to prepare notes about the site, which would pave the way for a full-scale excavation at a later time. While Lawrence was a lover of archaeology, he was even more fascinated by military strategy. He and Woolley were participating in an ongoing project to map western Palestine. By 1913 everything had been mapped west of the Jordan River valley with the precision and attention to detail for which the Royal Engineers were justly famous.

The Negev was of particular interest, as it would have to be crossed by any Ottoman army en route to Egypt. By June 1914, Woolley and Lawrence had filed a report on their archaeological findings, but more important were the maps the two produced of the area, especially designating water sources.[48]

Although war had been anticipated, it was on June 28, 1914, that anticipation became reality. Shortly after noon crowds had gathered in Sarajevo, the capital of the Austro-Hungarian province of Bosnia, to see the heir to the Hapsburg throne, Archduke Franz Ferdinand and his wife Sophie. As their open touring car drove the royal couple past their cheering subjects, a young man, Gavrilo Princip, ran from the crowd, leaped onto the car's running board and fired two shots at the archduke at point-blank range. Franz Ferdinand's pregnant wife took a third bullet in the stomach. Both were dead by the time they reached the governor's residence.

When the assassination was investigated by Austrian authorities, it was discovered that Princip, a Bosnian, had lived in Serbia for several years. The investigators deduced that he had acted as an agent of the Serbian government. That same day, Austria declared war on Serbia. By the end of October 1914, the Central Powers—Austria-Hungary, Germany, and the Ottoman Empire—were at war with the Allies—Belgium, France, Great Britain, Russia, and Serbia.

In the Middle East, Lawrence and Woolley were quickly called back into service in the Negev. They would be vital to the British Army stationed in Egypt. Meanwhile, the Turkish VIII Corps had set up headquarters in Jerusalem, where the German-Turkish High Command under the leadership of General Friedrich Freiherr Kress von Kressenstein made plans to attack the Suez Canal. By mid-January 1915, some one hundred thousand troops were stationed in and around Beersheba. Kressenstein sent his troops across the Sinai in a human wave assault against the well-entrenched and heavily armed British and Indian troops. British machine guns and artillery crushed the Turks and sent survivors limping back to Palestine.

Assessing the situation and redoubling his efforts, Kressenstein realized his troops needed to be combat hardened and better trained to take on the Brits. He called in help from Berlin, where the importance of the Suez mission was recognized and understood. Germany sent machine gunners, heavy artillery, and even aircraft to the Sinai front. During the summer of 1916, British defenders repelled two more desperate attempts to pierce their lines around the canal.

On the Western Front in Flanders, English blood was being spilled at a ghastly and alarming rate in places with names like Ypres and Somme. Had the government not suppressed the casualty rate, the public outcry would have likely forced Britain out of the conflict. One man, Marshal Horatio Kitchener, devised a plan to break the stalemate in the trenches of France. Kitchener believed a full-fledged expeditionary force in Egypt for the purpose of achieving a stunning victory against the Turks would help the war effort and lift morale. He died in 1916, but newly elected Prime Minister David Lloyd George saw the merit in Kitchener's plan and took the necessary steps to implement it. If it failed to achieve the goal of breaking the stalemate in France, it would at the very least secure the Suez Canal. That alone was a worthy goal.

Under the command of Sir Archibald Murray, the Egyptian Expeditionary Force of the Royal Army struck out across the Sinai in December 1916. Following the coastline as Napoleon had in 1799, they took Al-Arish and Rafah with little opposition. From there the EEF moved up into southern Palestine.

In Gaza, they found the Turks heavily entrenched. Murray hurled his troops at the line, but victory eluded them. Heavy casualties drove them back, and Murray was faced with the predicament that had beset Kressenstein in 1915. The English leader responded just as his German counterpart before him had: He replenished his troops and attacked the fortress at Gaza again in April 1917. The results were the same. Gaza sand soaked up the blood of the Englishmen and Indians. The Turks had prepared by bringing in troops from the German Asienkorps.

Lloyd George was livid. He was certain his plan had been foiled by an incompetent leader. Another event that same month gave him a new perspective on the war. The United States declared war on the Central Powers. It appeared that the stalemate would be broken after all.

Murray was relieved of command of the EEF and replaced by General Edmund Allenby, a dogged and tenacious fighter nicknamed, "The Bull." Before embarking for the Middle East, Allenby was summoned to No. 10 Downing Street, where Prime Minister George made it abundantly clear that the British had no intention of suffering a third defeat in Palestine. Allenby was to marshal his strength, his wisdom, and his troops to present the British people with a Christmas present—Jerusalem.

Allenby arrived in Egypt in June 1917 and went directly to the front near Gaza. He quickly recognized that another frontal assault would be a suicide mission. He set about to devise a better plan. While he was working on his plan, unexpected news arrived. T. E. Lawrence and a handful of Bedouins whose loyalty he had gained had managed to cross what had been thought to be an impassable desert to reach Aqaba by land. Aqaba's heavy guns faced the Persian Gulf waters, the only anticipated avenue of attack. Lawrence, however, was able to enlist a group of local Bedouins to help him drive the Turks from the port city. He took the town by complete surprise and accomplished his goal.

The effect of the capture of Aqaba was more than valuable for Allenby. It served to protect his rear and right flank should he accomplish his plan—to break the Ottoman line at its eastern point, Beersheba. On October 31 a British fleet began to bombard Gaza unrelentingly. At the same time, a British scout allowed himself to be spotted by Turkish sentries. In his flight, he dropped a courier pouch. Inside, the sentries found what appeared to be secret British plans for an imminent and massive assault on Gaza, not unlike those employed by General Murray.

The Turks took the bait. To ready for the attack, they pulled a sizeable body of troops from Beersheba to Gaza to help man the trenches there. Only a small garrison was left at Beersheba. Meanwhile, a large complement of British troops moved to within easy striking distance of the town. They were guided by maps compiled four years earlier and by up-to-date intelligence reports from a network of Jewish spies living in Palestine. When the troops received the signal to attack, they swarmed over Beersheba with lightning speed and accuracy. The Turkish garrison was stunned and quickly retreated to Gaza.

Now was Allenby's moment to take Gaza. Fortified with naval support, aircraft for reconnaissance and support—a first for the EEF—and with tanks (the first deployment in the Holy Land), Allenby drew up his battle plan. Within nine days, Gaza had fallen.

On November 2, in the midst of that momentous battle, something even more significant and historic was happening in London. It began earlier, in January 1916, before Lloyd George had become prime minister. British representative Sir Mark Sykes and French representative Francois Georges-Picot concluded an agreement that allocated postwar spheres of influence in the Middle East to their two nations. Britain would supervise Mesopotamia, most of Transjordan, and southern Palestine. France would take southern Turkey, Syria, northern Palestine, and the Mosul area of upper Mesopotamia.

The area around Jerusalem in central Palestine would require special treatment. The Russian Czar exercised a protective role over various Orthodox monasteries and churches. The French had a similar interest in regard to Catholic institutions. The British represented the somewhat smaller Protestant interests in the area, along with the Germans. However, Britain's prime interest had been the Suez Canal. Consequently, they all had their hands in the pot when it came to central Palestine.

Lloyd George was appalled to learn of the Sykes-Picot agreement. He wanted Britain to be the sole protector of Palestine—all of Palestine. He turned to an Anglo-Zionist alliance that had been taking shape over the previous several years. The main reason for its existence and strength was a man named Chaim Weizmann. In 1914, the Russian-born Weizmann, then a forty-year-old instructor in chemistry at the University of Manchester, had already proven himself a lucid and convincing propagandist for the Zionist movement. He had begun to win a hearing in the high echelons of British society.

Two newspaper editors introduced him to Lloyd George, Arthur James Balfour, Winston Churchill, and Lord Robert Cecil. Weizmann was a man of unusual charm and charisma. With his commanding physical appearance and his charming English laced with a Russian accent, he adapted his arguments to each listener with unusual skill. With Britons and Americans he could use biblical language to awaken deep emotions. With Lloyd George, a Welshman, he emphasized Palestine's topography, which was much like that of Wales. With Balfour, who came from an evangelical background, he explored Zionism, and with Lord Cecil he spoke in terms of a new world organization. With other British leaders he stressed the extension of British imperial power inherent in the plan.

The evangelical heritage of many of Weizmann's listeners worked in his favor. These men had read the Old Testament and were familiar with it to a degree unparalleled by their Catholic allies in France and Italy. To them the children of Israel and the land of Canaan were to be venerated.

So it was that Weizmann's talk of a "British protectorate over a Jewish homeland" began to interest government officials more and more. Several officials in particular began to advocate a partnership with the Zionists. Among them was Mark Sykes, who had concluded the Sykes-Picot agreement with France. That was before he met the charismatic Mr. Weizmann. Through him and other influential spokesmen, Sykes had become convinced that a Jewish national presence in Palestine was in the best interests of the British Empire. He was, however, hampered by the agreement he had signed with the French, which he could not disclose to the Zionists.

He had hinted that the government was not a free agent in the Middle East, that it needed the endorsement of Paris and Rome before it could officially sponsor the Zionist cause. Sykes asked Weizmann if he and his cohorts would secure the endorsements needed in Europe. He and his fellow Zionists left for Europe only to find Sykes at every turn, carefully stage-managing the entire enterprise.

Sykes' plan succeeded. The French gave the Zionists a letter to assure that they were sympathetic to the Zionist cause. A bigger surprise was the cordial welcome from Pope Benedict XV. It was easily explained: The British were preferable to the Russians and their Orthodox Church when it came to who was going to replace the Turks in Palestine.

Other factors moved Lloyd George and his government steadily toward the fateful step they would take on November 2, 1917. Even with the U.S. entry into the war, France's strength was all but spent. No American troops had yet reached the trenches, Italy had suffered a major setback, and German submarine warfare was taking an enormous toll on Allied shipping. The prime minister's two greatest needs were to get the Americans fully engaged and committed and to keep Russia from dropping out altogether.

Weizmann kept up his campaign for a statement from the British government. He was finally rewarded on June 17, 1917, when Balfour urged the Zionists to draw up an appropriate declaration. He promised he would submit the document to the cabinet with his endorsement.

Weizmann's two closest associates, Harry Sacher and Nachum Sokolow, set to work. Their final version of the paper was presented to Balfour the following day. The statement read:

His Majesty's government views with favour the establishment in Palestine of a national home for the Jewish people, and will use their best endeavors to facilitate the achievement of this object, it being clearly understood that nothing shall be done which may prejudice the civil and religious rights of existing non-Jewish communities in Palestine, or the rights and political status enjoyed by Jews in any other country.[49]

When the letter was presented to the cabinet, most ministers heartily approved it, with the exception of one. Joined in his efforts by Lord George Curzon, Secretary of State for India Edwin Montagu persuaded the other members to take no action on the proposal. Montagu, a Jew, felt it had taken a long time for him to win full acceptance in the high levels of government in which he now moved. He took exception to the phrase, "a national home of the Jewish people." He felt that if he were to endorse that, it would call into question his own loyalty as an Englishman. He told his fellow cabinet officers that Zionism was "a mischievous political creed"[50] and that endorsement of the statement would alarm the Muslims of India and embarrass the Jews of England.

A second hearing on October 4 convinced the pro-Zionists in the cabinet that a milder text was needed. Weizmann and his friends didn't like it, but decided it was the best they could get. Now only one hurdle remained. Lloyd George had sent the first draft to President Woodrow Wilson. The prime minister knew he would require Wilson's support for a British protectorate in Palestine after the war. Wilson thought the Sacher-Sokolow text had made too big a commitment. When he saw the second, milder draft, he asked his closest advisor, Colonel Edward House, to advise the British that he "concurred in the formula suggested." House informed British intelligence, who cabled London that day:

Colonel House put formula before president, who approves of it but asks that no mention of his approval shall

be made when His Majesty's Government makes formula
public, as he had arranged that American Jews then ask him
for his approval, which he shall give publicly here.[51]

The cable arrived at Whitehall on October 16 and gave the pro-Zionists the muscle needed to override Montagu's and Lord Curzon's objections.
On October 31, the War Cabinet gave the document, which would become
known as the Balfour Declaration, a solid majority vote.

On November 2, 1917, Balfour sent a letter to Lord Lionel Walter
Rothschild, president of the British Zionist Federation:

> Dear Lord Rothschild,
>
> I have much pleasure in conveying to you, on behalf
> of His Majesty's Government, the following declaration of
> sympathy with Jewish Zionist aspirations, which has been
> submitted to, and approved by, the Cabinet.
>
> "His Majesty's Government view with favour the estab-
> lishment in Palestine of a national home for the Jewish
> people, and will use their best endeavours to facilitate the
> achievement of this object, it being clearly understood that
> nothing shall be done which may prejudice the civil and
> religious rights of existing non-Jewish communities in Pal-
> estine, or the rights and political status enjoyed by Jews in
> any other country."
>
> I should be grateful if you would bring this declaration
> to the knowledge of the Zionist Federation.
>
> Yours sincerely,
>
> Arthur James Balfour

By the time Lord Rothschild received the letter, Allenby's troops were
pursuing Turks and Germans northward along the Palestinian coastline. On
November 11 they overran Tell el-Hesy. A week later a different contingent
of Allenby's force cleared Germans from the trenches at Tell Gezer. The same

day, Allenby's main force captured Jaffa. From there, he turned eastward and began to concentrate on his primary objective—Jerusalem.

The Turkish-German High Command in Jerusalem was in a state of panic. Prisoners of war and wounded soldiers from both sides crowded a city already threatened with starvation. When Djemal Pasha, the ruler of that region of the Ottoman Empire, realized British forces were marching on the city from the north, south, and west, he ordered an evacuation. Officers grabbed whatever they could find—autos, wagons, carts, camels, and horses—and loaded them with furniture, records, gold, and silver, and frantically retreated to Damascus. Valuables that could not be transported were destroyed or hidden.

By December 9, the Turks and Germans were gone. The residents of Jerusalem were left to fend for themselves in the face of an impending British attack. They could not know that Allenby, a religious man, was unwilling to damage the Holy City. He consulted with the War Office and with the king about how to take Jerusalem. His sovereign counseled him to make it a matter of prayer. Presumably he did just that. He decided to drop leaflets on the city from an airplane. They addressed the absent Turkish authorities and invited them to surrender.

Jerusalem's civilian mayor, Haj Amin Nashashibi, decided to accept Allenby's offer. He borrowed a white sheet from an American missionary and walked outside the city through the Jaffa Gate toward the southwest. He assumed it was the direction from which the main body of the troops would come. He and his associates were accompanied by a small group of boys before and behind them.

Not far down the road the small entourage encountered two British scouts, Sergeants Hurcomb and Sedgewick of the London Regiment. With hand signals, the mayor made his intentions of surrender clear to the two men. Within hours British troops had marched into the city. The Jews, the largest segment of the population, had heard of the Balfour Declaration. The arrival of these troops signified to them the seriousness of the declaration to give them a national homeland.

Arabs were cheering too. They were all familiar with the exploits of
Lawrence of Arabia and the way in which he represented the British support for the Arab desire for national independence. Of course, the Christians
cheered with the knowledge that Jerusalem's Holy Sites would no longer be
under Muslim domination.

Two days later, on December 11, Allenby arrived at the Jaffa Gate to mark
the beginning of a new regime. A fierce Turkish counterattack on November
25 had slowed his progress into the Judean Hills from Jaffa. His troops had
fought hard to reach that point. Allenby dismounted, reached for the visor
of his cap, and removed it from his head. Humbly he entered the Holy City
as the bells of various churches and the clock tower rang a joyous welcome.

Once inside, he mounted the steps of the Turkish citadel and read a
proclamation, which assured the city's inhabitants that the rights of the religious communities would be preserved and their various shrines scrupu-
lously protected. He also gave formal greetings to the chief rabbis, the mufti,
the Latin and Orthodox patriarchs, and other religious leaders.

An official report revealed:

> From 2 to 7 that morning the Turks streamed through
> and out of the city, which echoed for the last time their shuf-
> fling tramp. On this same day, 2,082 years before, another
> race of conquerors, equally detested, were looking their last
> on the city which they could not hold; and inasmuch as the
> liberation of Jerusalem in 1917 will probably ameliorate the
> lot of the Jews more than that of any other community in
> Palestine, it was fitting that the flight of the Turks should
> have coincided with the national festival of the Hanukah.[52]

Winter rains held up further advances by Allenby's troops, so the Turks
remained in control of Palestine above a line running north of Jaffa and
Jerusalem. Consequently, Jewish residents of Galilee suffered bitterly because
the Turks believed them to be firmly aligned with the Allied cause. Ottoman
troops confiscated Jewish farms, and Turkish Army deserters terrorized

Jewish settlements, looting and murdering the populace. In addition, hunger, illness, and exposure also took a toll. By September 1918, Jewish settlers in Palestine were reduced by thirty thousand men, women, and children.

Also by September, Allenby reached Megiddo and scored yet another striking victory. His conquest of the Holy Land was complete. Before the end of the year he captured Damascus and Aleppo. He had succeeded where Richard the Lionhearted had failed.

CHAPTER ELEVEN

THE POLITICAL
MANDATE

For the Lord has chosen Zion; He has desired it for
His habitation. —PSALMS 132:13

A fter General Allenby marched into Jerusalem, the most important issue had not changed. Jerusalem was still "trodden down by the Gentiles." Some Englishmen were enamored of the notion that the Anglo-Saxon tribes that had moved into Britain long ago were actually the lost tribes of Israel. They wanted to believe the mandate over Palestine awarded to Britain in 1920 represented the fulfillment of Jesus' words in Luke 21:24:

> *And they will fall by the edge of the sword, and be led away*
> *captive into all nations. And Jerusalem will be trampled by Gen-*
> *tiles until the times of the Gentiles are fulfilled.*

In order to understand what happened to bring about the British Mandate for Palestine, we must take a look back to a meeting in Cairo in 1914. An Arab, Abdullah ibn Hussein, and an Englishmen, Horatio Kitchener, met in February of that year. Abdullah was a sharif, or governor, of Mecca and descended from Mohammad. His father, Sharif-Hussein, had recently been appointed Grand Sharif of Mecca by the Young Turks, who had taken over the Ottoman government in Istanbul. Abdullah would attend the meeting as a representative of Hejaz, the mountainous coastal district of the Arabian Peninsula that extended from near Mecca toward Sinai in the north.

Abdullah was thinking, however, of more than just having a voice in parliament for Hejaz. He had stopped off in Cairo to discuss with Lord Kitchener an all-out Arab revolt against the Turks. Kitchener was interested but noncommittal.

In 1915 the same conversation was taken up by two different men, Abdullah's father, Hussein, and Sir Henry McMahon, Britain's high commissioner in Egypt. In a letter dated October 24, McMahon revealed his country was ready to recognize and support Arab independence throughout Syria, Arabia, and Mesopotamia, with the exception of districts in Damascus, Homs, Hama, and Aleppo. In return for this pledge, Hashemite Arabs would help the British fight the Turks. Although no formal agreement was signed, Hussein's son, Feisal, led an Arab revolt in June 1916. With the full support of the British army, Feisal became a quasi-constitutional king.

Feisal and Chaim Weizmann met in Aqaba. Feisal entertained the Zionist cordially and was receptive as Weizmann stressed that there was plenty of room for everyone and that a lot of Arabs would undoubtedly be enhanced by the work of the Jewish settlers. That winter Sir Mark Sykes invited both Weizmann and Feisal to a meeting in London. At a luncheon hosted by Lord Rothschild, Feisal addressed the guests with remarks prepared for him by T. E. Lawrence, in which he said, "No true Arab can be suspicious or afraid of Jewish nationalism."[53]

Emir Feisal later wrote to Felix Frankfurter, Harvard Law School Dean and later Supreme Court Justice:

> We feel that the Arabs and Jews are cousins in race, having suffered similar oppressions at the hands of powers stronger than themselves, and by a happy coincidence have been able to take the first step towards the attainment of their national ideals together.
>
> We Arabs, especially the educated among us, look with the deepest sympathy on the Zionist movement. Our

deputation here in Paris is fully acquainted with the proposals submitted yesterday by the Zionist Organization to
the Peace Conference and we regard them as moderate and
proper. We will do our best, insofar as we are concerned,
to help them through: we will wish the Jews a most hearty
welcome home.[54]

Not long after, Weizmann and Feisal signed a formal agreement that
guaranteed, among other things, unlimited Jewish immigration and settlement in Palestine so long as Arab tenant farmers and their plots were safe-
guarded and received economic aid from their Jewish neighbors. Feisal,
however, noted on his Arabic copy of the agreement that he would concur
only if the Arabs were granted independence in accordance with his memorandum to the British foreign office.

Within a month, Feisal made it clear that what he really wanted from the
Jews in exchange for his goodwill was their support in his struggle against
the French. In July 1919, he presided over an Arab congress in Damascus
that called for recognition of the kingdom of Syria, which would include
Palestine with Feisal as sovereign, repudiation of the Sykes-Picot Agreement
and the Balfour Declaration, and foreign assistance, preferably from the U.S.,
not France.

The French had no intention of acquiescing to Feisal's demands. Before
the end of 1919, French troops occupied Lebanon, and by July 25, 1920,
they were in full command of Damascus. Feisal was forced to flee, and his
coveted Arab state evaporated. The British found a place for Feisal in its
mandate in Mesopotamia, which in 1921 renamed itself Iraq. Feisal was proclaimed king. Most of the men who had surrounded the king in Damascus,
however, found refuge from the French in Jerusalem. That has played a critical role in the unfolding of events to this day, but especially in the period
from 1920-1940.

The Arab leaders, who fled to Jerusalem and began to set up their
nationalistic headquarters, saw the issues as these: Neither the British nor the
French were going to be leveraged out with ease. The Jews were a minority

settlement on land that seemed to be shrinking by the day, and the Jews had no great army. They were much more vulnerable to Arab muscle than were the French or British. Therefore, the Jews were their first target.

In early April 1920, Arabs convened in Jerusalem to celebrate an annual Muslim pilgrimage holiday, Nabi Musa.[55] It was short work to whip the crowd into a frenzy against Zionists, who threatened the permanent establishment of the kingdom of Feisal. Arab police stood by silently while crowds began to attack Jews. One hundred sixty were injured in three hours of rioting. When British troops arrived, the rioters were jailed overnight. When released the following morning, the riots resumed. It took three days to quell the uprising. By then, a number of Jews and Arabs were dead, and hundreds had been injured.

The aftermath of the rioting was as appalling as the riots themselves. British authorities dismissed the Arab mayor of Jerusalem and gave stiff sentences to the two leading Arab agitators. Most rioters got off with light sentences. Vladimir Jabotinsky and several other Jews who had organized the Jewish self-defense were given fifteen-year jail terms. This obvious favoritism produced such an uproar in England that the government decided to set up a court in Jerusalem to investigate the matter. The British officers defended their actions during the hearings by declaring the Jews guilty of having started the riots.

The Jews accused the British officers of encouraging Muslim unrest. The chief intelligence officer in Cairo, Colonel Richard Meinertzhagen, took the stand and was able to show that the military administrators in Palestine clearly favored the Arabs to the detriment of the Jews, which was in violation of the Balfour Declaration.

In late April an announcement came from London that the military government in Palestine would be dismantled and a civil administration placed in control. Lloyd George tapped Herbert Samuel as the civil high commissioner. Samuel, a leader of George's Liberal party and former cabinet member, was a Jew and a loyal Zionist.

Feisal was angered by the appointment and alarmed Allenby, who then warned of Arab violence. Samuel was dispatched to Jerusalem on June 30,

1920, under heavy guard. The early days of his administration demonstrated his determination to strengthen the Palestinian economy, to encourage Jewish immigration, and to be utterly impartial. It was his impartiality that ultimately caused problems.

In order not to offend the Arabs he eventually restricted Jewish immigration and imposed other measures that impeded Zionist progress. He hoped to appease the Arabs, but instead it encouraged them to want more and to compromise less. Winston Churchill was serving as colonial secretary during this time. It presented him with some of his most taxing issues. One such quandary was the rise of Feisal's older brother, Abdullah, who undertook a crusade to restore his brother to the throne in Damascus.

Feisal and his retinue journeyed from Hejaz in the summer of 1920 to Amman in Transjordan. No one had taken much interest in that area since the flight of the Turks. That left Bedouin tribes free to raid settlements in Palestine and take booty. Churchill revived a suggestion put to him by T. E. Lawrence: Invite Abdullah to be king of Transjordan as a British protégé. If he accepted, it would keep him from troubling the French and embarrassing the English. It would also provide much needed administration in the area.

Churchill and Abdullah met in Jerusalem on May 26, 1921, for a day and a half conference. The proposal was made. The terms were simple: Abdullah would desist from any further action against the French; he would set up an orderly government in Amman; he would recognize Transjordan as an integral part of Britain's Palestine Mandate and govern the area in the name of the Mandate. On their side, the British would pay Abdullah a monthly subsidy, provide him with trained advisors, and guarantee him eventual independence.

After an all-night session with his advisors, Abdullah met with Churchill and informed him he would accept the offer and abide by its terms. Churchill was delighted and returned to London rife with self-satisfaction. Writing about the event at a later time, Abdullah spoke of the miracle Allah had provided him by getting the British to separate Transjordan from the Palestine Mandate. The terms of the Mandate, as finally approved by the League of Nations, included the exact wordage found in the Balfour Declaration.

Neither the Jews nor anyone else had expressed a particular interest in that largely barren land. Churchill seems to have drawn on the correspondence between Sir Henry McMahon and Abdullah's father, Hussein, in 1915. The Arabs had been promised autonomy over significant tracts of real estate. A year later, Herbert Samuel traveled to London to secure a definitive interpretation of the Balfour Declaration in order to dispel Arab fears once and for all. Churchill accepted Samuel's argument and told him to draft such an interpretation. He would sign it once the details were hammered out.

Later known as the Churchill White Paper, it said that the Jewish national home was restricted to the area west of the Jordan, that the Balfour Declaration had not meant to envision a predominately Jewish state, and that Jewish immigration should be limited to the economic capacity of the country. The Zionist Organization signed the paper with great reluctance and only because it did not wish to lose British support altogether. The Arabs rejected it flatly, establishing a pattern that would be repeated incessantly in years to come. That pattern is still followed today.

After the Churchill White Paper was released, the House of Commons ratified the Mandate just five days later. The Council of the League of Nations followed suit on September 29. With the Mandate in place, the British needed a basic document of law under which Palestine would be governed. Interestingly, while the Syrian and Iraqi mandates called for the mandatory regime (by France and Britain respectively) to foster self-government in those countries, nothing of the sort was envisioned in Palestine. The League's goal there was to ensure a Jewish homeland. Self-government in the 1920s in Palestine would have meant another Arab state, because the Arabs formed the majority.

Consequently, in Palestine Britain was vested with full legislative and administrative powers. After King George V signed the law into being, Herbert Samuel declared it from Jerusalem. Under the law Palestine operated as a Crown colony in all but name, with the headquarters for its own sector and the capital of the entire country in Jerusalem. Samuel completed his term as high commissioner in June 1925, after bringing many positive changes to the region. When Hebrew University on Mount Scopus opened, Allenby came from Cairo to attend, and Arthur Balfour traveled from London. He was moved to tears by the abundant evidence of progress.

Samuel was followed by Herbert Viscount Plumer. He carried on Samuel's record of achievement in a soldierly and forthright manner. Jerusalem's Jewish population doubled between the years of 1924-1928. The era was referred to as the Fourth Aliyah (wave of immigration) spawned by a nasty wave of anti-Semitism in Poland. About seventy thousand Polish Jews left their country and traveled to Palestine. As sad as their story was at the time, one can only marvel at how blessed they were to escape Poland before the Nazi invasion in 1939.

While the Zionists were making progress in Palestine, another man entered Jerusalem's story—Haj Amin al-Husseini. Haj Amin was one of the instigators of the Nabi Musa riots in Jerusalem in 1920. Although convicted and sentenced in absentia, he managed to slip across the Jordan and disappear. His exile didn't last long. In 1921 Grand Mufti Kamal al-Husseini died. Herbert Samuel began to look for a replacement for the office. He called on Ernest T. Richmond, responsible for formulating Arab policy, to assist him with his task. Richmond persuaded Samuels that Haj Amin was the man for the job. He convinced the high commissioner that the young Arab firebrand would gain a sense of responsibility in the post of Grand Mufti. In the short term, Richmond's plan worked; in the long term, it failed drastically.

Haj Amin worked quietly and steadily for seven years to build his power base. His most significant achievement was to rise to the presidency of the supreme Muslim Council. With that post went unrestricted control of all Muslim religious funds in Palestine. He controlled schools, courts, mosques, and cemeteries so that no teacher or official could be appointed who had not demonstrated unswerving loyalty to Haj Amin. The Mufti made sure his most loyal following was based among the illiterate residents of the villages and farms in Palestine.

Finally, on Yom Kippur in 1928, Haj Amin was ready to make his move. He found a pretext for violence at the Western Wall. As the Jewish holy day approached, the sexton who kept the area of pavement in front of the wall so as to separate the men from the women set up a portable screen running perpendicular to the wall. It was a minor change, but in Jerusalem any change in the status quo can quickly achieve major significance. The Mufti carefully orchestrated a series of protests and counter-protests over the following year. He fed the fire by suggesting that the Jews were trying to take over Arab property—their sacred property. The British tried vainly to keep everyone happy. On August 23, 1929, the weekly Muslim Friday Sabbath service came around. At noon Haj Amin mounted his pulpit in the Dome of the Rock to preach a commonplace sermon to the faithful gathered there. The "faithful" had been carefully chosen by the Mufti, armed and ready to carry out their mission.

As the Jews began to congregate at the Western Wall late that afternoon in preparation for the Shabbat, Haj Amin went to his little garden just above the Western Wall. From there he could watch the Jews writhe and scream in the early twilight as they were pounded with the fists and clubs of Allah's servants. That night the rioting spread to the Jewish Quarter and across nearly all of Palestine. The Arab Police were of no use. A contingent of the Royal Air Force stationed in Amman could not restore order. By the time troops arrived from Cairo and restored order five days later, 133 Jews had died and 399 were injured. Arab casualties were significantly lighter: eighty-seven dead, ninety-one injured. Haj Amin had become the undisputed ruler of the Palestinian Arabs.

Back in London, in spite of waning interest in Zionism, Jewish immigration grew persistently, and especially as Hitler tightened his grip in Germany.

- ✧ 1932 — 12,500
- ✧ 1933 — 37,000
- ✧ 1934 — 45,000
- ✧ 1935 — 66,000

The trend continued through 1939 and became known as the Fifth Aliyah. Much of it was overseen by High Commissioner Sir Arthur Wauchope, a Bible-reading Scot, who regarded Zionism with much the same benevolence exhibited by his fellow Scot, Arthur Balfour.

By 1936 the tide had begun to turn. Britain was preoccupied with Hitler. Nazi propaganda in the Middle East was playing heavily on the anti-Semitic fears of the Arabs. Germany was manipulating the Arabs to Hitler's cause much as Britain had done during World War I. England's response was to become increasingly friendly towards the Arabs in an attempt to win their favor. One of the chief means was to limit Jewish immigration.

Haj Amin took advantage of the opportunity. He instigated a strike that lasted six months and was accompanied by an armed uprising among the Arabs aided and abetted by the Iraqis, Syrians, and other groups. The Jews and British suffered losses, but the real bloodletting was among the Arabs. Haj Amin saw an opportunity to destroy his enemies, particularly in the rival Nashashibi clan, but he didn't stop there. The Mufti had a rabid fear of anyone who was literate, especially in English, and targeted landowners, teachers, clerks, and the like. Men were gunned down in the marketplace and in their beds. The Mufti's goons became so adept at these executions, they began to be hired out for the use of others. Today we call them terrorists.

More than two thousand Arabs died in the melee. Haj Amin's grip on the Arab community was firmer than steel. It was a grip that choked the life out of the community. Those who might have led the Arabs into vital and dynamic growth were gone or cowed into silence. This was not the case with the Jewish community, where a generation of leaders and thinkers was being carefully nurtured and groomed.

In the midst of the slaughter, Haj Amin's own decorous and refined behavior was a strange anomaly. However, he lived in no dreamland. He never ventured out into the streets without a bulletproof vest and the company of his six Sudanese bodyguards. His automobile was armor plated, and he never arrived at an appointment on time—he would be either late or early.

During 1937 Nazi broadcasts into the Middle East greatly increased. Zionism was portrayed as the handmaiden of French and British imperialism, increasing Arab unrest. In July of that year, the Peel Commission issued a report detailing the British despair of ever finding a solution to the

Arab-Jewish conflict. Britain had made irreconcilable commitments to both groups. Since the British were unwilling to turn over four hundred thousand Jews to Arab domination, or conversely to put nearly a million Arabs under Jewish rule, the only solution was partition—to divide the territory into two separate states. Jerusalem and Bethlehem, said the Royal Commission, should be set aside in a British enclave with access to the coast.

The League of Nations rejected the partition idea. King Abdullah of Transjordan and his friends the Nashashibis likely favored the move but were afraid to say so. The Mufti and his followers were contemptuous in their rejection, which assured that the Arab Higher Committee would also turn it down. The Jews were willing to accept it as the least undesirable alternative. It was all a moot point; the status quo would continue. That would mean more fighting.

Also in July, Haj Amin stopped in to see the German consul-general in Jerusalem. He wanted to tell the Nazi official how much he admired the Third Reich, and how he would appreciate a little help in his struggle against the British and the Jews. From there the negotiations progressed until Admiral Wilhelm Canaris, head of German intelligence, delivered quantities of weapons from German manufacturers to the Mufti via Iraq and Saudi Arabia. Finally, in the wake of the assassination of some British officials in Galilee by Arab gunmen, the British deposed the Mufti and abolished the Supreme Muslim Council and the Arab Higher Committee. The Mufti retreated to the sanctuary of the Dome of the Rock.

On October 15, 1937, Haj Amin slipped past British police disguised as a beggar. He got to Jaffa by auto and then was smuggled aboard a fishing boat to Lebanon. He kept retreating north until, by 1941, he was the honored guest of Adolph Hitler in Berlin. He was convinced that the Nazis held the key to the two great goals of his life—to destroy the Jews and to drive the British out of the Middle East.

During the war the Mufti lived in Europe and helped the German war effort in any way possible. He recruited Arabs to sabotage the British behind their lines. He helped raise two divisions of Balkan Muslims for the S.S., and his agents provided useful intelligence.

His greatest zeal was spent in destroying Jews. When the "Final Solution" was invoked in 1941, the Mufti was one of its most enthusiastic supporters. He worked diligently to ensure that none of the Jews destined for the gas chambers and ovens were mistakenly diverted to Palestine or other places of refuge. Haj Amin got word that four thousand Jewish children from Bulgaria were to be allowed to emigrate to Palestine in 1943. They never left Europe thanks to the Grand Mufti.

After the war, Haj Amin narrowly escaped arraignment before the court in Nuremberg. Thanks to the French, he made his way to Cairo to resume leadership of the Arab cause in Palestine. It was he who would determine the Arab response to the momentous events of 1947 and 1948.

For the Jewish community in 1938 Jerusalem, the primary problem was trying to persuade the British to increase the immigration quotas. The British, however, saw increased allotments only as putting a match to the Arab fuse—and a short one at that. So we read the agonizing accounts of Jewish refugees escaping Hitler's iron fist only to perish in the waters of the Mediterranean in unseaworthy ships that could find no safe harbor.

In October 1943 three men—Winston Churchill, Chaim Weizmann, and Clement Atlee—sat down in London to discuss the latest partitioning plan. Named the Morrison Plan, it called for Jerusalem to be a separate territory under a British high commissioner. The plan would have to be kept secret until after the war, Churchill explained, but he wanted the other two men to know that Israel had a friend in him. He explained that when Hitler had been crushed, the Jews would have to be established in the land where they belong. Churchill added, "I have an inheritance left to me by Balfour, and I am not going to change. But there are dark forces working against us."[56]

The prime minister probably didn't know how dark and powerful were those forces working against him. No matter how firm his commitment to Zionism, the British Foreign Office and the authorities in Jerusalem who had charge of the Mandate hindered him from stating his position. The all-too-familiar story of the bitter struggle and disappointment for the Jewish people continued—Palestine was not open to the hapless survivors of the concentration camps.

Life became intolerable for the British in Palestine due to the rise of extremist groups. One, the Haganah, later became the basis for the Israeli Defense Forces in 1948. The Irgun was a Zionist paramilitary organization founded in 1931 and later absorbed by the IDF in 1948. Another was the Lehi, or "Fighters for the Freedom of Israel." These groups were determined to wrest control of Palestine from the British. They achieved that goal in 1947, when the hot potato was tossed into the lap of the United Nations. The English informed the UN that something needed to be done quickly, as it was withdrawing soon.

After studying the situation, the UN special committee recommended what had been suggested ten years earlier: partition. Jerusalem, instead of becoming a British colony much like Hong Kong, would be established as an international zone administered by the UN.

The Jews were blackmailed into accepting the idea of Jerusalem's internationalization by the Vatican. At its urging, the Catholic nations of Latin America made it plain to the Jews that they would cast their votes at the UN in favor of partition only if the Jews let the city go. It was an incredible price to pay—after all, the name of their movement, "Zionism," was directly linked to the city—but what could they do? They said yes and hoped God would overrule.

On November 29, 1947, the Latin Americans delivered their vote in the General Assembly and the necessary two-thirds majority in favor of partition was achieved. The next day Haj Amin's Arabs went into the streets of Jerusalem, and the next fight began.

CHAPTER TWELVE

JERUSALEM
DIVIDED

I am jealous for Jerusalem and for Zion
with a great jealousy. —ZECHARIAH 1:14 KJV

The two leaders—Golda Meir and King Abdullah—would rendezvous late at night in an out-of-the-way spot, where the Jordan flows into the Sea of Galilee. Golda was an American, although she had been born in Kiev in 1898. When she was eight, her family moved to Milwaukee, Wisconsin, where she grew to womanhood and became a schoolteacher. However, when she was seventeen she discovered her Zionist faith—the doctrine to which she gave the rest of her life.

In 1921 Golda and her husband, Morris Myerson, immigrated to British Mandate Palestine. By 1924, Golda was immersed in the political scene. She became an official in the Histadrut Trade Union. In the early 1930s Golda returned to the United States as the trade union's emissary. After many of the Jewish leaders in Palestine were imprisoned in 1946 she was appointed to lead the Jewish Agency's Political Department as the main liaison with the British. She actively raised funds to support Israel's War of Independence.

Golda's silver-tongued oratory caught the attention of Prime Minister David Ben-Gurion who appointed her a member of his government. In early May 1948, Ben-Gurion had her masquerade as an Arab and dispatched her to a meeting with Jordan's King Abdullah.

Ironically, Meir and King Abdullah met on the little stretch of the east bank of the Jordan River, the site of a hydroelectric station built and run by the Jews. It was from this facility that the king's palace received electricity. The meeting was on the eve of the UN partition vote, and as head of the Jewish Agency, David Ben-Gurion had sent Golda to meet with Abdullah in the home of the plant's director. They greeted one another as old friends with a common enemy—the Mufti Haj Amin. Abdullah confided that in the event of partition, he would prefer simply to annex the Arab sector to his kingdom.

Meir thought that sounded much better than a separate state led by Haj Amin. She pledged that the Jews would leave the Arab sector to its own devices, and the Jews would devote themselves entirely to the establishment of their own sovereignty within the borders assigned them by the UN. Abdullah was not anti-Semitic. He recognized the Zionists as fellow Semites returned to their homeland after a long exile. Their presence in Palestine had already profited him and his people immensely. He knew better than to think he could put a stop to the establishment of a Jewish state.

The Mufti, on the other hand, was a foolish man who thought of the Jews in terms of the pale rabbinical students so easily cowed by his ruffians' clubs. Abdullah knew the Zionists for what they were: a vigorous and capable people who could put up a stiff fight. In the months between November 29, 1947, when the UN General Assembly voted for partition, and May 14, 1948, when the last British troops left and the state of Israel was reborn, Jerusalem was the scene of interminable conflict. It was Haj Amin's opportunity to seize final control and turn Palestine into an Arab state with him at its helm.

To lead this crusade he selected a kinsman, Abdul Khader Husseini. Abdul Khader was a uniquely charismatic leader who aroused the admiration and zeal of his fellow Arabs. His father had been mayor of Jerusalem— the same one deposed and exiled by the British in 1921 following the Nabi Musa riots. Khader was a small child at the time, but he grew up fighting the British. He was wounded twice during the Arab revolts from 1936-1939. Under Haj Amin's sponsorship, he had received considerably more education than most of the Mufti's lieutenants, including training with explosives in Germany during World War II.

In December of 1947 Khader slipped back into Palestine and began to organize the holy war his cousin had called against the Jews. The centerpiece of his strategy was Jerusalem, and his goal was to strangle the city. Before Khader's arrival, the Mufti had already launched his crusade by calling for a three-day strike in the immediate wake of the partition vote. The Arabs opposed partition because it acknowledged the right of the Jews to exist unmolested in the Middle East. Haj Amin denied that right with his very being. After the strike relations between the Jews and Arabs grew even more strained and distant. Jewish and Arab workers who had co-existed peacefully for years were now compelled to search each other for weapons at the beginning of each day.

The UN had called for internationalization of the city, but its inhabitants—Jew and Arab—knew that no country, not Britain, not the U.S., not France, not anyone, was willing to back the UN policy with its own troops. It was probably the greatest victory for the Arabs that winter—the admission that the United Nations' Palestine resolution could not be implemented without armed force. Only the Jews and Arabs were willing to shed their blood for Jerusalem. They rest of the world stood by and said so be it.

David Ben-Gurion's strategy was simple and applied to the whole Yishuv—the Jewish community in the land of Israel, including Jerusalem: Every Jew should stand fast. Not one shred of territory that they had gained should be given up. In Jerusalem, where the Jews were in the clear majority, this meant harassing the Arabs in an effort to get them to back off first. Sometimes it worked.

Abdul Khader's first thrust was a desultory raid against a house where a detachment of Haganah men was stationed. He brought in a truckload of 120 men from Hebron, an Arab center thirty miles south of Jerusalem. The brief skirmish was broken up by a British armored car, and there were no casualties. Meanwhile, the Jews were doing everything possible to strengthen their hold on their most vulnerable and isolated population center—the Jewish Quarter of the Old City, which was surrounded by walls. Living inside the Jewish

Quarter were rabbis, sages, and students. Pale and stooped from long years of studying the Torah, they were not sturdy recruits for the Haganah. Instead, the task of the Haganah was to smuggle as many fighting men into the Quarter as possible, past the watchful eyes of both the British and the Arabs.

Another thing the Haganah lacked was arms. The Arabs had access to arms by way of shipping routes from all around the Middle East. Military hardware could only reach the Jews through the Mediterranean ports, where British agents maintained a close watch. Smuggling became a fine art. Rifles, mortars, machine guns—all sorts of materiel—arrived disassembled and disguised. The arms were then assembled and carefully hidden in secure storage areas pending the departure of the British. Meanwhile, Golda Meir made a memorable trip to the U.S. to raise money to pay for all this—entirely from private funds.

The man appointed by Ben-Gurion to defend Jerusalem was David Shaltiel. He had gained his military training in the French Foreign Legion fighting Arabs in Morocco. Shaltiel later settled in France and only really became involved in Zionism in the late thirties, with the rise of Nazi anti-Semitism. He was captured by the Gestapo, tortured, and sent to Dachau and Buchenwald. It was there, ironically, that his leadership skills began to shine. When released from the camps, he managed to return to Palestine just before war was declared on Hitler's Germany. In Palestine Shaltiel continued war efforts as a Haganah counterintelligence operative.

As Shaltiel rose through the ranks of the Haganah, his background in the French military became apparent. He was a spit-and-polish disciplinarian in what was then and still is today the most egalitarian army in the world. He was a man who would put the starch into the Jewish defense of Jerusalem. And starch it would need! Shortly after he arrived, Shaltiel got a taste of the way things would be in Jerusalem. A British sergeant major arrested four Haganah men, who had been exchanging gunfire with the Arabs. He simply took the four into the Arab sector and turned them over to the mob. One was shot to death. The other three were stripped, beaten, emasculated, and hacked to death.

Abdul Khader Husseini was after bigger game. His chief demolitions expert was Fawzi el Kutub, a graduate of an SS terrorism course in Nazi Germany. Fawzi blew up the offices of *The Palestine Post*, a Jewish newspaper, on February 1, 1948. Later in the month, with the help of two British deserters, he managed to plant an enormous explosive device on Ben Yehuda Street in the heart of Jewish Jerusalem. Fifty-seven died and eighty-eight were injured. His greatest accomplishment, from his point of view, was on March 11, when a U.S. consulate car carried a bomb into the headquarters of the Jewish Agency—the most heavily guarded building in the city. Thirteen people died.

The most severe threat to Jerusalem, however, was starvation. Abdul Khader's militia held Bab el Wad, Kastel, and other strategic points along the main highway between the coastal plain and the Judean hills on which Jerusalem sits. His tactic was working. Virtually every convoy bringing supplies was ambushed and sustained losses before reaching the city—if it reached Jerusalem at all. By the end of March, nothing was getting through. The city had only a few days' supplies left—the Jewish Quarter, that is.

On March 29, 1948, Ben-Gurion summoned his Haganah commanders to a meeting to determine how to reopen the road to Jerusalem. Yigael Yadin, an archeologist in civilian life but now chief of operations for the entire Haganah, put it plainly: The Yishuv, both in Jerusalem and in Galilee, was being strangled. Convoys and mere defensive measures were no longer getting the job done, and bolder measures were required. It was Ben-Gurion's most critical moment. The Zionist cabinet debated the situation for three hours. They would have gone longer had Ben-Gurion not said, "Enough!" The time had come to take action, and the cowed cabinet approved his plan.

The first requirement was for weapons in sufficient quantity to launch a sizeable operation. Ben-Gurion had already cabled Ehud Avriel, his agent in Prague. A Dakota transport plane arrived at a deserted British airstrip less than twenty miles south of Tel Aviv on April 1. Two days later the main shipment arrived via freighter off a coastal inlet loosely patrolled by British guards. Hundreds of machine guns and thousands of rifles were ferried ashore. From there they went by truck directly to the untested troops who would use them. The men had to use their own underwear to wipe the packing grease from the new weapons. By April 5, three battalions of five hundred men each started clearing the way for a convoy of 250 trucks to bring relief to Jerusalem.

During the fighting a very decisive thing happened—Abdul Khander was killed. Caught in the crossfire of a more intense Jewish assault than he had ever experienced, Khader called on Fawzi al-Kaukji, an Iraqi leader on his northern flank, to send help. Kaukji was Khader's rival. Haganah agents monitoring the conversation heard his terse lie in response, "Ma'fish—I have not any!" Abdul Khander was betrayed and died in the fighting soon after the conversation.

When his body was found the following morning, unprecedented mourning and wailing broke out in the ranks. Such was the nature of his leadership that, with his passing, Haj Amin's cause was lost. Never again would the Palestinian Arabs offer so serious a threat to the Haganah. As the Arabs mourned Abdul Khader, the Jews of the New City were rejoicing. Truckload after truckload of supplies arrived. The siege had been broken, at least for the moment. Before long, the Arabs would resume the ambush of the convoys and supplies would begin to dwindle again.

Added to the starvation tactics was increased shelling of the city. As the British continued to withdraw, they turned over their arms and other material to the Arabs. In this way the Palestinians came to possess more and more artillery with which to fire on the Jewish sectors of Jerusalem. In the midst of all this, the final day of the British withdrawal arrived— May 14, 1948. While Ben-Gurion read the independence proclamation, Sir Alan Cunningham, the last British high commissioner, left his residence in Jerusalem and was driven to Haifa, where he boarded a British cruiser.

Years later Menachem Begin described the scene eloquently in an address to the Knesset:

> One day after our independence was renewed, in
> accordance with our eternal and indisputable right, we were
> attacked on three fronts, and we stood virtually without

arms—few against many, weak against strong. One day after the declaration of our independence, an attempt was made to strangle it with enmity, and to extinguish the last hope of the Jewish People in the generation of Holocaust and Resurrection.[57]

Arab armies from five nations were poised on Palestine's borders, waiting for this moment to drive the Jews into the sea. That objective has not changed to this day. They had exerted as much pressure as could be brought to bear to keep the U.S. from recognizing the new state of Israel. It had come mostly through the Arab American Oil Company (Aramco) to the state department: If the West wanted Arab oil, it had better not try to help the Jews. Oil is still the leverage of choice against support for Israel.

In America, President Harry S. Truman was being urged by his foreign policy advisers to give in to Arab pressure. Nevertheless, after an emotional encounter with his old business partner in Kansas City, a Jew named Eddie Jacobson, he had decided to meet with Chaim Weizmann. A cordial meeting between Truman and Weizmann took place on March 18, 1948. Truman assured Weizmann that America was for partition and would stick to it. The next day, however, Truman was embarrassed by remarks the American ambassador to the UN made in the Security Council:

> On March 19, 1948, Warren Austin, U.S. ambassador to the United Nations, without the president's knowledge or White House clearance, announced on national radio as well as to the UN Security Council that the U.S. government opposed the partition of Palestine. On March 20, Secretary of State George Marshal made a similar announcement. Truman was furious. According to [White House Council Clark] Clifford, Truman said, "I assured Chaim Weizmann that we were for partition and would stick to it. He must think I am a plain liar." He quickly contacted Jacobson and Weizmann

to reassure them that Austin had misrepresented the U.S. position.[58]

Truman later wrote in his diary:

> What is not generally understood is that the Zionists are not the only ones to be considered in the Palestine question. There are other interests that come into play, each with its own agenda. The military is concerned with the problems of defending a newly created small country from attacks by much larger and better trained Arab nations. Others have selfish interests concerning the flow of Arab oil to the U.S. Since they all cannot have their way, it is a perfect example of why I had to remember that "The Buck Stops Here."[59]

Truman was embarrassed because he was certain Weizmann would think him a double-crosser. He was deluged with communications from Zionist and Jewish communities that objected vehemently to the change in U.S. policy, which would postpone partition and Israel's independence. As it turned out, on May 14, a very short while after Ben-Gurion read the declaration of Israel's independence, Truman extended American recognition to the new government.

Now the man in the middle was King Abdullah, who was sitting with a newspaperman in Amman. He supposedly told the reporter:

> The Arab countries are going to war, and naturally, we must be at their sides, but we are making a mistake for which we will pay dearly later. One day we will live to regret that we did not give the Jews a state to satisfy their demands. We have been following the wrong course, and we still are."[60] King Abdullah smiled faintly at the newspaperman and added, "If you quote me on that, I will deny it publically and call you a liar.[61]

Abdullah's army, the Arab Legion, led by British officer Lieutenant-General John Bagot Glubb, was the only professional army in the Arab Middle East at that time. He identified what he believed to be the chief weakness of Arab military establishments. He felt Arab armies tended to be over-staffed with the over-educated elite and political theorists, rather than with officers whose first interest was in soldiering. Glubb Pasha, as he was known in Arab circles, had managed to expunge this tendency from the ranks of his Arab Legion. They would be the only Arab army to prove durable against the Haganah.

On May 11, three days before the end of the Mandate, Golda Meir, disguised as an Arab peasant woman, slipped across the Jordan at Naharayim to meet again with King Abdullah. Abdullah was pale and seemed to be under great strain. Golda asked him if he had broken his promise to her—the one made during their visit the previous November. He told her that when he had made that promise he thought he was in control of his own destiny. He had since learned otherwise. He informed Mrs. Meir that he thought a war could be averted if the Jews were not in such a rush to proclaim statehood.

Golda replied that the Jews had waited two thousand years, and she didn't think they were being impatient at all. The time of statehood had arrived; it would not be postponed. The king sadly informed her that war was inevitable. Golda assured him that the Jews would fight...and they would win. When the king and the future prime minister parted company, Golda expressed a desire that they meet again. It was not to be. Abdullah was assassinated by an Arab in Jerusalem three years later, on July 20, 1951.

In the early years of the war to retain their independence, Jewish authorities in Tel Aviv had to put Jerusalem on hold while they gave their attention and manpower to ward off an Egyptian onslaught coming up through the Negev. This gave Abdullah's forces an advantage in Jerusalem. Because of the Dome of the Rock, it had become the third holiest shrine in Islam. Also, Abdullah's father had lost Mecca and Medina to the Saudis in 1925, so Jerusalem would serve as compensation for his family as well—a vindication of the Hashemite dynasty.

Glubb was reluctant to commit his Bedouin soldiers to street fighting in Jerusalem. If he had known how poorly defended the city was at that point, he might have felt differently. The first units of the Legion—a small detachment—arrived in the Old City on May 19. At the same time 2,080 of his soldiers invaded the heights north of the city and began to advance on the New City—the center of Jewish population with roughly 100,000 inhabitants. Their approach struck terror. This was a real army, not an undisciplined bunch of irregulars.

David Shaltiel had roughly the same number of men under his command, but they were virtually weaponless. A group of teenagers armed with Molotov cocktails, a bazooka, and an armored car encountered Glubb's first column of the Legion. The Jordanians had made a wrong turn near the Mandelbaum Gate and were taken completely by surprise in the ambush. Before the Arabs withdrew, the teenagers had managed to knock out three of their armored cars. The victory gave new heart to the Israelis. They would need it.

While the New City was momentarily safe from capture by the Arabs, the Jewish Quarter remained in grave danger. On May 18, a second company of Haganah men had managed to fight its way into the Quarter to join the lone company that had been defending the Jews there. Here, however, Glubb's Legion held the real advantage. Its artillery prevented further reinforcement by the Jews, and the Arab death grip tightened. The Quarter was forced to surrender on May 28. It was an enormous symbolic loss not only to the inhabitants of Israel but to the Jewish community worldwide.

Ten days of savage fighting followed, during which the Jews turned back the Arab assault. On May 28, Glubb called off his attack. His men had been seriously mauled in the fighting. Besides, the strategy for his assault was wrong. The battle for Jerusalem would be decided on the heights of Latrun, which overlooked the supply road from Tel Aviv. David Shaltiel only knew he had done what he could in the Jewish Quarter and that his primary responsibility was the New City.

The Egyptian threat from the south had been lessened by the end of May, and the Israeli high command could focus its attention on getting relief to Jerusalem. By early June the Jewish sector had been the recipient of more than ten thousand rounds fired from Jordanian artillery. Two thousand homes had been destroyed and twelve hundred civilian casualties reported. The city was entirely cut off from supplies, and the people were on the verge of starvation.

Haganah operations chief Yadin and Ben-Gurion summoned General Yigal Allon, who had been leading the fighting in Galilee, to head the assault on Latrun and break the Arab stranglehold on Jerusalem's supply route. Haganah troops had been augmented with large numbers of raw recruits, many fresh off the immigrant ships. These men were rushed to the front by bus and taxi. In the blistering heat, these untrained troops were tossed into a direct frontal assault on the entrenched Jordanians without artillery support or even adequate reconnaissance. The Arabs raked them with artillery and mortars. The Jews were forced to withdraw with heavy losses.

In the midst of the campaign to take Latrun, Ben-Gurion assigned a new and special volunteer to oversee the assaults. He was David Marcus, a Jewish American, a West Point Graduate, a Normandy veteran, and a colonel in the U.S. army. Marcus had left his prestigious post at the Pentagon to help his brothers in Israel. He joined with Shlomo Shamir, the commander of the first assault against Latrun, and together they tried harder to make the next assaults successful.

In spite of reinforcing their operations considerably, the Fourth Regiment of the Arab Legion stood firm in the face of the next Israeli attack. More Jewish bodies littered the slopes in front of their positions. It seemed that the hope of relieving Jerusalem was being bled dry at Latrun. An upcoming deadline made their task even more urgent. A UN ceasefire was due to go into effect on June 11. When that happened, if the road to Jerusalem was not open, it would be too late.

Marcus began to search for a different route. There was a path by which the troops had been getting to Jerusalem on foot. Marcus got two young officers, Vivian Herzog and Amos Chorev, to take a jeep ride with him, and together they discovered it was quite possible to traverse this path from Tel Aviv to Jerusalem on wheels. Now, all they needed to do was make it passable for trucks. Dirty and unshaven from their trek across the mountainous terrain, the three men headed directly for Ben-Gurion's office as soon as they arrived back in Tel Aviv. The prime minister listened carefully to the report. Maybe, just maybe, if a jeep could get through...

A searing heat wave continued across Palestine as hundreds of workers set out from Tel Aviv to begin the daunting task of building a road in the wilderness. Given the shortage of heavy machinery, it was a mind-boggling job. Meanwhile, in Jerusalem the situation was growing more desperate by the hour. Only a few days' supplies remained. The ordnance officer estimated that enough ammunition remained for a sustained battle of no more than twenty-four hours.

Dov Joseph, a Canadian Jew and civilian governor of Jerusalem during the crisis, could take much of the credit for the orderly and disciplined way of life in the city. The people were remarkably steadfast and courageous. On Saturday, June 5, Joseph was still reeling from the death of his daughter, who had died fighting in the south a few days before. Now he was forced to cut the citizens' rations once more. He and his fellow Jerusalemites would subsist on four thin slices of bread each day, supplemented by half a pound of dried beans, peas, and groats each week. He waited in anticipation of news from what many were calling the "Burma Road," the proposed Tel Aviv to Jerusalem route. It was named after the path hacked out of the jungle-covered mountains in Burma by Chinese coolies in order to provide supplies to Chiang Kai-shek's troops during World War II.

Marcus began the excavation with just one bulldozer at his disposal. The work inched forward at an agonizing pace. Each hundred yards of progress toward Jerusalem required three hundred yards of winding roadway. Alternate crews worked day and night. Then a second bulldozer became available. By then conditions in Jerusalem were desperate. On Monday, June 6, Joseph had cabled Ben-Gurion that the city couldn't hold out beyond the following Friday. Ben-Gurion weighed his alternatives. Marcus had three miles to go. Could he make it in four days?

Ben-Gurion decided he could not afford to risk the wait. He called out the Home Guard and sent them on foot with forty-five pound packs loaded with food for Jerusalem. Three hundred middle-aged men were bused to the end of the Burma Road and set out to hike the three miles over ridges and through ravines until they reached the point where they could offload their packs onto a truck bound for the Holy City.

On June 9, David Marcus and his two bulldozers emerged from the wilderness through which they had been digging since the end of May. The first trucks, filled with food and water, made their way over that primitive roadway to be greeted in Jerusalem with tears and cheers of joy. Two days later, at ten a.m., the UN ceasefire went into effect. It was just the breathing space Israel needed to rearm and replenish itself for the completion of the War of Independence.

In Jerusalem, the war was over. The Jordanians held half the city— including the Old City with the Holy Sites, the Western Wall, the now-abandoned Jewish quarter, and all the surrounding countryside north, south, and east. The Israelis held the New City and a secure western corridor leading to the coast. Jerusalem now had a knife thrust through her heart: for the first time in her history, she was a divided city.

CHAPTER THIRTEEN

JERUSALEM
REUNITED

Great is the Lord, and greatly to be praised
In the city of our God. —PSALM 48:1

After the 1948 armistice was declared between Israel and Jordan, it was thought Jerusalem was permanently divided. The armistice provided for Israeli access to two important Jordanian-controlled areas of Jerusalem: Mount Scopus, where the campus of Hebrew University and Hadassah Hospital were located, and the Western Wall and synagogues of the Old City. The only good to come of this agreement was that the Jews were allowed to maintain a police outpost on Mount Scopus.

In November 1949, Jerusalem again appeared on the agenda of the United Nations. The Israelis argued against internationalizing the Holy City. They instead offered to sign an agreement which would guarantee access to all holy sites in their portion of the city. This was not to be. On December 10, the UN General Assembly passed a resolution calling for internationalization under UN trusteeship.

The government of Israel reacted promptly. In December 1949 it announced the immediate transfer of offices from Tel Aviv to Jerusalem and proclaimed Jerusalem the eternal capital of Israel. Faced with Israel's actions and Jordan's vehement opposition to the resolution, the UN Trusteeship Council recognized it was unenforceable except by armed intervention. The resolution was set aside.

By January 1950, all government services that had been housed in East Jerusalem during the British Mandate were transferred to Amman. King Abdullah annexed the city and the West Bank, the hill country of Samaria and Judea that lie north and south of Jerusalem. He then changed the name of his country from Transjordan to the Hashemite Kingdom of Jordan. East Jerusalem was heralded the "second capital" of Jordan, although it meant little in actual practice. The city was cut off from access to the Mediterranean and somewhat isolated up in the hills.

For several years following the armistice, East Jerusalem was without electricity and water was in short supply. The economy was based on tourism and institutions devoted to religious research. Its only significant manufacturing was a lone cigarette plant. Under Jordanian oversight, building projects were near nonexistent, confined to a few hotels, churches, and hospitals.

On the other side of the wall separating Israeli and Jordanian oversight, the times were very different. The Israelis were much more aggressive in their allotted portion of Jerusalem, even though it was situated at the end of a long corridor and surrounded by hostile Arabs. Larger water pipelines replaced circa 1948 conduits. An immense reservoir for water was constructed south of the city. The already-functioning electrical network was connected to the national grid, and train service in and out of the city resumed in May 1949.

Major highway construction and other building projects got underway quickly. Both Hadassah Medical Center and Hebrew University required new campuses to replace the facilities on Mount Scopus, which lay vacant. The complex multiplied to include a medical school, training school for nurses, dental school, and a wide range of specialty clinics.

The university added a stadium, synagogue, planetarium, and a major national library. A convention center for concerts, dramatic performances, exhibitions, and conferences was erected on the western outskirts of the city. In 1951 the Twenty-third Zionist Congress assembled in the center. It was the first to be held in Israel.

To the southwest of Jerusalem, Mount Herzl was turned into a national memorial park in honor of Theodore Herzl's work. It was he who, in the nineteenth century, had ignited the spark of modern Zionism. Since then many noted Zionists and Israeli leaders have been honored by burial there.

Israeli government buildings were raised in the late 1950s. The Knesset building, financed by the Rothschild family, was completed in 1966. These structures, including the Shrine of the Book and the Jerusalem Museum, lent credence to the belief that Jerusalem was indeed the capital of Israel. Most nations, including the U.S., refused to recognize the validity of the claim and established embassies or legations in Tel Aviv.

After Israeli president Chaim Weizmann died in 1952, the presidential residence was moved permanently to Jerusalem. It was there that foreign diplomats were compelled to present their credentials as well as to confer with the prime minister or foreign minister. By 1961 West Jerusalem's population had reached 166,300.

Life on the west side of the dividing wall was occasionally disrupted by sniping incidents instigated by Jordanian soldiers. A major point of contention was the Israeli police garrison on Mount Scopus. Each fortnight, a convoy passed through the Mandelbaum Gate under UN supervision to bring the relief shift and resupply the garrison with food and water. In one incident Jordanian troops fired on Israeli patrols, killing a UN observer and four Israeli policemen. Dag Hammarskjöld, then secretary-general of the UN, and his envoy, Ralph Bunche, shuttled from Amman to Jerusalem in an effort to resolve the problem. They were unsuccessful.

In 1965 Teddy Kollek was elected mayor of West Jerusalem. Two years later, following the reunification of Jerusalem, he became the first mayor of a united Jerusalem. During his tenure in office, the atmosphere between Jordanian East Jerusalem and the western part of the city was, while not cordial, relatively quiet. There were isolated incidents, but the real boiling cauldron was in Egypt and Syria, where the Soviets were pulling out all stops to court the two countries. Israel had been on the receiving end of the Soviets' courtship following World War II, but little came of it.

Both Egyptian President Gamal Nasser and Syrian President Amin al-Hafez were the recipients of an enormous amount of military and economic aid from Russia. In 1967 Soviet rhetoric reached a crescendo when the

Israelis were accused of fostering an ominous arms buildup along the Syrian border and the Golan Heights. It was a patent falsehood.

In mid-April 1967 Soviet Ambassador to Israel Leonid Chuvakhin complained to Prime Minister Levi Eshkol about the purported buildup. Apparently Ambassador Chuvakhin had no need to learn the truth; the abounding rumors were enough for him. Eshkol offered to drive him to the Syrian border to show him that the accusations were untrue. It was a useful diplomatic tool. If the rumors of Israeli aggression failed to materialize, the Soviets could brag that it was their support of the Syrian Ba'athist regime that saved the day.

The Soviets, however, stoked the fire just a tad too long, and it would soon boil over and scald them. Nasser amassed an army on the Sinai Peninsula, opposite Israel's border. He closed the Strait at Sharm El-Sheikh at the mouth of the Gulf of Aqaba. It was the classic provocation. Israel had already notified the UN Security Council that if measures warranted, it would act in its own self-defense. UN Secretary General U Thant failed to act forcefully to impose the conditions of the truce that had existed since 1956. The UN peacekeeping forces standing between Nasser's army and the Israelis timidly packed up their tents and left town. On May 19, 1967, nothing stood between the Egyptians and the border of Israel.

In an amazing display of self-assurance, Levi Eshkol and Defense Minister Moshe Dayan remained cool, not acting until every alternative to avoid a confrontation had proved fruitless. On May 30 King Hussein of Jordan flew to Cairo to mend fences with Nasser and sign a mutual defense pact. Israeli intelligence, headed by Isser Harel, had spent a considerable amount of time studying the Arab character. They knew, for instance, that collective efforts among Arabs were seldom cohesive for any length of time. The best the Israelis could hope for was that the pact would be Hussein's lone demonstration of Arab solidarity—and he would leave the fighting to Egypt and Syria.

Israel launched a lightning attack against the Arab states at ten minutes after seven on the morning of June 5th. Well before noon nearly the entire Egyptian aircraft fleet was a flaming wreck. Their air force was destroyed on the ground by Israeli fighter jets as God blinded the eyes of the Egyptians. In similar attacks, Israel destroyed Syrian jets and Jordanian planes.

Simultaneously, Israeli ground forces struck the Egyptian army amassed in the Sinai with a fist that virtually demolished Egypt's capacity to respond. As an important part of Israeli strategy for victory, Dayan had ordered a complete blackout of news. None of the stunning victories of June 5 were acknowledged for a twenty-four hour period. They allowed loudly proclaimed Egyptian announcements boasting it had destroyed Israel's armed forces to go unchallenged. The Israelis wanted to forestall a Soviet move toward a cease-fire if it thought its client states were winning.

Dayan's ploy had one unexpected drawback: King Hussein also heard Radio Cairo's bizarre and whimsical interpretation of the facts and believed the reports. Israel had already contacted the king and offered not to infringe on his territory if he would stay put. Perhaps out of a desire for self-glory, Hussein ignored Israel's proposal and instructed his troops to begin shelling West Jerusalem. Hoping that was the limit of Hussein's military action, Dayan ordered the front commander in Jerusalem, Uzi Narkiss, to hold his fire. But just to be on the safe side, Israeli jets destroyed Amman's air force of twenty Hunter jets the same day.

At one o'clock that afternoon, the Jordanians made their move to overrun Government House on the south side of the city. It was the headquarters of General Odd Bull, the Norwegian chief of the United Nations Truce Supervision Organization. Surrounded by seven hundred acres, it would give Hussein easy access for his Patton tanks to invade Israeli Jerusalem.

An hour later Dayan gave the signal for Israeli troops to secure Government House. The Jerusalem Brigade drove the Jordanians from their objective and even further south from "The Bell," a series of entrenchments. By midnight the brigade had accomplished its mission with the loss of eight men.

About the time Dayan had ordered the Jerusalem Brigade to attack, Uzi Narkiss issued the command to Uri Ben-Ari, leader of the Harel Mechanized Brigade—tanks and motorized infantry—to take the ridges north of the corridor. He was then to intercept Jordanian tank columns advancing on Jerusalem south through Ramallah. Ben-Ari's men and tanks advanced into the Jerusalem corridor. He then began to send units into the ridges controlled by the Jordanians.

Ben-Ari chose four separate routes to ensure that at least one column would break through and reach the objective—Tel el-Ful. It was the place where the road south from Ramallah and west from Jericho met and formed one road into Jerusalem. It was a strategic point. The main obstacles to their advance were Jordanian troops and a minefield that stretched the entire length of the border in the area. The ground had been mined for so long, no one knew where the mines were located. Uri Ben-Ari and his troops would find them before the battle had ended.

At five o'clock the command was given to commence firing. The Israeli tanks—supported by jet fighter-bomber attacks—blasted the Jordanian bunkers blocking their way. The infantry moved forward while engineers set out to find the mines equipped only with bayonets, cleaning rods, and other improvised equipment. Many of the men lost legs that grisly night.

As dawn crept over the battlefield, Ben-Ari's units had managed to reach the outskirts of Tel el-Ful. They had only four Sherman tanks, some half-tracks, and a few vehicles from the reconnaissance unit. They soon spotted three Patton tanks moving toward them from Jericho and opened fire. They scored direct hits, but to their astonishment the 75mm shells bounced off the Pattons' heavy armor plate. Supplied with 90mm guns, the Pattons returned fire and scored a direct hit on one of the Israeli tanks. With its commander wounded and its main gun destroyed, the Sherman withdrew. The firing pin on the second Sherman cannon broke, leaving two Israeli tanks to level ineffective fire at the advancing Jordanian Pattons. If the three Jordanian tanks kept coming, there was little the Israelis could do to stop them. Lying just behind the three advancing Patton tanks were twenty more awaiting orders to advance.

Suddenly, the Jordanian tanks began to turn and withdraw behind Tel el-Ful. The cessation of fire gave the Israelis an opportunity to crew the tank with the damaged gun and rejoin the operative Sherman tanks. Soon thereafter, the Patton tanks came from behind Tel el-Ful to rejoin the fray. The Israelis resumed firing only to see their shells bounce off the Jordanian tanks.

Sitting in the turret of the tank with the disabled cannon was Sergeant Mordechai Eitan. He had been studying the Patton tanks through his binoculars when he spotted metal containers mounted on the backs of the Jordanian tanks. Could they be auxiliary fuel tanks?

There was only one way to find out. He cocked the heavy machine gun on the tank's turret and opened fire toward the containers. A direct hit on one of the containers caused the Patton to burst into flames. The terrified crew of the tank beside it bailed out and ran for their lives. One Jordanian tank kept coming toward the Israeli line. Just as its commander broke through, Israeli air support arrived and directed a well-aimed round at the Patton tank. The remainder of the Jordanians turned and headed back to Jericho. Ben-Ari's troops had secured the road to Jerusalem and firmly blocked it.

In Tel Aviv, Colonel Mordechai Gur and his 55th Paratroop Brigade had been scheduled for deployment in the Sinai. Things were going so well there, however, that the high command offered their services to Narkiss. Colonel Gur and his staff arrived in Jerusalem a few hours ahead of their paratroopers. The greatest difficulty facing Gur's plan to penetrate the Green line—as the border with Jordan was called—was whether to attack at night or wait for dawn. Since Dayan had ruled out air support because of the holy sites, it made little sense to wait for daylight; launching a night attack might even give the Israelis an advantage.

The battle for Jerusalem was bloody and costly. The Jordanians had withdrawn to entrenched positions on Ammunition Hill. Here, the Israelis encountered massive resistance. In the early morning hours, two prongs of the paratrooper attack crossed just north of the Mandelbaum Gate. One unit headed toward the Old City, the other toward several Arab strongholds. Both groups encountered fierce street-to-street combat. By noon, however, Jordanian resistance had ended.

Perhaps the most critical struggle for Jerusalem was not fought on the battlefield but in the cabinet of Prime Minister Eshkol. Defense Minister Moshe Dayan and Menachem Begin were in favor of surrounding the Old City and choking it into surrender. Others in Eshkol's cabinet were in favor of liberating all of Jerusalem. Dayan's plan remained in effect until he and

Narkiss drove to Mount Scopus to survey the area. As Dayan gazed out over the Old City—Jerusalem the Golden—he realized the city had to be taken or it would be lost.

At the cabinet meeting that night, Eshkol issued orders through Chief of Staff Yitzhak Rabin to take the city. Colonel Mordechai Gur arranged for detachments to enter the Old City through its gates. The main thrust would be through the Lion's Gate opposite the Mount of Olives. Resistance was minimal. The remainder of the day was relegated to rejoicing and the costly work of eliminating the last pockets of Jordanian opposition.

At the same time the Western Wall was being liberated, columns of Israeli tanks and infantry continued pressing the Jordanians throughout Samaria and Judea—called the West Bank by Arabs. My beloved friend General Mordechai Gur, who was a 37- year-old colonel at that time, led his 55th Paratroopers Brigade to defend Jerusalem. Years later in his office in Jerusalem he told me, "On Wednesday morning, June 7th, I and my paratroopers stormed into the Old City and advanced on the Temple Mount. I wept as I shouted over my communications system, 'The Temple Mount is in our hands!'"[62]

Gur said to me of that experience:

> I had long looked forward to liberating Jerusalem as something sublime. For me it was the culmination of my most personal goals as a youngster, as a Jew, and as a soldier. To me, the Temple Mount was more important than the Western Wall because the Temple was the center of religion, the center of tradition. It was also the center of the kingdom, of the state, of all our hopes. The day we took it, I wrote in my diary, "What will my family say when they hear we again liberated Jerusalem just as the Maccabees once did?" Jerusalem has only been a functioning capital when the Jews have ruled it.[63]

By sundown on June 7, the Israelis had reached the Jordan River. King Hussein had paid dearly for his gamble and his choice to believe the Egyptian propaganda. He suffered over fifteen thousand casualties—dead, wounded, missing—in his army. His air force had been decimated and half his tanks destroyed. He had lost his dynasty's last claim on the Islamic holy places. He had, however, lost more than that. The West Bank had been his richest agricultural land. The tourist income from Jerusalem and Bethlehem had accounted for 40 percent of Jordan's revenue. His only consolation was that the Jews had suffered more casualties against his army (1,756) than they had in the much larger Sinai campaign (1,075). One-fourth of Israel's losses had come in Jerusalem.

Few Israelis found room for mourning. Chief Rabbi Shlomo Goren said to me:

> I managed to reach the Western Wall even before the firing had died down. Like one of Joshua's priests, I was running with the ram's horn, the shofar, in my hand. When I placed it to my lips and blew, I felt like thousands of shofars from the time of King David were blowing all at once.[64]

Jews from every nation were dancing and weeping as they touched the Western Wall. They sang, "Yerushalayim Shel Zahav"...Jerusalem of Gold. Yitzhak Rabin told me years later when he was prime minister:

> This was the most holy day of my life. I heard rabbis crying that the Messiah was coming soon, and that ancient prophecy was fulfilled that day. You would have thought King David had returned with his harp and the Ark of the Covenant.[65]

Hardened veterans ran to touch the ancient wall, tears flowing down their faces in gratitude. "Next year, Jerusalem," was no longer a heartrending cry; it was reality. To pray at the Western Wall was no longer a yearning;

it was a certainty. The Temple Mount, on which stands the Dome of the Rock—an Islamic mosque, still remained closed to the Jewish people, but they could at least stretch out their fingertips and touch a portion of it.

Most importantly, Jerusalem was united in Jewish hands.

CHAPTER FOURTEEN

JERUSALEM
RESURRECTED

The Lord is rebuilding Jerusalem and bringing the exiles back to Israel. —PSALM 147:2 NLT

On the morning of June 9, 1967, Mayor Teddy Kollek bounded out of bed with an entirely new portfolio. His responsibilities had increased one hundred fold! He was now mayor over all of Jerusalem, including some 67,000 Arabs who were opposed to the new oversight. Kollek was unclear as to their legal status as Jerusalemites and his responsibility towards them.

Given the condition of East Jerusalem, it would have been understandable had the Jews sought revenge against the Arabs in their midst. Upon inspection, the Jews discovered not a single usable synagogue in the old Jewish Quarter of the city. Jewish shrines and cemeteries had been desecrated shamefully. Given the hatred and vitriol spewed at the Jews by their Arab neighbors, retaliation might have been foremost in their minds. The choice by the Israelis, however, was not retribution but mercy.

Mayor Kollek realized that it was the Jordanians who were the true perpetrators of the defilement in the Jewish Quarter. He determined that under Israeli administration, all the city's inhabitants, no matter their nationality or religion, were entitled to law and order, freedom of religion, and efficient and humane public services. He went to work that very day—even before the ceasefire was announced.

Municipal employees crossed into East Jerusalem to repair broken water pipes and electrical circuits. They tore down and hauled away the barriers, roadblocks, and barbed wire that had divided the city. The electrical grid and telephone systems were integrated. Water from West Jerusalem reservoirs ended the chronic shortages that had plagued Arab Jerusalem since 1948. The physical quality of life for the Arabs improved immeasurably overnight.

The chief goal of Mayor Kollek and the Israeli government was to incorporate Arab Jerusalem as thoroughly as possible into the fabric of Israeli life. They wanted it understood unmistakably that Jerusalem was now united, and they had come to stay. This was apparent in Kollek's enthusiasm to share his staff's talents with the Arabs, and also in the way he incorporated hundreds of Arab municipal employees and inspectors into the united city's enlarged administration. It was also apparent in the tough measures taken to remove squatters from the Jewish Quarter and to clean out the bedraggled warren of flats that abutted the Western Wall in order to make room for the Jews to worship there.

The mayor wrote me a letter expressing his concerns for Jerusalem:

> Now it is more important than ever that we rally support for Jerusalem...international opinion is being swayed in favor of two capitals in one city. We know that is not the solution and that two capitals in Jerusalem will only lead to a redivided city.

Every evicted Arab was offered compensation and alternative housing, but the move was inevitable. The Israelis were determined to remove every temporary, ramshackle lean-to in the area. The course for the future of the city was permanent change.

The Knesset passed into law a bill amending the Law and Administration Ordinance of 1948 to say that the government could, by order, extend the law, jurisdiction, and administration of the state to any part of the Land of Israel so designated. An order accompanying this bill placed East Jerusalem and its environs under Israeli law, jurisdiction, and administration. Another bill authorized the minister of the interior to, at his discretion, enlarge by proclamation the area of a particular municipality by the inclusion of a designated area.

Following the passage of that second bill, the interior minister enlarged the Municipality of Jerusalem to include the city's holy places in an effort to protect them from desecration and insure equal access to all—Arabs, Christians, and Jews. The UN saw this move as the Israelis having annexed East Jerusalem. The General Assembly voted 99 to 0 that the changed status of Jerusalem was invalid and that Israel should rescind its actions. Israel responded by informing the UN that the measures adopted by the Knesset related only to the integration of East Jerusalem in the administrative and municipal spheres, and served only to provide for the protection of the holy places in the city.

What the UN General Assembly members failed to understand was that the Jordanians had taken the land in 1948 not by international law but by force. It had been incorporated into their state. Israel had taken back their land in an act of self-defense. It was an argument any person should have been able to understand and respect.

There was one chief legal problem, however. The Arabs of Jerusalem were Jordanian citizens who now lived in the State of Israel. This technicality didn't seem to bother them at all. They mingled freely with the rest of the population. Arabs visited homes they had abandoned nineteen years before. In a show of solidarity on Friday, June 30, Mayor Kollek attended the prayer services at Haram esh-Sharif (the Noble Sanctuary located on the Temple Mount).

Jerusalem's Arabs didn't turn up their noses at the many improvements the Jews had brought to their area. True, the Israelis could be imperious and unaccommodating, but the Arabs were not indifferent to their essential physical security. By year's end, Kollek had provided fifteen miles of newly-paved streets, twelve hundred new street lights, thousands of trees planted in city gardens, new waste-removal equipment, and Arab homes were being connected to the municipal water system at the rate of fifty per week. The mayor was spending three times more on East Jerusalem than had the Jordanians.

Israelis poured into the Old City to spend their hard cash on virtually everything the Arabs had for sale. It was a far cry from the sinister brutality they had been warned to expect from the Jews. The West Bank and Jerusalem Arabs were enjoying economic prosperity such as they had never known.

In the early years there were some incidents of strikes and violence. Eight hundred buildings were leveled in a West Bank village that was a base for terrorists. Convicted terrorists were jailed or deported. In Jerusalem, violence has remained the monopoly of imported terrorists.

Since the Israelis regained control of the Old City in 1967, Hebrew University resumed activities on its Mount Scopus campus, and was expanded and improved. Hadassah Hospital was reopened. Today the modern facility serves Arabs and Jews alike, as it did before 1948. The Jewish Quarter in the Old City has undergone a total restoration and is once again a thriving part of the city. The Muslim Quarter, as indicated, has been upgraded. Throughout the Old City, television cable has all but eliminated unsightly antennas.

Streets and alleyways have been improved, and the Via Dolorosa—the traditional route taken by Jesus to His crucifixion on Calvary—has been resurfaced with ancient paving stones from the time of Herod. The Old City's crenellated walls were renovated, and a walkway permits citizens and visitors to stroll along its ramparts. The marketplace received a thorough cleaning and painting, and the ancient Roman thoroughfare that bisects the city— the Cardo—has been excavated, restored, and turned into a shopping mall with souvenir shops that cater to the tourist trade.

Outside the walls of the Old City, the Israelis expanded the water districts, built twelve elementary schools, four vocational schools, three dental schools, two community centers, twelve adult and youth clubs, three childcare centers, and four libraries. An average of one million tourists visit Jerusalem each year, among them a multitude of people from Arab states that maintain no diplomatic relations with Israel.

A Saudi Arabian king is said to have complained that he did not feel free to visit Al-Aqsa Mosque because it stood on ground occupied by Israel. That seems contradictory when neither he nor his predecessors visited the mosque when it was under Jordanian control. This points to one important detail: The Arabs are united only in anti-Semitism. They all can agree that the Jews are the "Little Satan," but here their unity ends. They talk openly about replacing Israel with a Palestinian state but distrust each other, and well they should. The Syrians really want Lebanon, Israel, and Jordan. The Jordanians want the West Bank and Jerusalem. The PLO wants all of Israel, preferably with every Jew slaughtered, and anything else that can be wrested from Jordan, Syria, and Lebanon.

Today Americans and Europeans tend to take the Arabs at face value. None seem to understand that it is deemed perfectly acceptable, even preferable, to lie to an infidel—and every non-Arab is an infidel. The U.S., EU, UN, and Russia continue to call for a negotiated settlement, believing the Arabs to be reasonable people who are willing to negotiate a compromise by which Israel will be allowed to live in peace. Unfortunately, some Israeli leaders have bought into this fatuous dream. In the hard reality of daylight, however, Israel has little choice but to retain sovereignty over all of Jerusalem.

Teddy Kollek wrote of Jerusalem:

> Let me be perfectly candid. The thing I dread most is that this city, so beautiful, so meaningful, so holy to millions of people, should ever be divided again; that barbed wire fences, mine fields, and concrete barriers should again sever its streets, that armed men again patrol a frontier through its heart. I fear the re-division of Jerusalem not only as the mayor of the city, as a Jew, and as an Israeli, but as a human being who is deeply sensitive to its history and who cares profoundly about the well-being of its inhabitants...It must never again be divided. Once more to cut this living city in two would be as cruel as it is irrational.[66]

The treaties with terrorists that have been forced on Israel are nothing more than an attempt to divide the Holy City of Jerusalem, which God Almighty gave to Abraham and to David. Jerusalem became David's capital over three thousand years ago. A journalist for *U.S. News and World Report* wrote: "Peace is more than the mere absence of war...the path to Middle East peace remains as perilous as Moses' forty-year trek through the desert."[67] Peace has continued to be elusive, but there can be no doubt that the moment the Jews took Jerusalem back, that holy city was resurrected and began to thrive.

CHAPTER FIFTEEN

SURROUNDED
BY THE ENEMY

From the wicked who oppress me,
   From my deadly enemies who surround me.
Arise, O Lord,
   Confront him, cast him down;
   Deliver my life from the wicked with Your sword.

PSALM 17:9,13

After all Israel had done to incorporate the Arab residents in Jerusalem and the West Bank, it was still not enough for the enemies that surrounded the tiny nation. It seemed none would be satisfied until Israel ceased to exist.

In September 1970, Egyptian President Gamal Abdel Nasser died. His successor, Anwar Sadat, was determined to regain the territory lost during the Six Day War. Through a UN intermediary, Sadat let it be known that he would sign a peace treaty with Israel if the nation agreed to withdraw to the pre-1967 boundaries. Israel responded: "Israel will not withdraw to the pre-June 5, 1967 lines."[68]

Sadat's plan was to cause just enough damage to the Israelis to alter their decision. The leader of Syria, Hafiz al-Assad, had no such aspirations. He was only determined to reclaim the Golan Heights militarily. The Syrians had launched a massive upsurge along their border with the Golan Heights, and they planned nothing short of a decisive victory against the Israelis. Al-Assad had another goal in mind as well: to establish Syria as the supreme military force among Arab countries. He was certain that with Sadat's assistance, the two allies could strike a convincing blow against tiny Israel and insure that the West Bank and Gaza would once again be in Arab hands.

Sadat was plagued by economic ills that he thought would be forgotten by a war with Israel, the nemesis of all Arabs:

> The three years since Sadat had taken office...were the most demoralized in Egyptian history... A desiccated economy added to the nation's despondency. War was a desperate option.[69]

The Egyptian people had been put to shame by the rout of their troops during the Six Day War. If Sadat was successful militarily, he might be able to persuade the population that reforms were necessary. University students protested against Sadat and saw war as the only way to regain respect in the region. They were upset that Sadat had waited so long to retaliate against the Israelis.

King Hussein of Jordan, on the other hand, was hesitant to join a coalition to attack Israel. His country had lost much in 1967, and he was afraid of even more losses in another attempt. While Sadat backed the PLO in its claims to the West Bank and Gaza, King Hussein was fighting his own battles against the terrorist organization. After several hijackings, attempts to assassinate the king, and efforts to wrest the Irbid—the area with the second largest city in the Hashemite Kingdom—from Hussein, Jordanian troops expelled the PLO from the country during what became known as Black September 1970.

In the bloody fighting that followed the king's decision, terrorists murdered Major R. J. Perry, military attaché at the U.S. embassy in Amman. Then they occupied two hotels, the Intercontinental and the Philadelphia, and held thirty-two American and European guests hostage. The leader, George Habash, announced they would kill the hostages and blow up the hotel if Jordanian troops did not retreat. An uneasy quiet ensued, but that was broken in September when Habash's men hijacked SwissAir and TWA jets, ferrying them to Dawson Field in Jordan. Three days later, a BOAC plane was hijacked and flown to Dawson. The group then had 445 hostages.

By September 12 only fifty-four hostages remained captive, and by September 16, King Hussein announced a military government to restore order to Jordan. The following morning he unleashed the Bedouin Arab Legion in a full-scale operation against the PLO. Tanks demolished every building in Amman from which gunfire erupted. Before Hussein had regained control, an estimated three thousand Palestinian terrorists had been killed. PLO power in Jordan had been broken.

As the king's troops battled the PLO, Syria intervened, sending forces across Jordan's border. The Syrians greatly outnumbered Jordanian forces in both tanks and aircraft. When the king realized his predicament, he requested that "the United States and Great Britain get involved in the war in Jordan,"[70] asking the U.S., in fact, to attack Syria. Some transcripts of diplomatic communiqués show that Hussein requested Israeli intervention against Syria: "Please help us in any way possible."[71] The following missive sent from King Hussein pled for assistance:

> Situation deteriorating dangerously following Syrian massive invasion. I request immediate physical intervention both land and air. . . to safeguard sovereignty, territorial integrity and independence of Jordan. Immediate air strikes on invading forces from any quarter plus air cover are imperative.[72]

Israel and the United States mobilized their forces, giving notice to Syria that if she launched a full-scale invasion she would encounter more than Jordanian troops. It worked. Syria held back, and the Jordanians were able to drive them out.

From Jordan, the PLO moved to Lebanon, the only Arab nation with a significant Christian (Syrian Orthodox and Catholic) population. When the French pulled out of Syria and Lebanon in 1946, the Christian majority in Lebanon worked out a delicately balanced arrangement with the Muslim minority under a democratic constitution. Beirut became a bustling and prosperous commercial center. Its citizens enjoyed the highest per capita income in the Middle East.

After Israel became a state in 1948, several thousand Palestinian Arabs were admitted to Lebanon—not more, lest the Christian-Muslim balance of population would shift disastrously. Disturbing the balance was always a matter of grave concern to the Christians who stood to lose the most.

When the French left Lebanon, the Muslims pushed for unification with Syria. They had little regard for Lebanon's pre-Islamic past—the days of the Phoenicians and the vast wealth of Tyre and Sidon. For them, significant history commenced with the advent of Islam in 632 C.E. As a result, tension boiled beneath the surface.

The Palestinians, however, did disturb the balance in Lebanon—far out of proportion to their actual numbers. PLO agents worked actively in the refugee camps and established bases within them from which to launch terrorist attacks into Israel. The Lebanese government was faced with a serious dilemma. If the PLO were driven out, it would anger the Muslim population. To let them stay would enrage the Christians. The Lebanese prime minister began a delicate tightrope walk—he denied the existence of the PLO in public while negotiating with Arafat to limit raids into Israel. His aim was not to provoke Israel retaliation against the PLO terrorists.

The arrangement worked only briefly. The PLO in Lebanon commandeered an EL Al airliner. Israel responded by dispatching fighter jets to Beirut's airport to destroy Arab airliners on the ground. While the Lebanese government was knocked off balance, its Muslim neighbors pressed for the right of the PLO to supervise and police the refugee camps in Southern Lebanon. Additionally, PLO terrorists imprisoned for subversive activities were released from Lebanese prisons. The result: a burgeoning of terrorist activities inside Lebanon.

While Lebanon was dealing with the PLO problem, Egypt's President Anwar Sadat was busily planning an attack against Israel to gain a foothold and therefore a bargaining chip to retake the lands lost in 1967. On October 24, 1972, he announced his plan to the Egyptian Supreme War Council. He also sought the assistance of Syria and Jordan. Both declined to join Egypt in an attack, as did Lebanon:

> Egypt and Syria had both lost territory in 1967 but their aims were now different. Egypt had accepted Resolution 242 and was prepared to recognize Israel while Syria was not. Moreover, Sadat's war aims were directed at the recovery of the Arab territory lost in 1967. In contrast, Syria, in common with the Palestine Liberation Organization (PLO) which it harbored, was bent on Israel's destruction.[73]

Undeterred, Sadat made a diplomatic push to engage support for his plan to launch an offensive against Israel. By late 1973, he had been joined by approximately one hundred Arab states and had enticed several European countries into joining the Arabs on the UN Security Council in unifying against Israel.

On October 6, 1973, Yom Kippur, the holiest day of the Jewish year, the Arab coalition struck Israel with a sneak attack in the hope of finally driving the Jews into the Mediterranean. When the war began, Israel was tragically caught off-guard. Most of its citizen army were in synagogues, its national radio was off the air, and people were enjoying a restful day of reflection and prayer. Israel had no immediate response to the coordinated attacks by Egypt and Syria. Israeli intelligence had not seen the assault coming, and her military was ill prepared for war.

At the outset of hostilities, Egypt attacked across the Suez Canal. The battle raged for three days, and then the Egyptian army established entrenchments which resulted in an impasse. On the northern border, Syria launched an offensive at the Golan Heights. The initial assault was successful but quickly lost momentum. By the third day of fighting Israel had lost several thousand soldiers (more Israeli causalities were lost in the first day than in the entire Six-Day War), forty-nine planes, one-third (more than five hundred) of her tank force, and a good chunk of the buffer lands gained in the Six-Day War. The Israelis seemed to be again on the brink of a holocaust.

On the fourth day of the war, in an act of desperation, Prime Minister Golda Meir opened up three nuclear silos and pointed the missiles toward Egyptian and Syrian military headquarters near Cairo and Damascus. Army chief of staff Moshe Dayan was reported to have said, "This is the end of the Third Temple," in one of the crucial meetings. Later he told the press, "The situation is desperate. Everything is lost. We must withdraw."[74]

At that time Richard Nixon sat in the Oval Office. Earlier in his presidency, "Nixon made it clear he believed warfare was inevitable in the Middle East, a war that could spread and precipitate World War III, with the United States and the Soviet Union squaring off against each other."[75] He was now staring down the barrel of that war, so he authorized Henry Kissinger to put every American plane that could fly in the air to transport all available conventional arms to Israel. The supply to defend Israel was larger than the Berlin airlift that had followed World War II and literally turned the tide of the war, saving Israel from extermination and the world from nuclear war. Nixon carried Kennedy's agreement to militarily support Israel to the next logical level—a full military alliance.

The IDF launched a counter-offensive within the week and drove the Syrians to within twenty-five miles of Damascus. Trying to aid the Syrians, the Egyptian army went on the offensive all to no avail. Israeli troops crossed the Suez Canal and encompassed the Egyptian Third Army. When the Soviets realized what was happening, they scrambled to further assist Egypt and Syria. The Soviet threat was so real Nixon feared direct conflict with the U.S.S.R. and elevated all military personnel worldwide to DefCon III, meaning increased readiness that war was likely. However, a ceasefire was finally worked out between the U.S. and the U.S.S.R., adopted by all parties involved, and the Yom Kippur War was ended.

It was shortly after this, in 1974, that the United States finally decided to give formal military aid to Israel for the first time. The U.S. knew that if Israel were attacked again, we would do whatever necessary to protect her as a full ally. If a strong Israel could deter another possible war or even defend herself if necessary, it would save the U.S. higher direct expenditures in the long-run.

Congress voted for the first aid packages to Israel with part of it earmarked for defense. Before this time most aid to Israel was in the form of loans, all of which Israel repaid, or sales. There were some loans for defense reasons but no grants or gifts. Starting in 1976, however, Israel became the largest recipient of U.S. foreign assistance. Since 1974, Israel has received roughly $100 billion in aid, much of which were loans.

Israel had been continually surrounded by enemies since the rebirth of the nation in 1948, but at least for a while she found a strong ally in the United States.

CHAPTER SIXTEEN

GOD VERSUS HUMANISM

Now the Spirit expressly says that in latter times some will depart
from the faith, giving heed to deceiving spirits and doctrines of demons,
speaking lies in hypocrisy, having their own conscience seared
with a hot iron. —I TIMOTHY 4:1-2

I stated earlier that Israel has two enemies: Islam and humanism. Islam is the more obvious because it comes from without, and we have examined its relentless attacks on the city of Jerusalem through the ages. Humanism, on the other hand, is more subtle because it comes in the guise of sounding reasonable and "tolerant." This satanic projectile of deception was first launched at Jerusalem by Alexander the Great in the form of Hellenism. It is interesting to note that Alexander, like Mohammed, also had a demonic encounter that changed his life.

Alexander made a sojourn into the remote Libyan Desert to visit the temple and oracle of Zeus-Ammon. The oracle, nothing more than a demon spirit, convinced Alexander he was the son of the Greek god Zeus and would, as such, conquer the world. Hellenism, the acceptance of Greek culture including humanistic beliefs, became so popular in Jerusalem that it almost destroyed God's people from within.

Hellenism was a test both to the Jews that had been scattered abroad and those who remained in Palestine. Author Norman Bentwich wrote:

The interaction of Judaism and Hellenistic culture is... one of the fundamental struggles in the march of civilization...[76]

The nature of the enticement which beset the Jews in the midst of Hellenism may be noted from the writings of the ancient historian Posidonius:

> The people of these cities are relieved by the fertility of their soil from the laborious struggle for existence. Life is a continuous series of social festivities. Their gymnasiums they use as baths where they anoint themselves with costly oils and myrrhs. In the *grammateia* (such is the name they give to the public eating-halls) they practically live, filling themselves there for the better part of the day with rich foods and wine; much that they cannot eat they carry away home. They feast to the prevailing music of strings. The cities are filled from end to end with the noise of harp-playing.[77]

Many who had remained in Judah were concerned about the impact of Hellenism on the Jewish people. A movement against the Hellenists surfaced and expressed concern about materialism, including nudity in the gymnasiums, and the disregard for Jewish observances. The more pious Jews, the Hasidim, were prepared to stand up for their beliefs. Under Antiochus IV Epiphanes scores died for the faith they were willing to defend.

Today, this same evil spirit has a vise-like grip on government leaders throughout the Western world. It is expressed in terms such as "negotiated settlements" and "mediation for a just and lasting peace between Jews and Arabs." The real purpose, however, is to strip the ownership of Jerusalem from the Jewish people and return it to the Arab Gentiles. Were this to happen, Jerusalem would again be trodden underfoot by the Gentiles—contrary to Scripture. Jesus is not returning to a Jerusalem controlled by Muslims or a tri-partite commission. Luke 21:24 records:

> *And Jerusalem will be trampled by Gentiles until the times of the Gentiles are fulfilled.*

If Satan could, he would prevent the return of the Messiah by wielding his sword of destruction through the biblical prophecies. Satan has launched the two darts of Islam and humanism toward the very heart and soul of Jerusalem in order to bring the city back under Arab Gentile rule and thwart the return of Jesus the Messiah.

Islam is the demonic religious order that works in concert with humanism, deceiving and pressuring international leaders to reject biblical prophecy as inconsequential and superstitious—and most important, as causing all the problems in the Middle East. If Israel would just admit that all this prophecy nonsense is "extreme religious intolerance" and give up Jerusalem, "share" her land with the rest of the world, and be assimilated into the world's population as before—or form a Jewish state, say, in the United States—then all the world's troubles would disappear. That is the humanist view. It completely denies that the Bible is the Word of God and the prophecies about Israel are absolute truth, which the God of the Bible will see that they come to pass.

In the past ten decades, Jerusalem has been brought from the background of prophetic events onto center stage of history's most dramatic conflict. Its bloody and brutal chronicle did not end with the rebirth of the nation on May 14, 1948; quite the contrary, the attacks have become more diabolical. And the import of the assault has moved from the dusty back roads of an ancient land to the world arena.

In one of my numerous conversations with Prime Minister Begin, I asked him to speak to the controversial subject of what the world calls "the occupied territories." He began by sharing his first meeting with President Jimmy Carter:

> We were in the cabinet room and Mr. Carter asked me a question. In that question, however, there was a very negative statement. He said the settlements were illegal. I had prepared a counter question to propose to him. Like Winston Churchill, I was ready with a "prepared improvisation." I had asked our embassy in Washington, D.C., to ready a list of American cities with biblical names, i.e., Bethlehem, Shiloh, Hebron, and Bethel. I showed my long list to President

Carter and asked him if he could imagine the governor of Pennsylvania proclaiming that anyone could live in the city of Bethlehem except Jews. President Carter agreed that if a man did such a thing, he would be guilty of racism.

I pointed out that I was the governor of the state in which the original Bethlehem, and the original Jericho, and the original Shiloh were located. Did he expect me to say that everybody could live in those cities except Jews? Of course, he didn't; it would be absurd...This land we occupy is Eretz Yisrael, the land of Israel, since the days of the prophet Samuel 3,000 years ago. We had a downfall later, but even the Romans called us Judea until after the Bar-Kokhba revolt in the second century. Then, because the Jewish resistance had been so fierce and heroic, and because the Emperor Hadrian had suffered such severe casualties, he decided to try to delete all memory of the connection between the people and that land. The Romans had done it in Carthage, why not here? So he renamed the area Syria et Palestina, using the name of our ancient enemies, the Philistines.

So the word "Palestine" came into all languages. Thus the preamble to the British Mandate after World War I used these words: "recognition having been given to the historical connection between the Jewish people and Palestine." In spite of Hadrian, nobody forgot that it was our land. Every intelligent person understands that Palestine is a misnomer for the land of Israel. We have a right to live in Judea and Samaria...but that does not mean we want to evict even one Arab from his village or town. We never wanted to do that.[78]

The prime minister further stated:

A Palestinian state is a mortal danger to Israel and a great peril to the Free World. We never agreed to a Palestinian

state at Camp David. What we agreed to was autonomy as a
way to solve the problem of Palestinian Arabs...The Camp
David agreement calls for security for Israel and autonomy
for the Arab inhabitants, the right to elect their own ministers of council to deal with daily problems.

As we know from history, Jimmy Carter never did embrace Prime
Minister Begin's wisdom. Then, in 1982 and after President Reagan took
office, Prime Minister Begin was slated to meet with him. Dr. Reuven Hecht,
an advisor to Mr. Begin, called and asked if I could meet with them in New
York City. The prime minister and Reuven were concerned about how the
meeting with the president would be conducted. Dr. Hecht told me Reagan
thought Begin was a hardheaded Jew whose brain had been baked by the
Holocaust. He had heard from the attorney general that, in fact, a meeting
might not even take place.

When we met, I asked Reuven to tell me about the proposed meeting
with the president. He replied, "The cabinet members will meet with the
prime minister's advisers." Then I asked if the president would even meet
privately with the prime minister. Reuven replied that a fifteen-minute session was scheduled.

I looked at Reuven and said, "I believe I have a message from God's
Word for the prime minister. When I was in the Oval Office some time ago,
I saw a photograph on the president's desk. I was told the picture had been
given to him by the International Red Cross. It was a child with no arms.
Reagan had been told that the Israelis had caused the injuries to the little
boy. In actuality, he had been born deformed. Nevertheless, the president
thinks your countrymen did it.

"Mr. Hecht," I said, "Jesus said that if two or more agreed as touching
anything, God in Heaven would bring it to pass. Prime Minister Begin needs
to tell President Reagan that."

Dr. Hecht looked at me like I was crazy. I felt God wanted me to advise
the advisor. "The prime minister should say this to President Reagan: 'Both
our countries were founded on religious principles. They are both inhabited

by people with a belief in the God of the Bible. The peoples of both our lands offer prayers for divine intervention and protection. The peoples of both our lands believe God is in control of their destinies. Given all that we are in agreement on, how can our two countries not find a way to move together toward peace and security in the world? We both believe in God. We both believe God has a great plan for our lives. God has a great plan for our countries. We both have faced death. Would you pray, Mr. President that God's will be done in our meeting today?'"

I knew this was a "God-idea," and I thank God Mr. Begin did too. As a result, his meeting with President Reagan forged a new friendship between the men. After they prayed together in the Oval Office good relations between our countries were restored.

Through the power of intercessory prayer and the courage of Bible-believing people worldwide, God can change the hearts of our leaders just as He did the hearts of Harry S. Truman and Ronald Reagan. God has a prophetic plan for Bible-believers in this day, and He will use them to bring the leadership in this nation to honor God and obey His Word.

The strong arm of humanism can be broken by the faith-filled prayers and actions of God's people. Imagine. No longer would the president and his cabinet try to force Israel to the negotiating table to be humiliated by those who only seek her destruction. No longer would the man or woman in the Oval Office seek to appease Arab wrath by offering Israel as the sacrificial lamb. They would believe God's plan as outlined in His Word is for Jerusalem to be under Jewish control.

U.S. leaders often speak with two voices—our Indian ancestors called it "speaking with a forked tongue." At the same time, they often pursue differing policies regarding Jerusalem. Again and again proposals have been submitted—proposals which Israel has fulfilled and which the Arab leaders have rejected.

So what is the solution? The United States simply needs to recognize that Israeli lands belong to the Jewish people and that Jerusalem is, indeed, the capital of Israel—and has been ever since God declared it to be so. For at least a century, Jerusalem has boasted a Jewish majority, and the nation has paid dearly in lives for its defense of the Holy City.

The Oslo Accords, which were to be a framework to establish peaceful relations between Israel and the PLO, were signed in Washington on September 13, 1993. The ceremony was attended by PLO chairman Yasser Arafat, Israeli Prime Minister Yitzhak Rabin, and President Bill Clinton. In the years since the documents were signed, the PLO and its sister terrorist groups have initiated attack after attack. Over sixteen hundred Israelis have been killed, and over eleven thousand Israelis have been injured.[79]

As if contending with their borders lined with enemies isn't enough, Israel has also fallen victim to a current *en vogue* doctrine in the Church that was spawned in Hell. This doctrine supports the humanist view that biblical prophecy concerning Israel is irrelevant to the times in which we are living, thus making the issue of who lives and rules in the land called Israel and the city of Jerusalem irrelevant.

This particular canon teaches that the Church has replaced Israel in the plan and heart of God. It is known variously as replacement theology, progressive dispensationalism, or supersessionism. The early Church did not teach this. The root of this doctrine dates back to between 160 and 180 AD when Constantine brought paganism into the Church. He banned all things Jewish from the Church and replaced them with pagan traditions. For example, the Feast of Passover and Resurrection Day were replaced with Easter. It was taught that the Church has supplanted Israel in God's plan for the ages. Constantine's actions began to wash away the Jewish roots of the Church and opened the door for replacement theology which teaches that the Jews had been rejected. Israel failed God, crucified Jesus Christ, and as a result was replaced by the Church. The Church, it teaches, is the spiritual Israel and Jerusalem is any town in which there is a church. These heretical doctrines have done great harm to the Jewish people. If God has turned His back on them, it legitimizes the actions of Adolf Hitler and the fanatical Muslim jihadists, who seek to destroy the Jews.

From the earliest centuries the Roman and then the European Church failed to realize and honor the fact that our eternal salvation came through the agency of the Jews. The fingers of the physical descendants of Jacob wrote all but a small portion of the world's best-selling book: The Bible. Almost all of the prophets in the Bible were Jewish, as were all of the apostles, the parents of Jesus, and most importantly, the Messiah. How could the Church have overlooked such critical factors in supporting the Jewish people?

Today, many churches in America have embraced replacement theology. Because the Jews are seen to be responsible for Christ's death, these churches are relieved from any obligation to speak out against anti-Semitism. This insidious doctrine propagates the age-old practice of blaming the Jews for the world's ills, weighing them in the balance and finding them wanting. This frees the Church from any obligation to share the Good News of the Gospel of Jesus Christ with those whom He came to seek and to save.

When speaking to the Samaritan woman about eternal life, Jesus pointed out that His heavenly Father's free gift of eternal salvation had been brought to the world via the Jews:

> *"You worship what you do not know; we know what we worship, for salvation is of the Jews."*
>
> JOHN 4:22

If the most precious gift that Christians will ever possess came by means of the Jewish prophets, leaders, teachers, and in particular Jesus the Messiah, how can we have any attitude other than one of deep gratitude toward Jacob's offspring? We who were born Gentiles and became Christians should be extremely thankful that God, in His shining wisdom and gracious mercy, has allowed us as "wild olive branches" to be grafted into the rich Tree of Israel, as revealed in Romans 11:17.

In his New Testament letter to the Romans, the apostle Paul went on to point out that the "grafted in" Gentile believers do not tower over the Jewish people, as many have maintained over the centuries and still do today. Rather, regenerated Jews (including Abraham, our father in the faith) were the original covenant people that remain the bedrock "root" that supports every Christian's spiritual life.

> *But if some of the branches were broken off, and you,*
> *although a wild olive shoot, were grafted in among the others*
> *and now share in the nourishing root of the olive tree, do not be*
> *arrogant toward the branches. If you are, remember it is not you*
> *who support the root, but the root that supports you.*
>
> ROMANS 1:17-18 ESV

> *For I am not ashamed of the gospel of Christ, for it is the*
> *power of God to salvation for everyone who believes, for the Jew*
> *first and also for the Greek.*
>
> ROMANS 1:16

Many have said, "The reason I don't support Israel is because the Jews crucified Christ. They are under judgment because they rejected God's Word." John 10:17-18 tells us that Christ willingly gave His life. No one took it from Him.

> *"Therefore my Father loves Me, because I lay down My life*
> *that I may take it again. No one takes it from Me, but I lay it*
> *down of Myself. I have the power to lay it down, and I have the*
> *power to take it again."*

God Almighty will judge the person or group that embraces a doctrine of judgment, one that is given the Word and then rejects it through disobedience. Nations that reject God will be judged. Luke 12:48 says, *"For everyone to whom much is given, from him much will be required."*

There are more churches in America than in any other nation in the world. There are more Christian bookstores, radio and television stations, and Bible schools. The world views America, then, as a Christian nation. America has been given much, and judgment will be meted out accordingly. The truth is, God is much more merciful than mankind. Lamentations 3:22 states: *"Through the Lord's mercies we are not consumed, Because his compassions fail not."* Nowhere in His Word does God make eternal promises to

America, yet He continues to show mercy. Even wicked Sodom was to be the beneficiary of God's mercy. Why? Because Abraham appealed to God to spare the city if only ten righteous men could be found there. Regretfully, ten righteous men did not answer the call to stand in the gap.

Will you stand with Israel today? Will you stand on the truth of God's Word and defy humanism and any false doctrine in the Church that supports it? There could not be a more important or appropriate time in Jerusalem's history for Christians to join together in prayer and intercession for David's City. I encourage you to pray for Jerusalem. Pray for her children. Pray for her grandchildren. Pray for her neighbors, and pray that anger and hatred will be bound. This is not a matter in which we can afford to be indifferent or apathetic. Why? It matters to God.

CHAPTER SEVENTEEN

THREATS
FROM AFAR

*"Now therefore, O Lord our God, I pray, save us from his
hand, that all the kingdoms of the earth may know that You
are the Lord God, You alone."* —II KINGS 19:19

When God pronounced His blessing on Abraham in Genesis, chapter
12, He declared three immutable promises:

✧ I will make you a great nation.

✧ I will bless you and make your name great.

✧ I will make you a blessing to others.

God promised to make an investment in Abraham. Of his great nation
He said,

> *"...blessing I will bless you, and multiplying I will multiply
> your descendants as the stars of the heaven and as the sand which
> is on the seashore; and your descendants shall possess the gate of
> their enemies."*

GENESIS 22:16-17

God said He would bless Abraham's friends. He vowed to be a friend to
Abraham's friends and to consider any benevolence to Abraham as if it were

a kindness to Him. Not only that, God promised He would reward those who were Abraham's friends. No act of kindness, not even a cup of cold water, would be overlooked. Jesus extended that covenant to His followers in Mark 9:41: "For whoever gives you a cup of water to drink in My name, because you belong to Christ, assuredly, I say to you, he will by no means lose his reward."

James 2:23 reveals the extent of God's covenant with Abraham:

And the Scripture was fulfilled which says, "Abraham believed God, and it was accounted to him for righteousness." And he was called the friend of God.

Would it not be the highest accolade to be called the friend of God? Abraham became known as the father of many nations and the father of the Christian faith. God has, indeed, made his name great because of his faithfulness.

God also promised Abraham that when threatened by enemies, He would provide a way of escape. There are those who continue to curse the descendants of Abraham's son Isaac. It is not by accident that the promise to curse is upon the individual: "I will bless them...I will curse him." Their futile curses against Abraham were nullified by God's blessings upon him and his descendants.

While God's blessings rain on the just and unjust (Matthew 5:45), His curses are reserved for the perpetrator alone. Each man must stand before God, the righteous Judge, and give account for his deeds and actions. If we bless God's Chosen People, not only we but our families will be blessed. If we curse His people, we alone will stand before God in judgment. It is an individual choice.

I would much rather stand with the Jewish people and be among the blessed of the Earth. In Psalm 128:5, the Psalmist wrote: "The Lord bless you out of Zion, And may you see the good of Jerusalem All the days of your life."

The United States has not always blessed Israel. In Madrid, Spain, in 1991, I stood in shocked silence as President George H. W. Bush opened the conference at the end of the Persian Gulf War. Israel had not been allowed to join the coalition of nations fighting against Saddam Hussein to liberate Kuwait because the anti-Semitic Arab countries had screamed in protest. Our president had also asked Israelis not to retaliate when they were bombarded with thirty-four SCUD missile attacks, and they honored his request. They would be rewarded for their acquiescence to U.S. demands, right?

At the end of the war they were "rewarded" with a $10 billion dollar loan guarantee freeze. This money was needed to provide housing for refugees, mostly Russian Jews. Israel's enemies were again appeased when Prime Minister Yitzhak Shamir was unceremoniously summoned to Madrid to sign yet another land-for-peace agreement with Yasser Arafat and his murderous PLO. Did peace ensue? No. Peace still remains elusive.

Syria alone was given one billion dollars by the U.S. that was spent on the purchase of North Korean missiles to be used against Israel. Many of those missiles are in Lebanon in the hands of Hezbollah, a Palestinian terrorist organization. The missiles are aimed at the cities of Israel. Historically the U.S. has been Israel's closest ally, but the lure of O.P.E.C. oil and Arab goodwill has been chipping away at America's dedication to that alliance.

Was it only coincidence that as President George H. W. Bush was opening the conference at the Royal Palace in Madrid, the Perfect Storm (the one made famous in the movie) developed in the north Atlantic, creating the largest waves ever recorded in that region? The storm traveled one thousand miles "east to west" (as opposed to the normal west to east pattern) to crash onto the eastern coast of the United States. Thirty-five-foot waves smashed into the Kennebunkport, Maine, summer home of President Bush. This was one of the worst storms in American history and one of the top ten in insurance claims.

When the Madrid conference was moved to Washington, D.C., for a resumption of the land-for-peace talks, hurricane Andrew struck Florida. It wreaked havoc, causing an estimated $30 billion in damages, leaving 180,000 Americans homeless, and securing a spot on the top ten list for largest disasters in American history.

Other costly events have occurred on dates that correspond with the U.S. trying to force Israel to give up land-for-peace. The most devastating financially occurred the week of October 11, 1999. In Israel, Jewish settlers were being driven from the West Bank in order to satisfy world opinion. In the U.S., the Dow-Jones plummeted 266 points on October 15. On October 16, a magnitude 7.1 earthquake was registered in the California desert. On the East Coast, Hurricane Irene produced torrential rains of between ten and twenty inches in Florida and ten inches in North Carolina. It caused over $800 million in damages. Coincidence? Not if you believe the Bible!

Is it a coincidence that following President Obama's shabby treatment of Israel's prime minister and his insistence that the Israelis kowtow to his demands regarding both the construction in East Jerusalem and peace talks with the Palestinian Authority that a devastating oil drilling platform exploded in the Gulf? Numerous safety measures designed to stop the flow of oil failed. The platform collapsed, killing eleven workers and spewing untold thousands of barrels of oil into the ecosystem daily for months.

As if that weren't enough, savage storms tore through Mississippi and Tennessee, spawning tornadoes, causing major flooding, and killing more than two dozen residents. To add insult to injury, a crude car bomb was discovered in Times Square in New York City. And, on May 6, 2010—some say due to human error—the Dow Jones Industrial Average fell some 998.50 points in approximately fifteen minutes. The market had been down almost 300 points when the dive occurred. Although the market rebounded, it still closed down 347.80 points. One can't help but wonder if this was Obama's "Perfect Storm."

Every nation in history that has lifted a hand against Israel has been cursed. And every nation that has blessed them has been blessed. *"For he who touches you touches the apple of His eye"* (Zechariah 2:8). Just as He promised to curse him who curses Israel, so God has promised to bless those who bless Israel. So what can you and I do to bless Israel? Prayer is the most powerful weapon in Heaven's arsenal.

God answers prayer. Just ask Esther if prayer changes things. She came to the king in fear for her life but left with supernatural favor. She came with poverty but left with prosperity. She came in despair but left highly favored. She came representing a people who were marked for destruction and left the king's presence with a way of escape for her Jewish people.

Esther fulfilled all the requirements of II Chronicles 7:14: "If my people who are called by My name will humble themselves, and pray and seek My face, and turn from their wicked ways, then I will hear from heaven, and will forgive their sin and heal their land." The United States can be preserved, but all the conditions set forth in this verse must be met in order for God to bring revival and bless our nation.

Daniel engaged in intercession in Daniel, chapter 10, and changed nations. For twenty-one days, the prophet had immersed himself in prayer. As he sought the face of God, an angel appeared to him. The angel had startling news for him and for those of us who have prayed earnestly and diligently. The "prince of Persia," apparently one of Lucifer's fallen angels, had hindered the answer to Daniel's prayer. Why is it important to know this? Persistence in prayer pays dividends! Had Daniel not continued to intercede until the battle in the heavenlies was won, his prayers would not have been answered.

King Hezekiah was faced, as are we today, with the threat of annihilation. The king of Assyria had threatened the Israelites with destruction. He made the unfortunate mistake of thinking that Hezekiah trusted in horses, chariots, and his alliance with Egypt. Using the "town crier" method of communication, the commander-in-chief of the Assyrian army stood in the midst of the town square and taunted Hezekiah. He proclaimed that *Yahweh* himself had sent the Assyrians to defeat Judah. (Does this sound familiar? He must have heard about replacement theology!)

When the king's threats were delivered to Hezekiah in the form of a written dispatch, he did the one most important thing he could have done... he went to the Temple, spread the letter on the altar, and prostrated himself before God. Hezekiah prayed: "Now therefore, O Lord our God, I pray, save us from his hand, that all the kingdoms of the earth may know that You are the Lord God, You alone" (II Kings 19:19).

God spoke the answer to Hezekiah's prayer through the prophet Isaiah: "For I will defend this city, to save it For My own sake and for My servant David's sake" (Isaiah 37:35). The king could have heard no sweeter words than the promise that God would defend the City of David.

The epilogue to Hezekiah's prayer and God's answer did not bode well for the Assyrians:

> *And it came to pass on a certain night that the angel of the Lord went out, and killed in the camp of the Assyrians one hundred and eighty-five thousand; and when people arose early in the morning, there were the corpses—all dead.*
>
> **II KINGS 19:35**

Nehemiah also knew the power of prayer and intercession. He had been exiled to Babylon and elevated to the position of cupbearer to the king. Nehemiah received a delegation of visitors from Jerusalem and was given the devastating news of the poverty and destruction there. He "sat down and wept, and mourned for many days; and fasting and praying before the God of heaven" (Nehemiah 1:4). His heart was broken with the plight of his countrymen and of his beloved city.

God miraculously answered Nehemiah's prayer. He moved the heart of the king and gave Nehemiah great favor. Nehemiah was allowed to return to his homeland and rebuild the walls of Jerusalem.

The New Testament is rife with instances of prayer petitions answered and people delivered—Peter from prison, John the Revelator from death on the Isle of Patmos, Paul from drowning at sea. Paul's ringing declaration while being tossed to and fro on the ship resonates: "For there stood by me this night an angel of the God to whom I belong and whom I serve" (Acts 27:23). It is never too late for God to come to the aid of His children, and prayer is the means by which we touch Him.

Israel is the key to America's survival—and prayer is the hand that turns the key. September 11th would never have happened if America had stood with Israel over the years, rather than weakening her by rewarding terrorists like Arafat and the PLO, Hamas, and Hezbollah. We have sent signals to these terrorist groups that America is weak and crime pays huge dividends. In 1981 Israel stood up to the nations of the world and destroyed Saddam Hussein's Osirak nuclear reactor. Israel was condemned for her actions; however, Israel's courage may have saved millions of American lives on September 11th.

In 1980 I interviewed Isser Harel, head of Israeli intelligence (Mossad), from 1947-1963. On September 30, 2001, the *Jerusalem Post* published an article, "America, the Target," based on that interview. An excerpt from that 1980 interview below will help you understand the seriousness of the matter:

> On a September evening in 1980 in Tel Aviv, I sat with former Mossad chief Isser Harel for a conversation about Arab terrorism. As he handed me a cup of hot tea and a plate of cookies, I asked him, "Do you think terrorism will come to America, and if so, where and why?"
>
> Harel looked at this American visitor and replied, "I fear it will come to you in America. America has the power, but not the will, to fight terrorism. The terrorists have the will, but not the power, to fight America—but all that could change with time. Arab oil money buys more than tents."
>
> "As to the where," Harel continued, "New York City is the symbol of freedom and capitalism. It's likely they will strike the Empire State Building, your tallest building [which was true at that time] and a symbol of your power."
>
> With my Western mind-set, I replied that America was dedicated to fighting terrorism. Harel smiled and said, "You kill a fly and you celebrate. We live with flies daily. One dies and 100 flies come to the funeral."
>
> "If 'land-for-peace' happens," Harel continued, "I think it will mean America gets peace for a season, as the West pressures Israel into giving Arafat our land. But once you let the genie of appeasement out of the bottle, he will grow and eventually turn on you. In time America itself will be in the crosshairs.

"Hitler first killed Jews, and then he killed Christians. Our
culture and our democracies are the root of [the terrorists']
rage. If we're right, then they are wrong."

Twenty-one years later, the first part of Harel's prediction came true
except, of course, that the twin towers of the World Trade Center were
much taller than the Empire State Building and became the terrorist targets.
However, it was the second part of his doomsday prediction that came true
much earlier.

It was 1982 and Israel had declared her own war on terrorism by invad-
ing Lebanon to root out Arafat's terrorist infrastructure. I was summoned to
New York by Prime Minister Menachem Begin's aide, Reuven Hecht, who had
just met with former Secretary of State Alexander Haig in Washington. Haig
had informed Mr. Hecht that America had changed her mind and would no
longer support Israel's war against terrorism in Lebanon.

Begin was shocked. The West—whose planes had been blown out of
the sky, its diplomats, soldiers, and civilians murdered by terrorists—was
now fighting to save the primary organization responsible for these vile acts.
In the end, American pressure prevailed and Arafat's ten thousand PLO terrorists—rifles in hand—were escorted out of Beirut to safe bases in Tunisia
and other Arab countries. Israeli mothers whose sons had died in Lebanon
stood outside Prime Minister Begin's apartment screaming, "Murderer!" It
was more than he could bear, and he resigned a depressed and broken man.

In the ensuing years Israel has increasingly been the target of Iranian
trained and armed terrorists. Israeli prime ministers have endured arm-
twisting, veiled threats, and attempts by spineless world leaders to sacrifice
Israel on the altar of appeasement. Unfortunately, President Jimmy Carter set
a precedent with Iran that still proves true today. The U.S. cowers behind a
group of allies, which are as toothless a tiger as can be found on the planet.
Also, thanks in large part to Carter, the world is again being challenged by
what may be the best student to emerge from Khomeini's madrasas (Islamic
schools), Mahmoud Ahmadinejad.

This determined despot takes devilish delight in calling for the obliteration of Israel at every turn. He has labeled Jews as "the most detested people in all humanity"[80] and all but crows with exhilaration that the Holocaust is a myth. He blames the Nazi atrocities on the Jews, explaining that the rhetoric surrounding the Holocaust was implemented to produce a sympathetic response. He is not alone in his hatred for the Jews; his views are often supported by vitriolic diatribes from other Iranian leaders.

At the Sixty-fifth General Assembly in New York City in September 2010, Ahmadinejad again raised eyebrows and ire. Dressed in his obligatory pinstriped suit and an open-necked white shirt, Ahmadinejad almost looked the part of the statesman he believes he is. That image is quashed the moment he opens his mouth with yet another anti-Semitic rant. While making his rounds in New York City, he again denied the Holocaust by saying it "has been exaggerated as a pretext for war." Ahmadinejad's tirade to the General Assembly resulted in the United States delegation accompanied by several European delegations exiting the venue after the Iranian president claimed that U.S. government officials perpetrated the lie that terrorists brought down the World Trade Center Towers on 9/11. He then espoused a theory of his own that "some segments within the U.S. government orchestrated the attack to reverse the declining American economy, and its grip on the Middle East, in order to save the Zionist regime." He told the 192 representatives of the assembly that "The majority of the American people as well as most nations and politicians around the world agree with this view."[81]

In their response to Ahmadinejad's heinous theories, the U.S. delegation issued the following statement: "Rather than representing the aspirations and goodwill of the Iranian people, Mr. Ahmadinejad has yet again chosen to spout vile conspiracy theories and anti-Semitic slurs that are as abhorrent and delusional as they are predictable."[82]

After his tirade at the U.N., Ahmadinejad cancelled many scheduled meetings following the growing notoriety of his 9/11 speech. One particular sign of his entering panic mode was the sudden cancelation of an opportunity to get his message across to the American people. Shepard Smith, Fox News Channel's lead news anchor, was to host an exclusive interview with Ahmadinejad on Friday morning which I had been able to arrange. Ahmadinejad finally agreed to an interview with Eric Shawn, a Fox news correspondent.

Just before the Sudanese delegation (an ally of Iran) arrived at the hotel to meet with Ahmadinejad, President Barack Obama had hosted them. He told the Sudanese that if they would divide the country into two nations—north and south Sudan—and normalize conditions in their country the United States would support investments, agricultural development, expanded trade, an exchange of ambassadors, and would eventually lift sanctions which had been imposed. Russia and China, as well as the Pan African organizations, also endorsed a commitment to help the Sudanese if they would pursue peace.

When the Sudanese delegation which included the nation's president, vice president, foreign minister and secretary of state arrived at the hotel to meet with President Ahmadinejad they were extremely angry about his 9/11 statements. They realized that Iran could cost them everything the U.S. had laid on the table. They went into a demonic tirade in the hotel lobby. The two groups were literally pushing, shoving, swinging, and screaming obscenities at each other. Ultimately, the police had to handcuff one of the Sudanese diplomats who was quickly ushered out by the Secret Service and police.

In the hotel lobby I saw pure panic in the eyes of the Iranians. Ahmadinejad's aides would only repeat to me that their president had "bilateral problems, bilateral problems."

It was Iran's mullahs who overpowered many of their own diplomats in demanding Ahmadinejad attack America by accusing the U.S. of carrying out the 9/11 attacks. I met with the Iranian religious leaders and their diplomats in the hotel, and the inescapable conclusion was that the mullahs, Iran's real rulers, were seeking to use Ahmadinejad's speech to appeal to their followers in Iran. During the Fox interview the mullahs were seated next to the cameras; there were few Iranian diplomats in the room.

It is apparent that Tehran wishes to neutralize America's influence in the Middle East as a major step in the plan to defeat Western civilization.

Foremost in that effort is the funding, training, and arming of Hezbollah in Lebanon, and not just with pistols and ammunition.

Lt. General (Ret.) Moshe Ya'alon, Deputy Prime Minister of Israel under Benjamin Netanyahu, writes:

> " ... according to Iranian Supreme Leader Ali Khamenei and Iran's Syrian partners, the Second Lebanon War was in fact a hostile probe of U.S. reflexes, as determined through Israel, a state that Iran and Syria consider to be a direct extension of American power in the Middle East."[83]

For years Lebanon has played host to a group from the Islamic Revolutionary Guard Corps, the elite of the Iranian military, and is best at training other terror units. It is obvious to me that Iran has a long-term plan to take control of the Middle East region by using proxies: Hamas, Hezbollah, and Palestinian Islamic Jihad, not to mention Muktada al-Sadr's Shiite Mahdi Army in Iraq. Would the spread of such terrorist entities have been assured had Jimmy Carter worked with the Shah to correct human rights issues rather than replace the monarch?

Ahmadinejad is equally determined to destroy Israel. Recalling Khomeini's earlier rhetoric, in October 2005 he declared, "This regime that is occupying Quds [Jerusalem] must be eliminated from the pages of history."[84] He has threatened elsewhere to "wipe Israel from the map." Despite Ahmadinejad's hateful proclamation, Persian Jews continue to live in Iran. The Iranian Jews were content to remain there following the establishment of the State of Israel (only about eight thousand emigrated), but the safety of the Jewish population is no longer guaranteed under the radical regime of Mahmoud Ahmadinejad.

The Iranian government has had absolute freedom to fund and fuel terrorism on many fronts. It has had the liberty to import the materials to build centrifuges in order to acquire the resources needed to construct nuclear weapons, it has been free to kill Americans in countries around the world, and through its proxies it continues to kill Jews in Israel. Ahmadinejad has asserted that the resolutions passed by the Security Council are worthless and, in his words, "illegitimate." The Lilliputian leader continues to thumb his proverbial nose at the entire world, and its response is to bury its collective head deeper into the sand.

Attempts to rein in the Iranian leader with harsher sanctions against the Iranian government elicit a response such as the one he delivered in February 2009. He arrogantly alleged, "The Zionist regime (Israel) and its (western) backers cannot do a damn thing to stop Iran's nuclear work."[85]

Israel and America share the same democratic values and religious roots terrorists despise and seek to destroy. A war on terrorism categorizing some terror as good and some as bad is a guarantee of failure—a cruel spectacle in the theater of the absurd. For Americans to think otherwise does not negate the hatred of terrorists worldwide for the "Great Satan," the United States.

After my conversation with Isser Harel, I was so convinced he was on the right track, I wrote *The Jerusalem Scroll* in 1999. In the novel Osama Bin Laden obtains a nuclear bomb from the Russian mafia and attempts to blow up New York City and Los Angeles. Little did I know he would ultimately attempt both. Thank God, he did not have access to a nuclear bomb. That was a true blessing.

CHAPTER EIGHTEEN

BLESSINGS
AND CURSES

"I will bless those who bless you, And I will curse
him who curses you; And in you all the families of
the earth shall be blessed." —GENESIS 12:3

In Romans 15:27 NIV Paul wrote, "For if the Gentiles have shared in the Jews' spiritual blessings, they owe it to the Jews to share with them their material blessings." As Christians, we owe a debt of eternal gratitude to the Jewish people for their contributions, which gave birth to our faith. Our Lord, the Rabbi of Rabbis, said, *"Salvation is of the Jews"* (John 4:22). Following are but a few of the things the Jewish people have given to Christianity:

✧ The Word of God

✧ The Patriarchs

✧ The Messiah

✧ The Disciples

✧ The Apostles

An amazing scripture is found in Luke 7:5: "For he loves our nation, and has built us a synagogue." The Jewish elders made an appeal to Jesus to come and heal the servant of Cornelius in Capernaum, for he was close

He was a Gentile. The Jews said to Jesus, "He deserves a blessing because he has been a blessing. He has performed some wonderful deeds of compassion for our people."

A similar story is found in Acts 10. The first Gentile selected by God to receive the Gospel lived in Caesarea. Cornelius, a centurion of the Roman regiment, was "a devout man and one who feared God with all his household, who gave alms generously to the people, and prayed to God always" (Acts 10:2). To whom did Cornelius give alms? To the Jews! Acts 10:4 records of him: "Your prayers and your alms have come up for a memorial before God." And in Acts 10:31, Paul penned: "Cornelius, your prayer has been heard, and your alms are remembered in the sight of God." Three times in the same chapter, a godly Gentile expressed his unconditional love for the Jewish people in a practical way. Cornelius and his family were divinely selected to be the first Gentiles to receive the Gospel and the outpouring of the Holy Spirit.

There is no doubt that prosperity (Genesis 12:3 and Psalm 122:6) and healing (Luke 7:1-5) came to the Gentiles as a result of their having blessed God's Chosen People. The Jewish people and the nation of Israel were blessed in a practical way; they received a commanded blessing. Deuteronomy 28:8 reads: "The Lord will command the blessing on you in your storehouses and in all to which you set your hand, and He will bless you in the land which the Lord your God is giving you."

There is another biblical reason why Christians should wholeheartedly support the Jewish people and their beloved homeland, Israel. It is a selfish reason in some respects, but a valid one nonetheless. After promising Abraham that He would make his offspring a great nation, the God of Israel pledged that He would **"bless those who bless you"** (Genesis 12:3). Of course, Abraham's descendants include the Arab peoples through Ishmael and Esau, and there is every reason for Christians to bless the Arabs today. But God's eternal covenant was passed down to Isaac, Jacob, and the twelve tribes of Israel. This means that the blessing promised by the God of Israel would come to those who particularly blessed the Jewish people.

How can we bless the offspring of Isaac and Jacob? One of the most important and obvious ways is to support their God-given right to live in their biblical Promised Land, and especially in their eternal capital city, Jerusalem. The sad fact is that many governments, international organizations, Muslim groups, and even many Christians do not acknowledge that divine right. Some denominations have adopted replacement theology, which I discussed in Chapter 15. This is an unbiblical stand that weakens our testimony, weakens Israel, weakens America, and puts the very soul of our nation in harm's way.

Again, replacement theology is the belief that because the Jews rejected Jesus Christ as the Messiah, the promises made to Abraham, Isaac, and Jacob have been conferred upon the modern-day Church. If this is, indeed, a reality, then what of the promises that God made to Abraham in Genesis 12:1-7?

When Sarah conceived the "son of promise," Isaac, God conferred the same covenant on him as he had upon Abraham: "But My covenant I will establish with Isaac, whom Sarah shall bear to you at this set time next year" (Genesis 17:21). And, the covenant also was extended to Isaac's son, Jacob, in Genesis 28:10-15. God later changed Isaac's name to Israel.

God is no respecter of persons, and He knows the end from the beginning. He made this covenant available to the Gentiles, but only through conversion to Judaism and circumcision…that is, until Jesus Christ opened the way for all people to come to salvation through His blood sacrifice.

Romans 11:17 in the *New Living Translation* says: "Some of these branches from Abraham's tree—some of the people of Israel—have been broken off. And you Gentiles, who were branches from a wild olive tree, have been grafted in. So now you also receive the blessing God has promised Abraham and his children, sharing in the rich nourishment from the root of God's special olive tree."

Replacement theology led to rampant anti-Semitism, especially in the Church. For instance, the Jews were labeled "Christ-killers" because of the crucifixion. This led to attacks of every imaginable nature being launched against the Jews. They constantly faced lack, banishment, or eradication.

The Jews, particularly in Europe, were denigrated, shunned, forced into baptism upon threat of death, burned alive in their synagogues, refused medical and legal aid, stripped of their businesses and material possessions, and finally exterminated. My own great-grandfather, a rabbi, and his congregation were burned to death in a synagogue in Minsk, Russia. Orthodox Christians boarded up the building and set it afire while shouting, "Christ-killers!" We tend to think that during World War II, the Nazis invented anti-Semitism in its vilest forms. Not so. They merely built on the foundation laid down through the centuries.

Through the centuries the Church has been a willing participant in the genocide perpetrated against the Jews. From the early Catholic Church to the Crusades to Martin Luther's Reformation period to World War II, the Church has at times been duplicitous in the terrorizing of Jews.

God not only promised to reward individuals for blessing His covenant Jewish people, He also pledged in the same scripture to bless families, and by extension, entire nations: **"And in you all the families of the earth shall be blessed."** So the great Master of the Universe reveals that our personal, family, and national welfare is closely related to how we treat the Jewish people. Should anyone need any other reason to support the contemporary offspring of Abraham, Isaac, and Jacob, especially in their brave endeavors to establish a thriving modern state within their biblically designated, ancestral borders?

As we have seen, both the Old and New Testaments make abundantly clear that Christians must support Israel in every possible way. This does not mean that the Israeli people and their government are perfect; far from it. They are fallen human beings like everyone else on Earth, in desperate need of salvation. But the biblical prophets, including the apostle Paul, foretold that the restored Jewish remnant in the Lord's land would mourn over their sins in the last days and be grafted back into their own sacred tree (Romans 10-11).

While waiting, working, and praying for "all Israel to be saved," we must wholeheartedly support what the sovereign Lord is doing in returning His ancient covenant people to their God-given land. In doing so, we will be blessed as they are blessed. Best of all, we will make our Eternal Father happy by obeying His revealed will on a matter that is clearly close to His heart.

When we refuse to pray, we are saying simply, "God, I know better than You. I will not obey Your Word." God's Word says, "I have written my name there" (I Kings 11. 36). Almighty God has promised to dwell with them in the land (Zechariah 2:10), and He will determine blessings or curses on nations depending on how they treat Israel.

> *Thus says the Lord: "Against all My evil neighbors who touch the inheritance which I have caused My people Israel to inherit—behold, I will pluck them out of their land and pluck out the house of Judah from among them."*
>
> **JEREMIAH 12:14**

> *And it shall happen in that day that I will make Jerusalem a very heavy stone for all peoples; all who would heave it away will surely be cut in pieces, though all nations of the earth are gathered against it.*
>
> **ZECHARIAH 12:3**

We who bless Israel will reap the promises of the everlasting God.

> *Then the Angel of the Lord called to Abraham a second time out of heaven, and said: "By Myself I have sworn, says the Lord, because you have done this thing, and have not withheld your son, your only son— blessing I will bless you, and multiplying I will multiply your descendants as the stars of the heaven and as the sand which is on the seashore; and your descendants shall possess the gate of their enemies. In your seed all the nations of the earth shall be blessed, because you have obeyed My voice."*
>
> **GENESIS 22:15-18**

> *"There was a famine in the land, besides the first famine that was in the days of Abraham. And Isaac went to Abimelech king of the Philistines, in Gerar.*
> *Then the Lord appeared to him and said: "Do not go down to Egypt; live in the land of which I shall tell you. Dwell*

in this land, and I will be with you and bless you; for to you and your descendants I give all these lands, and I will perform the oath which I swore to Abraham your father. And I will make your descendants multiply as the stars of heaven; I will give to your descendants all these lands; and in your seed all the nations of the earth shall be blessed; because Abraham obeyed My voice and kept My charge, My commandments, My statutes, and My laws."

GENESIS 26:1-5

CHAPTER NINETEEN

THE EVIL OF
ANTI-SEMITISM

On the day that the enemies of the Jews had hoped to
overpower them, the opposite occurred, in that the Jews themselves
overpowered those who hated them. —ESTHER 9:1

The Old Testament book of Esther paints a beautiful picture of God's deliverance of the Jews from the menace of anti-Semitism. The story of Esther has all the elements of a modern-day love story. A beautiful young Jewish girl is torn from her homeland and taken captive to Persia, where a tyrannical ruler has banished his queen from the royal throne and has initiated a search for her successor. Like Cinderella, the king is taken with Esther and chooses her to be his new queen. Of course, there is also a dastardly villain, Haman, who desires to perpetrate genocide against her Jewish people.

> *Then Haman said to King Ahasuerus, "There is a certain*
> *people scattered and dispersed among the people in all the prov-*
> *inces of your kingdom; their laws are different from all other*
> *people's, and they do not keep the king's laws. Therefore it is not*
> *fitting for the king to let them remain."*
>
> ESTHER 3:8

Esther's uncle, Mordecai, challenges Esther to approach the king (a move that could be punishable by death) and ask for the salvation of her people. In encouraging her to do so, Mordecai confronts Esther with these timeless words:

> *"For if you remain completely silent at this time, relief and deliverance will arise for the Jews from another place, but you and your father's house will perish. Yet who knows whether you have come to the kingdom for such a time as this?"*
>
> **ESTHER 4:14**

Esther's response to Mordecai is magnificent:

> *"Go, gather all the Jews who are present in Shushan, and fast for me; neither eat nor drink for three days, night or day. My maids and I will fast likewise. And so I will go to the king, which is against the law; and if I perish, I perish!"*
>
> **ESTHER 4:16**

With great trepidation, Esther approached King Ahasuerus. Miraculously, he granted her an audience. The plan for the destruction of the Jews by the foul villain, Haman, was thwarted, and the king issued a decree throughout the land allowing Esther's people to defend themselves if attacked. Because of this decree, the Jews overcame every enemy and lived in peace (Esther 8-9).

Anti-Semitism is hatred against all Jews. Jesus was Jewish, as were the biblical prophets, priests, and kings of Israel—the chosen people of God. Anti-Semitism at its very root is hatred against God, His Son, His Spirit, and His Word. You cannot love Jesus whom you have not seen (who was Jewish) if you don't love the Jewish people whom you have seen. God says He will curse those who curse Israel (Genesis 12:3). If you refuse to bless the House of Israel when it is in your power to do so, what evidence of true Christian love do you have to present to a Holy God?

Martin Niemöller was a renowned Protestant pastor who became a vocal and public opponent of Adolf Hitler. When Hitler first came to power, Niemöller supported him. He soon learned that Hitler was nothing more than a dictator with a virulent hatred for the Jewish people. When that realization gripped the Lutheran pastor, he began to preach sermons critical of the Third Reich. He was soon arrested and remanded to a concentration camp, finally ending up in Dachau.

Niemöller is perhaps best known for this warning against misplaced complaisance:

> In Germany, they first came for the communists, and I didn't speak up because I wasn't a communist. Then they came for the Jews, and I didn't speak up because I wasn't a Jew. Then they came for the trade unionists, and I didn't speak up because I wasn't a trade unionist. Then they came for the Catholics, and I didn't speak up because I wasn't a Catholic. Then they came for me...and by that time there was nobody left to speak up.

In 1879 Wilhelm Marr, a German publicist and agitator, is said to have created the phrase "anti-Semite" to give the term "Jew-hatred" a more palatable name. The term was accepted and incorporated into dictionaries as meaning, "Theory, action, or practice directed against the Jews; hostility towards Jews as a religious or racial minority group, often accompanied by social, economic, and political discrimination." [86]

There is much truth in columnist Richard Cohen's take on the spread of anti-Semitism among Muslims:

> The Arab world is the last bastion of unbridled, unashamed, unhidden and unbelievable anti-Semitism. Hitlerian myths get published in the popular press as incontrovertible truths. The Holocaust either gets minimized or denied...This is sad stuff. It is sad because it is tolerated by governments throughout the Middle East, none of which is a democracy with freedom of the press. [87]

Anti-Semitism flourishes when Christians refuse to speak out in defense of the Jewish people, when hatred and revulsion are allowed to ferment, and when we refuse to become our brother's keeper. In every Arab state, you can buy Hitler's book, *Mein Kampf*, based on *The Protocols of the Learned Elders of Zion* (a fabricated, anti-Semitic book originating in Russia in 1903) and used as the excuse to murder six million Jews.

Unfortunately, many Arabs believe Hitler's teachings about the Jews—that mankind's problems are because the Jews control the world. Joseph Joffe, publisher and editor of *Die Zeit* and a research fellow at the Hoover Institution, points out that Israel is a pretext, not a cause, for the ills of the Arab world. He notes that some reformers in Arab countries have begun to realize that those who blame Israel for these self-inflicted wounds are keeping the wounds bleeding. In his article, "A World without Israel," the professor states:

> Since World War II, no state has suffered so cruel a reversal of fortunes as Israel. Admired all the way into the 1970s as the state of "those plucky Jews" who survived against all odds and made democracy and the desert bloom in a climate hostile to both liberty and greenery, Israel has become the target of creeping delegitimization. The denigration comes in two guises. The first, the soft version, blames Israel first and most for whatever ails the Middle East, and for having corrupted U.S. foreign policy. It is the standard fare of editorials around the world, not to mention the sheer venom oozing from the pages of the Arab-Islamic press. The more recent hard version zeroes in on Israel's very existence. According to this dispensation, it is Israel as such, and not its behavior, that lies at the root of troubles in the Middle East. Hence the "statocidal" conclusion that Israel's birth, with by both the United States and the Soviet Union in 1948, was a grievous mistake, grandiose and worthy as it may have been at the time. [88]

If the United States, the EU, UN, Russia, and the Arab League conspire to weaken Israel, they will risk any peace for which the world might hope because God has established that the road to world peace runs through Israel. Israel is the firewall between America and the anti-Semitic Islamic nations. America's ability to win the war on terrorism will be directly related to her willingness to support Israel's fight against terrorism. It is the only power that restrains Islamic terrorism from the West.

A lesser considered question might be: If Israel were no longer a major player in the Middle East, who would the Arab countries blame for the Palestinian unrest, for the unrepressed hatred between the Sunni and Shia factions, and for the terrorist attacks which circle the globe? Or, if the Palestinian issue were to disappear tomorrow, were all the Palestinian refugees absorbed by other Arab countries, would Israel be recognized by the Arab League as a legitimate Middle East state, or would another pretext be found to continue the onslaught against the Jewish people and their homeland?

If that were to happen, would the antipathy toward America, the "Great Satan" come to a halt? Would Israel still be the "Little Satan" and a target for terrorism? Fundamental Islamic terrorists consider America to be a Christian nation. Walid Shoebat, a former PLO member who now works to disseminate the truth about Israel and the Jews among Arabs, explained:

> The Israeli Arab Conflict is not about geography but about Jew hatred. Throughout the Islamic as well as Christendom's history Jews have been persecuted; the persecution of Israel is just the same as the old anti-Semitism…The Arab refugees are being used as pawns to create a terror breeding ground, as a form of aggression against Israel.[89]

Years ago Mother Theresa and I prayed together in Rome. As we prayed for Israel, I remember hearing her words: *"You cannot love Jesus without loving the Jewish people."* Her words are as true now as the day she spoke them.

The awful historical record shows that Jews have been the target of fierce discrimination and even persecution by Christians over the centuries. The first Crusades spawned a rash of anti-Semitic retaliations aimed at the Jews in Europe—initially in France and Germany. It was demanded that Jews convert to Christianity, and those who refused were "deprived of their goods, massacred, or expelled from the cities."[90] The barbaric Spanish Inquisitions were directed against the Jews in Spain. Many Jews were tortured to death or burned at the stake. A large number—the figure ranges from 80,000 to 800,000—were expelled from the country. For Spain, it constituted a self-inflicted wound from which the nation has never recovered.

The twentieth century was the time Tsarist and then Soviet regimes launched pogroms designed to rid Russia of the Jews. Today in fundamentalist Muslim countries under *Shariah* Law (the religious criminal code set forth by the Qur'an), the news media is rife with disdain for the Jews. These are the white-hot embers that keep the fire of anti-Semitism ablaze.

As evil as these anti-Semitic assaults were and are, they all pale by comparison to the Holocaust of World War II. Some six million Jews perished in "Christian" Europe, at least one million of them children. They were the victims of a cruel regime, which had sprung up in the very land where Martin Luther sparked the Protestant Reformation. A full one-third of the entire Jewish race was wiped off the face of the Earth by Hitler's Nazi forces. The utter horror of the Holocaust, as revealed by the testimonies of death-camp survivors and those who liberated them, cannot be overstressed.

> Liberators confronted unspeakable conditions in the Nazi camps, where piles of corpses lay unburied. Only after the liberation of these camps was the full scope of Nazi horrors exposed to the world. The small percentage of inmates who survived resembled skeletons because of the demands of forced labor and the lack of food, compounded by months and years of maltreatment. Many were so weak that they could hardly move. Disease remained an ever-present danger, and many of the camps had to be burned down to prevent

the spread of epidemics. Survivors of the camps faced a long and difficult road to recovery.[91]

The apostle Paul warned Christians not to act arrogantly against the physical descendants of Jacob. In Romans 3:1-2 NIV, he asked the question: "What advantage, then, is there in being a Jew, or what value is there in circumcision?" He answered: "Much in every way! First of all, they have been entrusted with the very words of God."

A show of arrogance would have been welcome in comparison to the ugly hatred and deadly violence historically aimed at the Jewish people in the name of Christ. This alone should be reason enough for contemporary Christians to stand with the Jewish people in their difficult struggle to rebuild their ancient homeland in the hostile atmosphere of the Middle East.

Too late, many Germans—indeed, most of the world—recognized the blessings the Jewish people brought to their society before Hitler's tragic rise to power. Jewish composers, scientists, doctors, teachers, writers, and others contributed their significant talents and intelligence to the land of Luther. They were repaid with Hitler's death chambers. American Christians should be the first to welcome the many blessings brought to this great land by our Jewish citizens.

Several years ago, in my discussion with a prominent Israeli government official, he said,

> I have a very deep conviction we are reliving the 1930s. The whole world has moved backward. In the 1930s the strength and the might of Nazi Germany was coal and steel. Now we have the Arabs with their oil. Their thrust is anti-Semitic now, just as it was then. And, the attitude of the Western democracies is one of appeasement now, as it was then.
>
> It was a fashionable intellectual mood in the West to appease the Nazis and say, "What do you know, they are making the trains run on time...and basically we need to

make sure that we have steel and coal for our economy, so we mustn't rock the boat. It they want to gobble up Czechoslovakia, why make a fuss…The idea of concocting a pseudonationalist movement like Hitler used against Czechoslovakia is being copied now…in the form of the PLO. Chamberlain was willing to sacrifice a nation to avoid confrontation; America just didn't want to get involved. An entire nation was lost to the Nazis without interference. Israel is just trying to get across to the world today that Jerusalem is not Czechoslovakia. We will not be sold out.

CHAPTER TWENTY

GOD'S IRREVOCABLE GIFT
OF COMPASSION

Can a woman forget her sucking child, that she should not
have compassion on the son of her womb? yea, they may
forget, yet will I not forget thee. —ISAIAH 49:15 KJV

D uring an afternoon in Jerusalem spent with Russian Jews who came
to Israel as refugees, one of the elderly ladies who had just buried
her second son as a result of a terrorist attack asked me, "Why are
the Christians killing us? I fled Russia to get away from the Russian Orthodox
Christians that hated us, only to run right into American Christians who
have divided our land and forced the terrorists on us." The House of Israel,
like the traveler on the road to Jericho, has fallen among robbers who have
not only stolen their land but their lives.

Where is the Good Samaritan in all of this?

> *"But a certain Samaritan, as he journeyed, came where*
> *he was. And when he saw him, he had compassion. So he went*
> *to him and bandaged his wounds, pouring on oil and wine; and*
> *he set him on his own animal, brought him to an inn, and took*
> *care of him. On the next day, when he departed, he took out two*
> *denarii, gave them to the innkeeper, and said to him, 'Take care*
> *of him; and whatever more you spend, when I come again, I will*

repay you.' So which of these three do you think was neighbor to
him who fell among the thieves?"

> *And he said, "He who showed mercy on him."*
> *Then Jesus said to him, "Go and do likewise."*

LUKE 10:33-37

We should heed the words of Jesus concerning the House of Israel. The story of the Good Samaritan has been so embraced by society that the name has come to mean, "A compassionate person who unselfishly helps others."[92] The narrative describes a concept of empathy and kindness that involves work and sacrifice. While others ignored the wounded traveler and passed by on the other side of the road, the Samaritan man rolled up his sleeves and provided first-aid. He then loaded the injured man on his animal and took him to the nearest place of shelter, an inn. He could have dumped the poor, injured traveler on the doorstep and high-tailed it out of town. Instead, he secured a room and ministered to the victim for a period of time. When it was time for him to depart, he still refused to abandon his charge and paid the innkeeper to keep watch over him until the Samaritan passed that way again.

So many down through the annals of time have turned a blind eye to the rabid anti-Semitism heaped upon the Jewish people. Like the priest and the Levite, people have pulled their proverbial robes around them and refused to extend a hand of compassion to the Jews. The Samaritan, hated for his ethnicity, did not see race or religion; he saw a man in need of compassion. He didn't stop to ask, like the rich, young lawyer, "And who is my neighbor?" (Luke 10:29). He saw a need, and he met it.

How do you react to the words "Jews," "Israel," or "the Jewish people"? Do your anti-Semitic hackles rise? Are you among those who grimace in hatred at the mention of the words? Do you feel the need to blame all the ills of the world on them, or do you respond as the Samaritan did? Do you react with mercy and kindness, with care and consideration? Are you a good neighbor like the Samaritan?

In Luke 10:27, Jesus said, "You shall love the Lord your God with all your heart, with all your soul, with all your strength, and with all your mind, and your neighbor as yourself." The Samaritan was a picture of the good neighbor Christ wanted his disciples to emulate.

God established a covenant with His chosen ones as Moses recorded:

> "For you are a holy people to the Lord your God; the Lord your God has chosen you to be a people for Himself, a special treasure above all the peoples on the face of the earth. The Lord did not set His love on you nor choose you because you were more in number than any other people, for you were the least of all peoples; but because the Lord loves you, and because He would keep the oath which He swore to your fathers, the Lord has brought you out with a mighty hand, and redeemed you from the house of bondage, from the hand of Pharaoh king of Egypt."
>
> **DEUTERONOMY 7:6-8**

This covenant still stands today. In Matthew 25, we find Jesus teaching on the Mount of Olives. He is painting a word-picture for his followers of what is to come upon them in the end times. As He neared the end of His discourse, Jesus said to them:

> "When the Son of Man comes in His glory, and all the holy angels with Him, then He will sit on the throne of His glory. All the nations will be gathered before Him, and He will separate them one from another, as a shepherd divides his sheep from the goats. And He will set the sheep on His right hand, but the goats on the left. Then the King will say to those on His right hand, 'Come, you blessed of My Father, inherit the kingdom prepared for you from the foundation of the world: for I was hungry and you gave Me food; I was thirsty and you gave Me drink; I was a stranger and you took Me in; I was naked and you clothed Me; I was sick and you visited Me; I was in prison and you came to Me.'
>
> "Then the righteous will answer Him, saying, 'Lord, when did we see You hungry and feed You, or thirsty and give You

drink? When did we see You a stranger and take You in, or naked
and clothe You? Or when did we see You sick, or in prison, and
come to You?' And the King will answer and say to them, 'Assuredly, I say to you, inasmuch as you did it to one of the least of
these My brethren, you did it to Me.'"

MATTHEW 25:31-40

Conversely, He will also pass judgment on those who refused to give a
cup of cold water in His Name:

> "Then He will answer them, saying, 'Assuredly, I say to you,
> inasmuch as you did not do it to one of the least of these, you did
> not do it to Me.' And these will go away into everlasting punish-
> ment, but the righteous into eternal life."

MATTHEW 25:45-46

As believers we are to have compassion upon those who are in trouble.
The fact that Israel, the apple of God's eye, is in the crosshairs of those terrorist organizations who wish only to see her destroyed should be argument
enough for helping Israel today.

Down through the ages, the Jews have been totally rejected by the world's
majority. This has been evidenced by their harsh and inhumane treatment.
This is not the response God expects from the followers of Jesus Christ. The
apostle Paul was grieved to intercede for his brothers in the House of Israel:

> "For I could wish that I myself were accursed from Christ
> for my brethren [the House of Israel], my countrymen according
> to the flesh, who are Israelites, to whom pertain the adoption, the
> glory, the covenants, the giving of the law, the service of God, and
> the promises."

ROMANS 9:3-4

In his first letter to the Corinthians, chapter 10, verse 32, Paul admonished them to "Give no offense, either to the Jews or to the Greeks or to the church of God." If God had forsaken the Jews, Paul would have known it. God's Word declares He will never forsake His chosen people.

Still, believers will say, "God has forsaken Israel because of her sins. He won't bless them." Jeremiah disputed that theory thousands of years ago. It would be wise for us to hear him today:

> "For Israel is not forsaken, nor Judah,
>   By his God, the Lord of hosts,
>   Though their land was filled with sin against the Holy One
>   of Israel."
>
> **JEREMIAH 51:5**

If God had truly revoked His promises and His covenant with Israel, why didn't John the Revelator know it? Why didn't our Lord, who gave the revelation to John, know it? It is impossible to read the book of Revelation and not be aware of Israel from chapters 7 through 21. Revelation 7:2-8 and 21:12 speak of the twelve tribes. Israel is, and will always be, God's miracle nation, His Chosen People.

Some like to deny their responsibility, saying the Jews are blind. They quote Matthew 23:39 NIV, which says, "You will not see me (Christ) again until you say, 'Blessed is he who comes in the name of the Lord.'" You cannot truly say you have been a blessing unless you have blessed the Jewish people. How can we expect them to listen to our message while we turn our backs on their pain?

The wounded man in Jesus' story of the Good Samaritan was in no condition to hear platitudes; he needed help. He needed someone to come alongside him, reach down, and provide physical assistance. James wrote in chapter 2,

> Suppose a brother or sister is without clothes and daily food.
> If one of you says to him, "Go, I wish you well; keep warm and

well fed," but does nothing about his physical needs, what good
is it? In the same way, faith by itself, if it is not accompanied by
action, is dead.

JAMES 2:15-17 NIV

Nowhere does it specify that we are to withhold support because a person happens to be Jewish. What we do speaks with greater clarity than what we say.

Sadly, even great numbers of real Christians did little or nothing to help during the Holocaust. Either through ignorance or fear, they were silent. If you were Jewish today, how would you feel hearing Christians sing about Moses, David, and Daniel, and talk about Jews in the end times—but do nothing to reach out in love to those who are perishing in the Holy Land? Too many professing Christians remain silent as America attempts to strong-arm Israel to give even more land-for-peace—a move that will not only expose the Jewish people to more terrorist attacks in Israel but also remove God's hand of protection from America.

In July 2000, President Bill Clinton invited PLO leader Yasser Arafat and Israeli Prime Minister Ehud Barak to Camp David for a summit. Clinton was insistent that the Israelis cooperate in order to reach a peace pact with Arafat. As a result,

> Barak submitted to Arafat 73 percent of the West Bank and all of the Gaza Strip as a Palestinian state. PLO autonomy would grow to 91 percent over a ten to twenty-five year interval. Israel would have traded portions of the West Bank housing Israeli settlements for an equivalent share of the Israeli Negev desert. A small number of Palestinian refugees would be given the right-of-return; those who were not offered that right would have been compensated. The arrogant Arafat rejected the prime minister's offer and declined a counter proposal.[93]

The PLO leader told President Clinton, "The Arab leader who would surrender Jerusalem is not born yet."[94]

Following Arafat's supercilious departure from the bargaining table, he launched the second intifada. His haughty refusal to accept Barak's offer has, since 2000, resulted in the death and mutilation of scores of innocent Jewish civilians. And, it has caused great grief and hardship to Arafat's own Palestinian people.

Many agree with Representative Eliot Engel of New York. Engel opined, "The Palestinian refugees have been used as political pawns for the past sixty years by people who don't want peace in the Middle East." While calling for changes in the United Nations Relief and Works Agency (UNRWA), Engel said, "The UN has been part and parcel of this conspiracy...Instead of resettling them, UNRWA keeps them in refugee camps. The Palestinians are in the refugee camps because the Arab nations want them in refugee camps in order to perpetuate political hatred against Israel."[95]

In 1949 UNRWA was activated as a short-term agency to aid the estimated 900,000 Palestinian refugees. Today, it is the only UN organization devoted solely to a specific group of people. Unbeknownst to most American taxpayers, large sums of their dollars are supporting UNRWA, and yet the organization reportedly fails to track the "recording, deleting, renaming, or manipulation of financial information by staff members or volunteers."[96] Your taxpayer dollars of over $3.4 billion have poured into UNRWA's coffers. In 2008 the U.S. State Department supplied $148 million to the agency. In February 2010 a $40 million contribution made its way into UNRWA's bank account to bolster its regular budget and for crisis intervention.

Columnist Lanny Davis, in an article for *The Hill,* asked some very provocative questions about UNRWA:

> Why haven't the Saudis, with all their oil money, contributed to finding homes for the great-grandparents, parents, grandchildren and great-grandchildren of the original Palestinian refugees over these 60 years?

Why doesn't the U.N. require an independent auditor to track all use of funds and put everything on the Internet for all to see — especially U.S. taxpayers?

Why do the Palestinians require almost four times the number of paid staff in the Middle East to serve less than one-half the number of people served…globally?[97]

Yet another question begs to be asked: Do the Palestinians really want a state? In his exceptional treatise, "The Power of Statelessness: the Withering Appeal of Governing," Jakub Grygiel wrote:

Many of the modern groups espouse radical ideas, tinted by religious and/or extremist views, making them less interested in the establishment of states… States require some sort of political compromise and, even if they are managed in an authoritarian or totalitarian style, they rarely can match the expectations of extremists who tend to become disappointed in political solutions.[98]

Grygiel did not single out the Palestinians as among the groups that have infinitely more power because of their "statelessness," but he could have. Were the Palestinians granted a state, it would involve compromise with the Arabs' sworn enemy, Israel. Proximity between the two groups—Palestinians and Jews—would require some semblance of civil interaction on the part of Hamas, Hezbollah, and the PLO. Playing the victim is apparently preferable to working intimately alongside the Israelis to create a stable Middle East.

As it now stands, the terrorist organizations that surround Israel can fire rockets across the border but continue to hoodwink the global society. Statehood would require accountability—which is now sadly lacking on the part of the PLO. The forging of a Palestinian state would end such lawlessness, for it would introduce a new measure of accountability.

The reality is that no government has the grit to challenge the Arab nations that support the terror organization threatening Israel and Jerusalem as her capital. This is just another illustration of lack of compassion, both for Jews and the Arabs who are used, and even killed, to further the terrorist aims. No one leader had the courage to take on Yasser Arafat and his band of goons; just as no one today has the tenacity to demand that the Arab League acknowledge Israel's right to exist and her citizens the right to live in the land that is rightfully theirs. So much has been conveniently forgotten in terms of what really belongs to Israel, it is ludicrous.

The Obama White House has so far been strangely reticent in even condemning the Palestinian Authority for the hateful attacks against Israel. A hand slap here, a wrist slap there, and it all adds up to the ridiculous. However, let Israel start construction on a new neighborhood in Jerusalem, and President Obama immediately summons Prime Minister Benjamin Netanyahu to Washington for a one-on-one session of diplomatic hand-wringing and arm-twisting.

Why doesn't Mr. Obama yank the chain of Hamas leader Mahmoud Zahhar and explain to him that one cannot make peace through murder? The answer is that the U. S., like most of the world, follows a double standard when it comes to Israeli-Arab conflicts. It's permissible to vilify Israel for any act that might appear to be an exercise of sovereignty, yet each Palestinian violation of the numerous peace agreements signed in the past receives no more than a wink and a nod.

For instance, when Yasser Arafat was still at the helm of the PLO, a fatwa from Mufti Ikremah Sabri was issued, urging the assassination of any Palestinian who sold land to a Jew. Ali Jamhour, a resident of a refugee camp east of Jerusalem, was found shot to death after he had been questioned by Arafat's security forces about allegedly brokering land sales to Jewish Israelis. Jamhour was the third Palestinian land dealer killed; all had been executed gangland-style with a bullet to the head. Shortly after his death, Israeli police foiled the kidnapping of a fourth broker, but at least seven land dealers were murdered. Ultimately, General Tawfik Tirawi, the leader of the Palestinian Authority's General Intelligence Service in the West Bank, acknowledged his underlings were guilty of the murders.[99]

A number of countries, particularly small countries surrounded by hostile neighbors, forbid the sale of land to outsiders; and Israel itself has restricted selling land to Arabs. It would be another thing, however, to kill those who violate the real estate restrictions. Imagine if Israel had announced it would impose the death penalty on anyone who sold land to Arabs. That would have been front-page news around the world, and the U. S. president would have issued a strongly worded statement taking Israel to task for such an outrage. The prime minister would have been summoned to the White House for a summit, and the U.N. would have instantly passed a resolution condemning the State of Israel.

Yet, when the Palestinian Authority actually made such a pronounce-ment and bodies started piling up, it took two weeks for President Clinton's administration to go on the record condemning the policy. It took longer still for the story to appear on the nightly news, and even then reporters passed along, without comment, the Palestinian's stock attempt to shift the blame: Perhaps the Israelis themselves were responsible, they suggested.

Prime Minister Netanyahu, by contrast, took swift action. When Israeli intelligence exposed a Palestinian Authority hit list of sixteen land dealers that included the names of the three already killed, Mr. Netanyahu called an emergency security session. His administration authorized the installation of alarm systems in the brokers' homes and increased police patrols in their neighborhoods. The prime minister also authorized an arrest warrant for a senior Palestinian official implicated in the land dealer executions.

Israeli security said it established that the murders were carried out with the participation, as well as the approval, of the Palestinian Authority. When Israeli police foiled the fourth kidnapping attempt, six armed men were arrested as they tried to flee to Ramallah, the Palestinian-controlled town just north of Jerusalem. Four of the would-be kidnappers were members of the Palestinian Authority security services. During the chase, the suspects ditched several weapons, one of which turned out to be the weapon that had been used in two of the recent murders.

Senator Jesse Helms, chairman of the Senate Foreign Relations Committee, and Representative Benjamin Gilman, chairman of the House

International Relations Committee, announced they would stall the delivery of $1.2 million in aid to the Palestinian Authority until the call to kill Arabs who sell land to Jews had been revoked.[100] Few then had the determination and compassion shown by the two Congressmen; it seems even fewer dare challenge the terror network surrounding Israel today.

More recently, as leader of the opposition in the Knesset in 2008, Benjamin Netanyahu met with Vice President Dick Cheney to discuss the Iranian threat. Netanyahu told Mr. Cheney:

> If we leave Jerusalem, Hamas, Iran and other forces affiliated with them will take control of it. They will threaten Jerusalem's wellbeing, Israel's security and the freedom of worship of millions of pilgrims and members of the different religions arriving in the city today.[101]

Nothing has changed since Mr. Netanyahu issued this admonition. We can only hope and pray that in the future our governmental representatives and the Church at large will become compassionate and wise like The Good Samaritan, reaching out to help and support the nation of Israel and God's chosen capital for her, Jerusalem, in tangible ways.

A GOD-GIVEN
MANDATE

Therefore He says: "Awake, you who sleep, Arise from the dead,
And Christ will give you light." —EPHESIANS 5:14

I t is time for Christians to stand up and be counted, to shake ourselves
in light of the biblical evidence presented here. We can only conclude
that Christians have a God-given mandate to honor the Jewish people,
wherever they are. How does this connect to modern Israel? Many Christians
seem happy enough to salute Jewish neighbors living with them in largely
Gentile lands, but they are indifferent or even hostile to the proposition that
we also have a duty to support the controversial Jewish State of Israel. Some
Believers bristle at the mere suggestion that God has anything to do with
Israel's amazing restoration in our era.

Centuries before the Jewish people first went into foreign captivity, God
revealed that they would be expelled from their covenant land because of
sin. He also pledged to eventually restore them to the Promised Land. This
prophecy came through Moses, a Levite, while he was in the process of hero-
ically leading the children of Israel out of the bondage of Egypt into Canaan:

> *The Lord your God will bring you back from captivity, and*
> *have compassion on you, and gather you again from all the*
> *nations where the Lord your God has scattered you.*
>
> Deuteronomy 30:3

This prophecy spoke of the return of the Jewish people from Assyrian and Babylonian captivity hundreds of years before the time of Christ. Yet the ancient Hebrew prophets also foretold that Israel's loving God would restore His people to the land promised them in the last days of history, in the days just before Messiah's reign in Jerusalem (Isaiah 11:11-12).

The prophets also foretold that the final Jewish ingathering would be from all over the globe, unlike the first return from lands directly to the east of Israel. It also would be a permanent return, meaning no additional exiles would follow. Most significantly, it would end with the spiritual revival that King Solomon prophesied in II Chronicles 7:14:

> If My people who are called by My name will humble themselves, and pray and seek My face, and turn from their wicked ways, then I will hear from heaven, and will forgive their sin and heal their land.

There are many prophetic scriptures about this important topic in the Bible. Let's examine a few of them:

> "I will bring back the captives of My people Israel;
>   They shall build the waste cities and inhabit them;
>   They shall plant vineyards and drink wine from them;
>   They shall also make gardens and eat fruit from them.
>   I will plant them in their land,
>   And no longer shall they be pulled up
> From the land I have given them,"
> Says the Lord your God."
>
> AMOS 9:14-15

> "'For behold, the days are coming,' says the Lord, 'that I will bring back from captivity My people Israel and Judah,' says the Lord. 'And I will cause them to return to the land that I gave to their fathers, and they shall possess it.'"
>
> JEREMIAH 30:3

"'Thus says the Lord God: "When I have gathered the house of Israel from the peoples among whom they are scattered, and am hallowed in them in the sight of the Gentiles, then they will dwell in their own land which I gave to My servant Jacob. And they will dwell safely there, build houses, and plant vineyards; yes, they will dwell securely, when I execute judgments on all those around them who despise them. Then they shall know that I am the Lord their God."'

EZEKIEL 28:25-26

He will set up a banner for the nations,
    And will assemble the outcasts of Israel,
    And gather together the dispersed of Judah
    From the four corners of the earth.

ISAIAH 11:12

For I will take you from among the nations, gather you out of all countries, and bring you into your own land.

EZEKIEL 36:24

And I will cause the captives of Judah and the captives of Israel to return, and will rebuild those places as at the first. I will cleanse them from all their iniquity by which they have sinned against Me, and I will pardon all their iniquities by which they have sinned and by which they have transgressed against Me.

JEREMIAH 33:7-8

Some Jews will still be living outside of Israel during the end of this age. However, this does not lessen or negate the fact that a large-scale return has occurred in our day. Nearly half the Jews on Earth have now returned to their biblical Promised Land. Christians around the world should be exuberant supporters of this prophesied restoration, for it confirms that the God of Israel exists, that He holds the future in His capable hands, that He is a covenant-keeping God, and that He is a merciful God who forgives the sins of His people.

Israel is a miracle nation because of its formation. When we stand with Israel, we are acknowledging God's prophetic plan for His Chosen People. Their very existence and the rebirth of Israel is a miracle. As Christians, we believe in miracles. The resurrection of our Lord was the greatest miracle. Just as He rose again, it is no problem for Him to restore the nation of Israel to its rightful place among nations.

Israel was not born in 1948; it was *reborn*. It was first born in the heart of God and revealed to Abraham many years before the birth of Isaac. God made a blood covenant with Abraham that the land of Canaan would be given to Abraham's seed through Isaac (Genesis 15:18). As part of that vision, God told Abraham that for four hundred years his seed would be strangers in a land that did not belong to them (Genesis 15:13). The seed of Abraham from Isaac spent four hundred years in Egypt before Moses led them out, and Israel, the nation, was born.

> *"Who hath heard such a thing? who hath seen such things? Shall the earth be made to bring forth in one day? or shall a nation be born at once? for as soon as Zion travailed, she brought forth her children."*
>
> **ISAIAH 66:8 KJV**

Unique as this religious centrality is, there is one reason above all others why committed Christians must stand with Israel: The God of the Universe, the God Whom we worship, has chosen to make an everlasting covenant with the physical descendents of Abraham, Isaac, and Jacob—the Jewish people.

The word "everlasting" has nothing temporary or conditional about it. It clearly means, "lasting forever." Although Jews are found today in North and South America, Australia, Russia, Europe, many parts of Africa—virtually every continent on Earth—their historic spiritual and physical center was and always will be Jerusalem and Israel.

God's eternal covenant with the descendents of Abraham featured the promise to give them the land of Israel as an everlasting possession. This is recorded in the very first book of the Bible, Genesis, in chapter 17:

When Abram was ninety-nine years old, the Lord appeared to Abram and said to him, "I am Almighty God; walk before Me and be blameless. And I will make My covenant between Me and you, and will multiply you exceedingly." Then Abram fell on his face, and God talked with him, saying: "As for Me, behold, My covenant is with you, and you shall be a father of many nations. No longer shall your name be called Abram, but your name shall be Abraham; for I have made you a father of many nations. I will make you exceedingly fruitful; and I will make nations of you, and kings shall come from you. And I will establish My covenant between Me and you and your descendants after you in their generations, for an everlasting covenant, to be God to you and your descendants after you. Also I give to you and your descendants after you the land in which you are a stranger, all the land of Canaan, as an everlasting possession; and I will be their God."

GENESIS 17:1-8

It is true God reveals in these verses that many peoples will eventually emerge out of Abraham's loins, and so it has been. The Arabs, scattered in over twenty countries throughout the Middle East and North Africa, trace their ancestry to the biblical patriarch who traveled to Canaan at God's command from the town of Ur in Chaldea. Their lineage comes through Abraham's first-born but illegitimate son, Ishmael. However, the Scriptures go on to reveal that the special, eternal land covenant would come through the lineage of Isaac, Jacob and his twelve sons—the forefathers of the modern Jewish people. This is summarized in Psalm 105, verses 8 through 11:

He remembers His covenant forever,
 The word which He commanded, for a thousand generations,
The covenant which He made with Abraham,
  And His oath to Isaac,
 And confirmed it to Jacob for a statute,
  To Israel as an everlasting covenant,

Saying, "To you I will give the land of Canaan
As the allotment of your inheritance."

The belief that God has revoked His solemn land covenant with the Jewish people due to their sin and rebellion against Him is widespread in the Church today. It is certainly a fact that living peacefully in the land was conditional upon obedience to God's Law. Jacob's offspring were warned that they would be removed from the land if they disobeyed God's commands. The Bible also foretells that a Jewish remnant would be restored to the Promised Land after a worldwide exile, as is wonderfully occurring in our day:

> *For I will take you from among the nations, gather you out*
> *of all countries, and bring you into your own land.*
> *'Thus says the Lord God: "On the day that I cleanse you*
> *from all your iniquities, I will also enable you to dwell in the cit-*
> *ies, and the ruins shall be rebuilt. The desolate land shall be tilled*
> *instead of lying desolate in the sight of all who pass by. So they*
> *will say, 'This land that was desolate has become like the Garden*
> *of Eden; and the wasted, desolate, and ruined cities are now forti-*
> *fied and inhabited.'*
>
> **EZEKIEL 36:24, 33-35**

Since the 1900s Jews have returned to the Promised Land from nations around the globe. Since the 1980s the Soviet Union and Ethiopia have been persuaded to release a number of Jews and have allowed them to emigrate to Israel. In May 1991 an astounding 14,500 Ethiopian Jews were airlifted to Israel in what would become known as "Operation Solomon." The Israeli government showed its eagerness to take advantage of the window to relocate the Jewish community in Ethiopia:

> The Likud government of Yitzhak Shamir authorized
> a special permit for the Israeli airline, El Al, to fly on the

Jewish Sabbath. On Friday, May 24, and continuing non-stop for 36 hours, a total of 34 El Al jumbo jets and Hercules C-130s—seats removed to accommodate the maximum number of Ethiopians—began a new chapter in the struggle for the freedom of Ethiopian Jewry.[102]

Those returnees have been joined by Jews from the U.S., China, Scandinavia, Australia, and South America, just to name a few.

The prophet Isaiah declared in 43:5-6:

> *Fear not, for I am with you;*
> *I will bring your descendants from the east,*
> *And gather you from the west;*
> *I will say to the north, 'Give them up!'*
> *And to the south, 'Do not keep them back!'*
> *Bring My sons from afar,*
> *And My daughters from the ends of the earth.*

This is exactly what Jehovah God has done and continues to do today.

CHAPTER TWENTYTWO

JEHOVAH,
KEEPER OF ISRAEL

Behold, he that keepeth Israel shall neither slumber nor sleep.
The Lord is thy keeper: the Lord is thy shade upon thy right hand.
The sun shall not smite thee by day, nor the moon by night.
The Lord shall preserve thee from all evil: he shall preserve thy soul.
The Lord shall preserve thy going out and thy coming in from this time
forth, and even for evermore. —PSALM 121:4-8 KJV

Although no people group has been targeted more than the Jews, God has not allowed them to be exterminated. Many horrific attempts have been made to annihilate them, but such attempts have ended in utter failure, defeat, and humiliation for the perpetrators. From Pharaoh to Haman to Hitler, their efforts to destroy the Jewish people have ended ignominiously. Haman was hanged on the very gallows he had built for Queen Esther's uncle, Mordecai (Esther 7:10). Pharaoh "commanded all his people, saying, 'Every son who is born you shall cast into the river, and every daughter you shall save alive'" (Exodus 1:22). This ruler, who ordered every Hebrew male child to be thrown into the river, was drowned with his own army in the Red Sea!

Satan's diabolical plan to annihilate the Jews during World War II was perpetrated through Hitler. He declared Jews were not the Chosen People, the Aryan race was. He said, "There is no room for two chosen people," and he inspired many to believe that the title of "divine elect" was the preserve of the Aryan Christian.[103] He had six million Jews murdered in concentration camps. When he knew his bunker was about to be overrun by the Russians, Hitler is said to have swallowed a cyanide capsule and then shot himself in the head. At the end of the war, Germany was divided and shortly thereafter Israel was reborn. Hitler's dream was a nightmare that crashed down around the German people. The Jewish people, however, were preserved and began to thrive again.

The preservation of Israel through all of its suffering, wars, and afflictions over the centuries is further evidence that Israel is God's miracle nation. Why have the Jews been so hated? It is because the only One who could defeat Satan would come through the Jews: The Messiah. Ultimately his adversary, Jesus Christ, would destroy the power of Satan, originally called Lucifer.

"How you are fallen from heaven,
Oh Lucifer, son of the morning!
How you are cut down to the ground,
You who weakened the nations!
For you have said in your heart,

'I will ascend into heaven,
I will exalt my Throne above the stars of God;
I will sit on the mount of the congregation
On the farthest sides of the north [the Temple site];
I will ascend above the heights of the clouds,
I will be like the Most High.'
Yet you shall be brought down to Sheol,
To the lowest depths of the Pit."

ISAIAH 14:12-15 [insert mine]

Lucifer rebelled against God—not a smart thing to do—and was soundly defeated. God changed his name to Satan, which simply means he became the evil enemy of everything good and of God.

Satan hates the Jews because they are God's covenant people. Our God is a covenant-keeping God. He remains faithful even when we are faithless (II Timothy 2:13). It is He who has decided to preserve the Jewish people as separate and identifiable before Him until the end of time, and then He will restore them to their biblical homeland. These truths are revealed in several scriptures. That the Jews would remain on Earth until the end of time as a distinct people group is foretold in Jeremiah, chapter 31:

> *Thus says the Lord,*
>> *Who gives the sun for a light by day,*
>> *The ordinances of the moon and the stars for a light by night,*
>> *Who disturbs the sea,*
>> *And its waves roar*
>> *(The Lord of hosts is His name):*
>>> *"If those ordinances depart*
>> *From before Me, says the Lord,*
>> *Then the seed of Israel shall also cease*
>> *From being a nation before Me forever."*
>
> **JEREMIAH 31:35-36**

Rather than turn a collective back on the Jewish people, Christians should rejoice. Why? God is a promise-keeper. He promised Israel a certain land, some of which the Jews have been allowed to occupy, and He has not gone back on His promise. This means He has not reneged on His promises to the New Testament Church—His promise of salvation, of provision, and the hope of eternal life. Numbers 23:19 says, "God is not a man, that He should lie, Nor a son of man, that He should repent. Has He said, and will He not do? Or has He spoken, and will He not make it good?" God cannot lie and His promises are faithful: "Let us hold fast the confession of our hope without wavering, for He who promised is faithful" (Hebrews 10:23). You and I can rest secure in the knowledge that God will keep His promises to us.

Many Bible teachers and denominations argue that Jewish sin, and particularly the general rejection of Jesus as their Messiah nearly two thousand years ago, was more than enough reason for God to erase the "everlasting" land promise. But the next verse makes crystal clear that the God of Abraham has no intention of ever forsaking His special covenant with Jacob's children, despite their many failures:

> *"I will direct their work in truth,*
> *And will make with them an everlasting covenant.*
>   *Their descendants shall be known among the Gentiles,*
> *And their offspring among the people.*
> *All who see them shall acknowledge them,*
> *That they are the posterity whom the Lord has blessed."*
>
> **ISAIAH 61:8-9**

In 1982 I founded the National Prayer Breakfast in Honor of Israel. Senator Billy Armstrong had the following "Proclamation of Blessing" placed in the Congressional Record. It states clearly why Americans must stand with Israel:

CONGRESSIONAL RECORD

Washington, D. C., Tuesday, March 16, 1982
"Proclamation of Blessing"

"As Bible-believing Americans, we believe there exists an iron-clad bond between the State of Israel and the United States. We believe that bond to be a moral imperative.

"Representing the vast majority of evangelicals in the United States, we have gathered together at this National Prayer Breakfast to reaffirm our support and prayers, that this bond not be weakened or diminished.

"We agree with the sentiments of our President: 'That a secure, strong Israel is in America's self-interest. Israel is a major strategic asset to America. Israel is not a client, but a very reliable friend. To weaken Israel is to destabilize the Middle East and risk the peace of the world, for the road to world peace runs through the Middle East.'

"We support Israel's right to their land spiritually and legally. History records that God deals with nations in accordance with how these nations deal with Israel. We rejoice that here in America, we have been committed to the Jewish people. The Jewish people have found refuge here; they have found a people who love them; and we can take pride in saying that Israel is not an exclusively Jewish issue.

"Bible-believing evangelicals consider the support of Israel a biblical mandate. Regardless of contrary opinion, we do not believe Israel has to offer an excuse for its existence. Israel lives today as a right! A right that has been hallowed by the Bible, by history, by sacrifice, by prayer, and by the yearning for peace!

I will bring back the captives of My people Israel; They shall build the waste cities and inhabit them; They shall plant vineyards and drink wine from them; They shall also make gardens and eat fruit from them. I will plant them in their land, And no longer shall they be pulled up From the land I have given them," Says the Lord your God (Amos 9:14-15).

"We believe one of the reasons America has been blessed over the years is because we have stood with Israel according to Genesis 12:3. So, for biblical reasons first and foremost, we support the State of Israel. For humanitarian reasons, we support the Jewish people. For historical reasons, believing that Palestine belongs to the Jewish people, we support the State of Israel. For legal reasons, dating back to 1948, and even further to the establishment of the British Mandate, we believe the land of Palestine belongs to the Jewish people.

"Israel and the United States are not separate and distinct—
we are one. We share common ideals and common democracy. What unites us across the ocean, and brings Jew and
Christian together, is the recognition that Israel is a nation
that is a manifestation of what America was and is.

"America has a strong interest in the Middle East. We affirm
our belief that the nation of Israel is the key to that interest because of our common bonds, our common values, our
common belief in social justice, and the godly principles on
which our two countries were founded.

"In affirmation of these beliefs, we hereby set our hands this
10th day of February, 1982."

It is imperative that we, as Christians, keep covenant with the Jews.
Jesus never denied His heritage; He was born a Jew. His family celebrated the
Jewish customs of circumcision, of taking Him to be presented in the Temple
at the age of thirteen. He studied and followed the Law of Moses. When
He was hung on the Cross, the very inscription above His head proclaimed
His Jewish roots: *"King of the Jews!"* The Jews were His people, and Israel
His land.

In Ezekiel 38:16 God calls the land of Israel, "My Land." He gave it to
Israel by a blood covenant that cannot be altered. God has assigned the land
of Israel to the children of Israel, and He has never cancelled His covenant
with them.

God declared that Israel would be scattered among the heathen,
and they were; but He also said they would be gathered again, and they
have been:

> *"Behold, I will gather them out of all countries where I have
> driven them in My anger, in My fury, and in great wrath; I will
> bring them back to this place, and I will cause them to dwell
> safely."*

"I will say to the north, 'Give them up!'
And to the south, 'Do not keep them back!'
Bring My sons from afar,
And My daughters from the ends of the earth."

ISAIAH 43:6

Thus says the Lord God:
"Behold, I will lift My hand in an oath to the nations,
And set up My standard for the peoples;
They shall bring your sons in their arms,
And your daughters shall be carried on their shoulders."

ISAIAH 49:22

It is of great interest to note that hundreds of years before the invention of airplanes, Isaiah prophesied the return of the people of Israel to their homeland by air: *"Who are these who fly* along like clouds, like doves to their nests?" (Isaiah 60:8 NIV). He also predicted that they would return by ships:

Surely the coastlands shall wait for Me;
And the ships of Tarshish will come first,
To bring your sons from afar,
Their silver and their gold with them,
To the name of the Lord your God,
And to the Holy One of Israel,
Because He has glorified you.

ISAIAH 60:9

God is fulfilling His promises to His people, Israel, and it is an unparalleled miracle. When one considers the extraordinary triumphs of the Israeli Defense Forces in 1948, 1967, and 1973, it is apparent that God was and is their Defender. Technology in that tiny nation is a wonder. One has only to drive the length and breadth of Israel to see the phenomenal agricultural achievements. Israel is a demonstration of God's rich and plenteous care for His people. As Christians, we should say with heartfelt love and compassion, "We stand with the people of Israel, with the Jewish people. We stand against the hostility shown to you by nations worldwide, against the ever-increasing hatefulness of anti-Semitism. We stand with you despite the onslaught of jihadists determined to 'wipe Israel from the Earth.' We stand with you against those who would, if allowed, drive Israel into the sea. We stand with you as friends, and we pray as David admonished, 'for the peace of Jerusalem'" (Psalm 122:6).

> "Rejoice with Jerusalem and be glad for her, all you who love her; rejoice greatly with her, all you who mourn over her.
> For you will nurse and be satisfied at her comforting breasts; you will drink deeply and delight in her overflowing abundance."
> For this is what the Lord says: "I will extend peace to her like a river, and the wealth of nations like a flooding stream; you will nurse and be carried on her arm and dandled on her knees."
> **ISAIAH 66:10-12 NIV**

PRAYER-WARRIOR
WATCHMAN

"I have set watchmen on your walls, O Jerusalem;
They shall never hold their peace day or night.
You who make mention of the Lord, do not keep silent,
And give Him no rest till He establishes
And till He makes Jerusalem a praise in the earth."

ISAIAH 62:6-7

In the Old Testament, the word "watchman" is often used for those called to intercessory prayer for their people. Just as a watchman in a city stood at the gate to warn the people of a coming enemy and was, therefore, the first line of defense, so intercessory prayer warriors are the first line of spiritual defense for our nations and communities. What happens when the watchmen don't do their jobs?

'But if the watchman sees the sword coming and does not blow the trumpet to warn the people and the sword comes and takes the life of one of them, that man will be taken away because of his sin, but I will hold the watchman accountable for his blood.'

EZEKIEL 33:6 NIV

Yes, in many ways the blood of those killed in suicide bombings is on our hands, just as the blood of Christians was on Paul's hands. So what did Paul do about it? What did he say?

Therefore I testify to you this day that I am innocent of the blood of all men. For I have not shunned to declare to you the whole counsel of God.

A C T S   20:26-27

Paul declared himself sinless because he turned from his killing ways to saving ways. He repented and followed God. We must turn from apathy to steadfast prayer in the same way! Nothing is more important to God than prayer. God will do nothing without prayer. The fuel that moves the engine of humanity is prayer.

God has a purpose and a plan for our lives. The lives of our nation and the nation of Israel are dependent on prayer. His will and His blessings are bound up in prayer. Almighty God created the world, and He created the nation of Israel. His purposes and plans are more important than anything that man can do:

'Call to me, and I will answer you, and show you great and mighty things, which you do not know.'

J E R E M I A H   33:3

As Jeremiah prophesied to the Jewish people during their captivity in Babylon, he was given this promise. The Jews were ultimately delivered from captivity, and revival came to Israel.

Thus says the Lord,
  The Holy One of Israel, and his Maker:
  "Ask Me of things to come concerning My sons,
  And concerning the work of My hands, you command Me."

I S A I A H   45:11

God takes prayer so seriously, He even says we can command Him! Although this may sound like heresy, it is His Word to us.

After the children of Israel were carried captive to Babylon, God had a plan in place for their deliverance before they went into captivity. The reality was that over seventy years later, they were still in captivity. What had happened? Had God forgotten to set His alarm clock? Had he slept through freeing His people? Absolutely not!

Although God had a plan for their rescue and had even given them the timetable for it through Jeremiah, nothing would happen until someone prayed it back to God. God's people needed an advocate on Earth to ask for the fulfillment of God's Word. James 4:2 says, "Yet you do not have because you do not ask." God's ear has always been attuned to the sound of intercessory prayer from His children.

Nebuchadnezzar, King of Babylon, had decreed that no one could ask any petition of any God or man for thirty days. Daniel, a Hebrew in Babylon (Iraq), refused to obey the decree of the king. He continued to pray three times a day (Daniel 6:1-23), just as he had done before the decree. Daniel honored God; and when his worship led to his being thrown into a den of lions, God responded by shutting the mouths of the lions. Daniel's prayers prevailed in the midst of Israel's captivity in Babylon:

> *For thus says the Lord: After seventy years are completed at Babylon, I will visit you and perform My good word toward you, and cause you to return to this place. For I know the thoughts that I think toward you, says the Lord, thoughts of peace and not of evil, to give you a future and a hope. Then you will call upon Me and go and pray to Me, and I will listen to you. And you will seek Me and find Me, when you search for Me with all your heart. I will be found by you, says the Lord, and I will bring you back from your captivity; I will gather you from all the nations and from all the places where I have driven you, says the Lord, and I will bring you to the place from which I cause you to be carried away captive.*
>
> **JEREMIAH 29:10-14**

Darkness flees when we pray! Demons tremble when we pray. Heaven moves when we pray, and angels receive assignments when we pray. Prayer affects three realms: The divine, the angelic, and the human. Without it, demons rule uncontested. (See Ephesians 6.) We cannot make contact with God without prayer. If we don't make that connection, no matter how sincere our intentions are we will not see a change in the circumstances of life.

God has watchmen on the wall. I call them Esthers and Nehemiahs… people like Corrie ten Boom and, hopefully, people like you. The world has figuratively been scratching its head trying to find an answer to the crisis in the Bible land. That answer is in your hands and mine—we just have to fold them together in prayer to hear from God.

Abraham is a striking example of the power of prayer. He interceded for Sodom for his nephew Lot's sake, and God delayed judgment. God would have spared Sodom for ten righteous souls (Genesis 18:20-33). Abraham thought surely Lot and his wife, their daughters, their sons, and their sons-in-law would be righteous and total more than ten. Unfortunately, he was wrong. Not all of Lot's family was righteous, and Sodom was destroyed.

Abraham was an intercessor. Wherever he pitched his tent and camped for a season with his household, he erected an altar of sacrifice and prayer. Even when he got into big trouble and told King Abimelech that his wife Sarah was his sister, God honored his prayers. Abimelech realized he had taken another man's wife, and God said to Abimelech, "Now therefore, restore the man's wife; for he is a prophet, and he will pray for you and you shall live" (Genesis 20:7). God heard Abraham's prayers, and He will hear ours. He wants us to be part of His dream and His team.

Moses prayed for forty days for Israel. The result of his prayers was a mighty deliverance for the nation of Israel after four hundred years in Egypt. God's movement to bring Israel from bondage had its inception in prayer. (See Exodus 2:23-25; 3:9.)

In Mark, chapter 9, the disciples came to Jesus, frustrated and downcast. A father had brought his child to them for healing. The little boy had what his father described as a "dumb spirit." After Jesus rebuked the spirit and the little boy was healed, the disciples privately asked Him why they could not heal the child. Jesus answered, "This kind can come out by nothing but prayer and fasting" (Mark 9:29).

September 11th was an assault from Hell, planned and executed by demon spirits. The terrorist holocaust in Israel is a result of the same dark spiritual powers. These powers cannot be defeated without prayer. Praying saints are God's agents to carry out His will on Earth. America is helpless without prayer, as is Israel. If Jesus said that He could do nothing without prayer, then we surely cannot hope to accomplish anything of eternal value and significance without prayer.

A Christian that refuses to pray is like a swimmer who refuses to enter the water. All the talk in the world about swimming will only bring skepticism and laughter if he never jumps in and begins to swim. For a Christian to refuse to make prayer the number one priority is like saying to Osama Bin Laden, "We have laid down our weapons of warfare. You win!"

Our weapons of war and our Commander in Chief are waiting to win the battle; we only need to speak the Word. God has given us the weapons we need to successfully war against the enemy of our souls (Ephesians 6:13-17), the means to become effective intercessors. It is Ephesians 6:18, however, that tells us why we need to use those tools: "...praying always with all prayer and supplication in the Spirit." Prayer is not for the faint of heart; it is hard work.

Only a barren woman can totally understand Hannah's petition for a son in I Samuel 1:11. She prayed in deep anguish—to a degree that Eli, the priest, thought she was drunk. James would call this a fervent and effectual prayer (James 5:16). Her petition began a great prayer movement for God in Israel. Hannah's prayers birthed Samuel the prophet, who would anoint a shepherd boy named David to become king of Israel and establish Jerusalem as the capital. Samuel was a man of prayer. He stood before the people on one occasion and said, "Far be it from me that I should sin against the Lord in ceasing to pray for you" (I Samuel 12:23).

We cannot make contact with God without prayer. If we don't make contact with God, no matter how sincere our intentions are we will not see a change in the circumstances of life. We must pray! James 4:2 tells us, "You lust and do not have. You murder and covet and cannot obtain. You fight and war. Yet you do not have because you do not ask." Paul encouraged the Philippians in chapter 4, verse 6: "Be anxious for nothing, but in everything by prayer and supplication, with thanksgiving, let your requests be made known to God."

During a dark hour of Israel's history, the Assyrians demanded heavy tribute from King Hezekiah. In response, Hezekiah stripped the Temple of its gold and silver in order to meet the demand. Still, that was not enough, and the Assyrians mounted an attack against the city. When King Hezekiah was informed in a letter from the king of Assyria that Israel would be destroyed if the demands were not met, he took the letter to the Temple. There, in the presence of God, he spread the letter on the altar and prayed:

> "O Lord God of Israel, the One who dwells between the cher-
> ubim, You are God, You alone, of all the kingdoms of the earth.
> You have made heaven and earth. Incline Your ear, O Lord, and
> hear; open Your eyes, O Lord, and see; and hear the words of
> Sennacherib, which he has sent to reproach the living God… Now
> therefore, O Lord our God, I pray, save us from his hand, that all
> the kingdoms of the earth may know that You are the Lord God,
> You alone."
>
> II KINGS 19:15-16,19

God responded with an amazing victory! The Bible says the angel of the Lord killed 185,000 Assyrian soldiers in one night. In great gratitude for God's mercy, Hezekiah cleansed, repaired, and reopened the Temple of God. Worship to Jehovah was restored, daily sacrifices were resumed, and the Passover Feast was celebrated by the nation.

Years earlier, when King Solomon had prayed at the dedication of the Temple, God came with great power and revealed His plan to Solomon:

> Then the Lord appeared to Solomon by night, and said to
> him: "I have heard your prayer, and have chosen this place for

Myself as a house of sacrifice. When I shut up heaven and there is no rain, or command the locusts to devour the land, or send pestilence among My people, if My people who are called by My name will humble themselves, and pray and seek My face, and turn from their wicked ways, then I will hear from heaven, and will forgive their sin and heal their land. Now My eyes will be open and My ears attentive to prayer made in this place. For now I have chosen and sanctified this house, that My name may be there forever; and My eyes and My heart will be there perpetually."

II CHRONICLES 7:12-16

Isaiah encouraged the Israelites with: "Then you shall call, and the Lord will answer; You shall cry, and He will say, 'Here I am'" (Isaiah 58:9). King Solomon prophesied that a national revival would come to Israel. It has not happened yet, and it can only come through the power of prayer. You and I can help usher in that revival through prayer. While the world attempts to find an answer to the crisis in the Middle East, you and I have the key in our hands: Prayer. That is why the apostle Paul admonished us to "pray without ceasing" (I Thessalonians 5:17).

You may be like Jonah, who did everything but pray. He knew what God wanted him to do but kept resisting. Jonah fled, and he ended up in the belly of a big fish. There he cried out to God against whom he had sinned. God intervened and caused the fish to vomit Jonah out onto dry land. Even the fish of the sea are subject to the power of prayer! When those in Nineveh saw this stinking, praying prophet, they repented quickly and God sent revival.

In the book of Revelation, the apostle John is shown the power of our prayers:

Then another angel, having a golden censer, came and stood at the altar. He was given much incense, that he should offer it with the prayers of all the saints upon the golden altar which was before the throne. 4 And the smoke of the incense, with the prayers of the saints, ascended before God from the angel's hand. Then the angel took the censer, filled it with fire from the altar,

*and threw it to the earth. And there were noises, thunderings,
lightnings, and an earthquake.*

REVELATION 8:3-5

In light of what we are discovering about the power of prayer, here are
two of the saddest scriptures in the Bible:

*So I sought for a man among them who would make a wall,
and stand in the gap before Me on behalf of the land, that I should
not destroy it; but I found no one.*

EZEKIEL 22:30

*He [God] saw that there was no man,
And wondered that there was no intercessor.*

ISAIAH 59:16 [insert mine]

No one to stand in the gap. No one to intercede. What a tragedy! Today
God is still looking for that man, woman, young person, or child, who will
commit to stand in the breach and pray. Will you, like Isaiah, say, "Here am
I! Lord, send me"?

When the children of Israel sinned in the wilderness and fashioned a
golden calf, danced before it, and denied God's sovereignty, God threatened
to destroy them. He told Moses that He would raise a new people from
Moses' offspring. Moses fell on his face before Jehovah God. The Psalmist
wrote in Psalm 106:23:

*Therefore He said that He would destroy them,
Had not Moses His chosen one stood before Him in the breach,
To turn away His wrath, lest He destroy them.*

The time has come for Christians everywhere to stand up and, "Blow the
trumpet in Zion, Consecrate a fast, Call a sacred assembly" (Joel 2:15). There
is a gap, a breach to be filled, and a price to be paid. Watchmen are needed

on every wall. God's Word is rife with examples of intercessors who prevailed against the enemy, the prayer warriors of Hebrews 11 who subdued kingdoms, shut the mouths of lions, set armies to flight, raised the dead, and secured the promises of God—all through prayer!

Daniel put his life on the line by praying three times a day despite the king's order to abstain. Prayer is a priority we cannot and must not overlook. Israel's, and indeed America's, future hopes lie in the hands of prayer warriors, those who will take up the banner and commit to prayer. It is not the last resort; it is the first step in winning the battle against the evil that stalks this world today.

If Daniel could pray and have mighty angels sent to do battle against demon spirits, so can we. Since Daniel lived in the Babylonian Empire, which is Iraq, it is quite possible that the prince of Persia he fought in the spirit was one of the same spirits we must battle today. But regardless of which spirits are now involved or how many there are, the clarion call is going out to God-fearing people everywhere to man the battle stations and fight the war in prayer.

Just as America has been forced to take the war on terrorism to the battlefields of the nations that sponsor it, we must take our fight to the battlefield in the spiritual realm to defeat the demons that sponsor it as well. We must take the battle to the enemy and defeat them through prayer in the name of Jesus!

Prayer is the only exploit that takes hold of eternity. It is the action that touches Heaven, and moves Earth. It pierces the heart of God, turns the head of God, and moves the hand of God. For a Christian, it is not the last resort...it is the first resort!

Through prayer, we must do everything possible to overthrow kingdoms of darkness, shut the mouths of the lions of terror, and quench the flames of Hell by the power of Almighty God! How you and I respond to God's call will determine whether we succeed or fail. The people of God have been called to intercede for and to comfort the Jewish people. Will you accept the call?

As Moses stood between the avenging angel and the children of Israel in the desert...as Ruth stood beside Naomi and cared for her...as Esther stood beside Mordecai and risked her life for her people…as Nehemiah stood upon the walls of Jerusalem and directed its reconstruction, so the Church needs to stand firm in support of Israel.

In Joel 2:17, we are admonished:

> Let the priests, who minister to the Lord,
>> Weep between the porch and the altar;
> Let them say, "Spare Your people, O Lord,
> And do not give Your heritage to reproach,
> That the nations should rule over them.
> Why should they say among the peoples,
>
> 'Where [is] their God?'"

The merciful are honored by God:

> He who oppresses the poor reproaches his Maker,
> But he who honors Him has mercy on the needy.
>> **PROVERBS 14:31**

If Christians who are able to bless the house of Israel withhold that blessing, especially by not reaching out to those who are suffering from terrorist attacks, how will the Jewish people ever know that real Christians are different from those who call themselves Christians but kill His people? To comfort the house of Israel is our duty and our privilege. Jesus was compassion personified:

> But when He saw the multitudes, He was moved with compassion for them, because they were weary and scattered, like sheep having no shepherd.
>> **MATTHEW 9:36**

God has always looked for volunteers to pray, to speak, and to do His compassionate work in the Earth. The story of Isaiah is a perfect example. King Uzziah had been a good king, a rare leader of God's people, and Isaiah was heartbroken when he died. It was at this time that God comforted Isaiah by showing him that the King of kings was still on the throne.

> *In the year that King Uzziah died, I saw the Lord sitting on a throne, high and lifted up, and the train of His robe filled the temple.*
>
> ISAIAH 6:1

When Isaiah realized the King of all kings, whose throne is elevated above every other, was still in charge, he was awed by the holiness of God and convicted of his own uncleanness. He fell on his face, repented, and the angel cleansed him of his iniquity.

> *Then one of the seraphim flew to me, having in his hand a live coal which he had taken with the tongs from the altar. And he touched my mouth with it, and said:*
>
> *"Behold, this has touched your lips;*
> *Your iniquity is taken away,*
> *And your sin purged."*
>
> ISAIAH 6:6-7

Then Isaiah was ready for his commission. Are you?

> *I heard the voice of the Lord, saying:*
>
> *"Whom shall I send,*
> *And who will go for Us?"*
>
> *Then I said, "Here am I! Send me."*
>
> ISAIAH 6:8

JERUSALEM,
GOD'S CHOICE JEWEL

"'Yet I have chosen Jerusalem, that My name might be there.'"
—II CHRONICLES 6:6

All God's expressions of Divine love for Israel still hold true today; none have been canceled. Israel is and always will be the apple of God's eye (Zechariah 2:8). She remains His joy and delight, His royal diadem (Isaiah 62:3), His firstborn, His chosen one, His beloved (Jeremiah 2:2, Hosea 11:1). Indeed, He says of His people,

> *For they shall be like the jewels of a crown,*
> *Lifted like a banner over His land.*
>
> **ZECHARIAH 9:16**

> *The Lord also will roar from Zion,*
> *And utter His voice from Jerusalem;*
> *The heavens and earth will shake;*
> *But the Lord will be a shelter for His people,*
> *And the strength of the children of Israel.*
>
> **JOEL 3:16**

> *Those who trust in the Lord*
> *Are like Mount Zion,*
> *Which cannot be moved, but abides forever.*

> *As the mountains surround Jerusalem,*
>   *So the Lord surrounds His people*
>   *From this time forth and forever.*
>
> PSALM 125:1-2

> *'For I,' says the Lord, 'will be a wall of fire all around her,*
> *and I will be the glory in her midst.'"*
>
> ZECHARIAH 2:5

When you sign your name to a check, it attests that you possess the amount indicated on that check. God wrote His name in Jerusalem, and He has the power to possess what His name represents:

> *This is the word of the Lord concerning Israel. The Lord, who stretches out the heavens, who lays the foundation of the earth, and who forms the spirit of man within him, declares: "I am going to make Jerusalem a cup that sends all the surrounding peoples reeling. Judah will be besieged as well as Jerusalem. On that day, when all the nations of the earth are gathered against her, I will make Jerusalem an immovable rock for all the nations. All who try to move it will injure themselves. On that day I will strike every horse with panic and its rider with madness," declares the Lord. "I will keep a watchful eye over the house of Judah, but I will blind all the horses of the nations. Then the leaders of Judah will say in their hearts, 'The people of Jerusalem are strong, because the Lord Almighty is their God.'*
>   *"On that day I will make the leaders of Judah like a firepot in a woodpile, like a flaming torch among sheaves. They will consume right and left all the surrounding peoples, but Jerusalem will remain intact in her place."*
>
> ZECHARIAH 12:1-6 NIV

In the last days
the mountain of the Lord's temple will be established
as chief among the mountains;
it will be raised above the hills,
and all nations will stream to it.

Many peoples will come and say,
"Come, let us go up to the mountain of the Lord,
to the house of the God of Jacob.
He will teach us his ways,
so that we may walk in his paths."
The law will go out from Zion,
the word of the Lord from Jerusalem.

He will judge between the nations
and will settle disputes for many peoples.
They will beat their swords into plowshares
and their spears into pruning hooks.
Nation will not take up sword against nation,
nor will they train for war anymore.

ISAIAH 2:2-4 NIV

If the revealed will of God and the record of history mean anything to followers of the Jewish Messiah—as they must—we can only conclude that Christians have a Heaven-ordained duty to love and support the Jewish people in every possible way. More than a duty, we should consider it our great privilege to bless the people who have blessed us, especially by being the channels through which our sacred Bible and our precious salvation have come to us.

Jewish men and women have made gigantic contributions to the world in chemistry, medicine, literature, finance, and so much more. We can thank people such as physicist Albert Einstein, Jonas Salk and Albert Sabin (polio vaccine), Selman Waksman (streptomycin), Julius Mayer (law of thermo-dynamics), Isaac Singer (sewing machine), Joseph Pulitzer (Pulitzer Prize).

of denim jeans? The achievement list goes on and on, for Jews discovered insulin, the analgesic effects of aspirin, and chloral hydrate that will halt convulsions.

One cannot help but consider that millions of Jews have been murdered through pogroms, inquisitions, the Holocaust, and in recent years, by terrorist attacks inside and outside the borders of their homeland. Imagine what may have gone undiscovered because of hatred for the Jewish people.

Jesus Himself said that the Son of Man would pass judgment on the nations when He comes to rule on His glorious throne as King of kings (Matthew 25:31). He went on to reveal that the main criteria for judgment would be how Gentiles treated His brothers (Matthew 25:40). Of course, all of us who are faithful followers of the Great Shepherd are the Lord's spiritual brethren. But Jesus' Jewish kin will always be His basic family stock, and thus His particular brethren. There is good reason to believe that these are the ones the Lord was referring to in the twenty-fifth chapter of Matthew.

Paul confirms that the Lord wants Christians to especially bless the Jewish people (Romans 15:26-27). Indeed, these verses reveal that Jewish believers in Jesus—who are once again greatly multiplying in our day—should be the direct recipients of financial blessings from Gentile believers:

> *For it pleased those from Macedonia and Achaia to make*
> *a certain contribution for the poor among the saints who are in*
> *Jerusalem. It pleased them indeed, and they are their debtors.* For
> if the Gentiles have been partakers of their spiritual things,
> their duty is also to minister to them in material things.
>
> **ROMANS 15:26-27 (emphasis mine)**

Christians have been blessed beyond words by being grafted into the rich olive tree of Israel. Therefore we must minister to our Jewish brethren in the Promised Land in many ways, but especially by actively supporting their right to live there. This is doubly important since widespread anti-Semitism has, in recent years, again reared its ugly head.

When I consider how the United States has dealt with Israel, and how some of Israel's prime ministers have responded, it greatly concerns me. When my dear friend Prime Minister Yitzhak Rabin was asked by President Clinton to take a "brave gamble" and sign the Oslo Accords in a White House ceremony, I appealed to the prime minister, both in person and by letter, not to believe a lie. My appeal was not heard by this beloved man.

The New York Times included a special edition on September 13, 1993, devoted to the historic meeting between Yasser Arafat and the prime minister:

> At 11:43 A.M. on the sun-splashed South Lawn of the White House, Foreign Minister Shimon Peres of Israel and Mahmoud Abbas, the foreign policy aide for the Palestine Liberation Organization, signed a Declaration of Principles on Palestinian self-government in Israeli-occupied Gaza and the West Bank. Three thousand witnesses watched in amazement, including former Presidents Jimmy Carter and George [H.W.] Bush.
>
> Moments after the documents were signed, Mr. Clinton took Mr. Arafat in his left arm and Mr. Rabin in his right arm and gently coaxed them together, needing to give Mr. Rabin just a little extra nudge in the back.[104]

Rabin paid with his life for acquiescing to Clinton's cajoling. On November 4, 1995, Yigal Amir, an Orthodox Jew and right-wing radical—incensed that Rabin had signed the Oslo Accords—shot Rabin in the arm and back. He suffered a punctured lung and died forty minutes after reaching the hospital.

At Prime Minister Rabin's state funeral there were 86 world leaders honoring him for taking that "brave gamble." Even Bill Clinton's eulogy for the fallen leader was a masterpiece of rhetorical legacy-building—his. In 2005 the former president was the keynote speaker at a rally to honor Mr. Rabin. He told those gathered, "Make no mistake about it, he (Rabin) knew he was risking his life." Or was he somehow coerced into signing a document the architects of which knew might cost him dearly?

Israel has been forced to the bargaining table time and time again. She has conceded land for peace, all to no avail. The PLO has been offered carrots that would have satisfied the most elite racehorse. Yet, Israel remains the target of terrorists worldwide, and there are those who maintain that the U.S. is targeted because of its support of Israel.

In a personal interview with Benjamin Netanyahu, he reminded me of the terrorists' true objective:

> They don't hate you because of us; they hate us because of you. They say we are the "Small Satan" and that America is the "Great Satan." It is important to understand that they could impose a direct threat to Europe and to the United States—and to Israel, obviously. They don't hide it. They don't even hide the fact that they intend to take on the West.[105]

September 11, 2001, was a tragic day in American history. The events of that day were no accident. It was a physical manifestation of a battle that had been lost weeks, months, and even years before because of a lack of prayer. Osama bin Laden had verbally attacked America for years, but the Church was asleep. The demonic powers that were influencing him needed to be violently confronted by holy angels on assignment through the power of prayer—as in the time of Daniel.

In Daniel, chapter 9, the prophet had been reading the prophecies of Jeremiah. He was aware that the Israelites would be held captive in a foreign land for seventy years, and that the days of that captivity were drawing to a close. Daniel fasted and prayed for God to honor His promise and allow His children to return to their homeland and to Jerusalem. "Then I set my face toward the Lord God to make request by prayer and supplications, with fasting, sackcloth, and ashes" (Daniel 9:3). God answered Daniel during the first year of the reign of Cyrus the Great.

In Daniel, chapter 10, the prophet is again on his knees agonizing before God to understand why so few Israelites had returned to their land. After days of struggling in prayer before God, Michael the archangel appeared to him. He assured Daniel that he had been heard by God on the very first day, but the answer had been delayed by the "prince of the kingdom of Persia" (v. 13). The Persians were the ruling kingdom, but Michael spoke not of a man but of a demonic being that held sway over Persia. His assignment was to manipulate actions in Persia so that God's plans for Israel would be hindered.

I believe Satan still has a company of demons whose solitary job is to manipulate leaders and rulers. We need only look at the hatred, strife, confusion, and warfare that reign in nations around the world. Such is certainly not the work of God the Father, but rather the work of Satan and his demonic minions. How do we know this? Jesus said in John 10:10, "The thief does not come except to steal, and to kill, and to destroy. I have come that they may have life, and that they may have it more abundantly."

In Isaiah 14:13 Satan had the audacity to challenge God:

> 'I will ascend into heaven,
> I will exalt my throne above the stars of God;
> I will also sit on the mount of the congregation
> On the farthest sides of the north.'

This is the Temple site. Satan's last threat to God was that he would sit on the Temple site on the side of the north and do battle against God. The result of this battle is devastation in the city of Jerusalem, the rage that is being manifested in Judea and Samaria, and the attacks on America.

When Nehemiah was told of the conditions in Jerusalem—the broken-down walls and fires burning in the city—he responded: "I sat down and wept, and mourned for many days; I was fasting and praying before the God of heaven" (Nehemiah 1:4). I believe I know how Nehemiah felt, having been in Israel when fires from rockets torched neighborhoods and people lay in the street dead or wounded. I too have fasted and prayed for God to answer my prayers and the prayers of the children of Jerusalem...Jewish, Christian, and Arab alike.

The nations of the world cannot solve the problem of Jerusalem; it has been tried numerous times. During many trips to Jerusalem, I have prayed that God would send a shield of protection over the city, over the Bible land, and over America. I have prayed that God would send a II Chronicles 7:14 revival to both nations.

The House of Israel is in a state of terror, as are all the children of the Bible land. In Psalm 20, David prayed a potent petition:

> *May the Lord answer you in the day of trouble;*
>   *May the name of the God of Jacob defend you;*
> *May He send you help from the sanctuary,*
>   *And strengthen you out of Zion;*
> *May He remember all your offerings,*
>   *And accept your burnt sacrifice. Selah*
>
> *May He grant you according to your heart's desire,*
>   *And fulfill all your purpose.*
> *We will rejoice in your salvation,*
>   *And in the name of our God we will set up our banners!*
>   *May the Lord fulfill all your petitions.*
>
> *Now I know that the Lord saves His anointed;*
>   *He will answer him from His holy heaven*
>   *With the saving strength of His right hand.*
>
> *Some trust in chariots, and some in horses;*
>   *But we will remember the name of the Lord our God.*
> *They have bowed down and fallen;*
>   *But we have risen and stand upright.*
>
> *Save, Lord!*
>   *May the King answer us when we call.*

The most important words of Jesus can be found in Matthew 28:18-20 NIV. We call it the Great Commission:

"All authority in heaven and on earth has been given to me. Therefore go and make disciples of all nations, baptizing them in the name of the Father and of the Son and of the Holy Spirit, and teaching them to obey everything I have commanded you. And surely I am with you always, to the very end of the age."

Acts 1:8 declares that Christians are to be a witness for Jesus in Jerusalem, Judea, Samaria, and the uttermost parts of the Earth. The Church was birthed in Jerusalem but has not been the witness for Jesus it was called to be—not in Jerusalem, Judea, or Samaria. The Church has not emulated the love for the Jewish people that Jesus did. Certainly you and I must first humble ourselves, pray, and stand in the gap. This is not an appeal to judge the Church but simply to say, "Lord, this is me in need of prayer."

God's Chosen People need the Lord to answer in their day of terror. They need the God of Jacob to defend them. They need help from the sanctuary and strength out of Zion. This is my prayer.

CHAPTER TWENTYFIVE

WELCOMING
THE KING OF KINGS

Then those who went before and those who
followed cried out, saying: "Hosanna! 'Blessed is He who
comes in the name of the LORD! —MARK 11:9

During a visit with Prime Minister Benjamin Netanyahu, we talked about the importance of biblical prophecies. This distinguished Israeli diplomat said,

> The truth of the matter is that if it had not been for the prophetic promises about returning to our homeland, the Jewish people would not have survived. There is something about reading the statements of the prophets in the original Hebrew language—the powerful impact of those words bore deep into your heart and are implanted in your mind. There is absolutely no question but that those ancient prophetic promises kept hope alive in the hearts of the Jewish people and sustained us over the generations during which we had nothing else to cling.[106]

With the survival of the Jewish people and the rebirth of Israel as a nation in the Promised Land, Ezekiel's track record as a prophet is convincing. He spoke in specific detail about future events, which would bring the world to the edge of Armageddon. In Ezekiel 38 and 39, the prophet gave a detailed account of a great military offensive that would be launched against Israel by Russia and a confederation of Arab and European countries. This will be the beginning of the "time of trouble" spoken of by Daniel.

The perilous position of our planet has world leaders talking about globalism, or a strategy of subjugating the interests of individual nations for the good of the entire world. At the much-touted UN Millennium Summit in 2000, UN Secretary-General Kofi Annan called for "benevolent globalization in the 21st century to insure that the information revolution does not leave billions of people behind in poverty."[107]

On his last day in office in 2000, President Clinton signed the Rome Treaty. It committed the United States to a global court without requiring Congressional approval:

> President Clinton has approved a treaty that would create an international court to try war crimes and crimes against humanity. He explained that, despite having concerns about the treaty, he signed on because he wants the United States "to remain engaged in making the ICC an instrument of impartial and effective justice." Signing was at best a tactical blunder, however. The treaty as it stands would further erode our diminishing sovereignty, and signing it removes our leverage in trying to fix its flaws. On December 31, with the country distracted by the New Year's revels, Bill Clinton announced that the United States would sign the treaty to establish an International Criminal Court. He characterized his decision as an act of "moral leadership." In other words, it was a betrayal of American interests.[108]

When then-Undersecretary of State John R. Bolton nullified the U.S. signature on the International Criminal Court treaty one month into President Bush's first term, he declared it the happiest moment in his years of service. Bolton referred to the court as a "product of fuzzy-minded romanticism . . . not just naive, but dangerous."[109]

Will President Barack Obama, in his quest for global acceptance, overturn Bolton's brave stance against placing America at the mercy of an international court? There are those who feel his inaugural address was a portent of what his choice might be. U. S. Ambassador to the UN Susan Rice was effusive in her praise for the court at her first official meeting: "[The International Court] looks to become an important and credible instrument for trying to hold accountable the senior leadership responsible for atrocities committed in the Congo, Uganda, and Darfur."[110] She garnered effusive praise from the French. Only time will tell what path we are forced to follow.

In Luke 21, Jesus told us that when we see certain events come to pass, we are to look up for "your redemption draws nigh." The time to pray for the peace of Jerusalem is now. When we pray for the peace of Jerusalem we are saying, "Maranatha! Come, Messiah!"

The Messiah is indeed coming back, and He is coming to Jerusalem. That is something on which both Jews and Christians agree. As Christians, we believe we know His name, while the Jewish people say they don't. But there is no question that when the Messiah comes, everyone will know His name.

Our Lord was asked by His disciples in Matthew 24:3 KJV, "What shall be the sign of thy coming, and of the end of the world?" He clearly gave them the signs, beginning with the destruction of the Temple. In verse 2 Jesus prophesied that the Temple would be taken apart stone by stone forty years before it happened.

The fig tree has always been a symbol of the nation of Israel. In Matthew 24:32-36, Jesus laid out the key sign of His return, that the sign of the end of the age would be the blooming of the fig tree. The fig tree of Israel bloomed on May 14,1948, in fulfillment of Isaiah 66:8: "Shall the earth be made to give birth in one day? Or shall a nation be born at once?" In Matthew 24:36 Jesus warned that we were not to set a date for His coming because no one would know the day or the hour. However, He also said in verse 34 that the generation that saw the blooming of the fig tree would not pass away until He came.

It was 597 B.C., in the days of Nebuchadnezzar in Babylon, that Israel was taken into captivity. In 1948 the prophecy of Matthew 24 knocked at the door. There is no question that we will not know the day or the hour, but Matthew 24 seems to indicate that we are very, very close to the Messiah's return. The events in the Middle East are surely lining up with this prophecy!

Our response to the war that began on September 11, 2001, will indeed echo throughout all eternity. You and I have a date with destiny! We are declaring that the Bible is true, that God is not a promise-breaker, and that the royal land grant given to Abraham and his seed through Isaac and Jacob was an everlasting and unconditional covenant.

By contesting the right of Jews to live in their covenant land and thereby going against God's holy Word, many are opening themselves up to be cursed! Therefore, anyone who seeks the blessings bestowed by our Heavenly Father should make sure they are. If we touch Jerusalem, God's time clock of prophetic events, America will lose the blessing of God and tragically lose the war on terrorism.

Only the saints of God, acting on God's direction, can impact America and Israel. We must have a vision for the future, like Nehemiah had when he saw Jerusalem with her walls destroyed and her people beaten down by their enemies. The Bible says that without a vision the people perish (Proverbs 29:18). I might add that without people the vision perishes.

The fact that the U.S. government refuses to recognize Jerusalem as Israel's legitimate capital is symbolic of the whole problem of America's current relationship with Israel. We who believe the Bible must surely believe that it is in the best interests of the U.S. to be a firm ally of Israel.

As Israel's enemies call for her destruction, we must remember the words of King David, "Is there not a cause?" Jerusalem, D.C., is David's capital, and there is a cause. It is a cause to show the Jewish people that Christians care, to rally behind them so their beloved city will not be divided.

If we bless Israel, God will bless us. If America blesses Israel, God will bless America. If we stand united, we can become a channel of God's love and grace to the Jewish people—not only in Jerusalem but also around the world.

CHAPTER TWENTYSIX

COMFORT YE, COMFORT YE
MY PEOPLE

*Comfort ye, comfort ye my people saith your God. Speak ye
comfortably to Jerusalem.* —ISAIAH 40:1-2 KJV

The passage of Scripture quoted above is often the springboard for
offering comfort to a person—in sickness, in death, and in other
tragic circumstances. It has become a catch phrase for cards, letters,
and emails. Once written or uttered, we feel our duty has been executed, and
we are free to go about our daily lives.

When we take a closer look at these two verses, however, we begin to
see some real truths that apply specifically to the Jewish people. These are
not the words of the prophet Isaiah; these are God's words of instruction to
him. This is God's instruction to his ministers—to those who carry the message of comfort to a lost and dying world.

There are times we are charged with comforting someone who, from the
human standpoint, really doesn't deserve our sympathy, our comfort, or our
words of hope and faith. Chapter 40 of Isaiah finds the prophet in exactly
this predicament. The children of Israel had been carried off to Babylon.
Isaiah prophesied that God would deliver them, but their freedom would not
come through a Hebrew prophet, priest, or king. It would come through a
Gentile man named Cyrus:

Thus says the Lord, your Redeemer,
And He who formed you from the womb:

> *"I am the Lord, who makes all things,*
> *Who stretches out the heavens all alone,*
> *Who spreads abroad the earth by Myself.*
>
> *Who says of Cyrus, 'He is My shepherd,*
>   *And he shall perform all My pleasure,*
>   *Saying to Jerusalem, "You shall be built,"'*
>   *And to the temple, "Your foundation shall be laid."*

ISAIAH 44:24,28

One hundred sixty years before the birth of King Cyrus, Isaiah prophesied that God would raise up this man to deliver them, return them to Jerusalem, and rebuild the Temple.

Not only did Isaiah prophecy Cyrus would come to the aid of God's people, he spoke words of comfort to them. He spoke of God's promise and the utter requisite of its fulfillment. God instructs His ministers to speak comfort to His children, and that command has not been negated. His message was and is, "I discipline, but I do not stop loving. There comes a pivotal point when wrath ceases and comfort is poured out." It is a promise that God will ultimately take up residence with His children. The preeminence of His presence is an indisputable promise.

This prophetic word is a God-given mandate to Christians to offer comfort, encouragement, and emotional and financial support to the House of Israel. If this scripture is not for Christians, then for whom is it? Nation after nation has turned its back on the Jewish people. First one Christian denomination and then another has abandoned God's people. Church organizations have taken Israel to task for refusing to surrender yet more land for peace and for not embracing the right of return for millions of Palestinians. Either option for Israel would place the Jewish homeland in great jeopardy.

As Christians, we are called upon to show God's love to all people and particularly the Jews, as did Corrie ten Boom and her family. The ten Boom family members were devoted Christians who dedicated their lives in service to their fellowman. Their home was always an open house for anyone in need. The family ten Boom started a weekly prayer meeting for the Jewish people in 1844, after an inspiring worship service in the Dutch Reformed Church of Reverend Witteveen. Willem ten Boom felt the need to pray for the Jewish people, so he started the weekly prayer meeting where the family, and others who stopped by, specifically prayed for the peace of Jerusalem (Psalm 122:6).

During the Second World War, the ten Boom home became a refuge, a hiding place for fugitives and those hunted by the Nazis. By protecting these people, Casper ten Boom and his daughters, Corrie and Betsie, risked their lives to save them. This nonviolent resistance against the Nazi oppressors was the ten Booms' way of living out their Christian faith. This faith led them to hide Jews, students who refused to cooperate with the Nazis, and members of the Dutch underground resistance movement.

During 1943 and into 1944, there were usually six to seven people illegally living in this home, four Jews and two or three members of the Dutch underground. Additional refugees would stay with the ten Booms for a few hours or a few days until another safe house could be located for them. Corrie became a ringleader within the network of the Haarlem underground. She and "the Beje Group" (the name of the clock shop) would search for courageous Dutch families who would take in refugees, and much of Corrie's time was spent caring for these people once they were in hiding.

On February 28, 1944, this family was betrayed, and the Gestapo (the Nazi secret police) raided their home. The Gestapo set a trap and waited throughout the day, seizing everyone who came to the house. By evening, over twenty people had been taken into custody. Casper, Corrie, and Betsie were arrested. Corrie's brother Willem, sister Nollie, and nephew Peter were at the house that day and were also taken to prison.

Although the Gestapo systematically searched the house, they could not find what they sought most. They suspected Jews were in the house, but the Jews were safely hidden behind a false wall in Corrie's bedroom. In this hiding place were two Jewish men, two Jewish women, and two members of the Dutch underground. Although the house remained under guard, the Resistance was able to liberate the refugees two days later. The six people had managed to stay quiet in their small, dark hiding place for all that time, even though they had no water and very little food. The four Jews were taken to new safe houses, and three survived the war.

Life in the concentration camp was almost unbearable, but Corrie and Betsie spent their time sharing Jesus' love with their fellow prisoners. Many women became Christians in that terrible place because of the sisters' witness to them. Four members of the ten Boom family died because of their commitment, but Corrie came home from the death camp. She realized her life was a gift from God, and she needed to share what she and Betsy had learned in Ravensbruck. In 1975 Dr. Billy Graham and World Wide Pictures released the movie version of *The Hiding Place*, starring Jeanette Clift George as Corrie ten Boom.

The arrests of the ten Boom family ended what had become a 100-year prayer meeting in their family home. On the day the Nazi soldiers came, the family was together for Bible study and prayer. Following the tradition of the ten Boom family, today the Jerusalem Prayer Team continues to pray for the peace of Jerusalem and encourages Christians to exercise their faith by helping the Jewish people—God's ancient people.

In September of 1986, I went to Holland to purchase and restore the ten Boom clock shop. It is now open as a witness to the love of Christians for the Jewish people. Corrie and her family saved eight hundred Jewish lives! The museum charges no admission, and its directors and board members accept no remuneration. It is a lighthouse to all because of the love of one Christian family for God's Chosen People. As the apostle Paul said, "Concerning the gospel they are enemies for your sake, but concerning the election they are beloved for the sake of the fathers [Abraham, Isaac, and Jacob]. For the gifts and the calling of God are irrevocable" (Romans 11:28-29 [insert mine]).

God's calling and His benefits are unalterable! He cannot and does not change His mind. Despite the horrors of the prison camp and the deaths of members of her family, I believe that were you able to ask Corrie ten Boom today, "Is God faithful?" she would respond with a hearty, "YES!" Her family paid the ultimate price for blessing Israel, but great is their reward in heaven.

We will be saved because of God's dependability to fulfill His Word. Numbers 23:19 NLT addresses God's veracity:

God is not a man, so he does not lie.
He is not a human, he does not change his mind.
Has he ever spoken and failed to act?
Has he ever promised and not carried it through?

The ten Boom family joined thousands of others who risked their lives to shelter tens of thousands of Jews during the Nazi occupation of the Netherlands. Among them were Miep Gies, the woman who sheltered Anne Frank and her family. She was, perhaps, the most noted because it was she who made Anne Frank's famous diary available to the world. She was joined by Geertruida Wijsmuller-Meijer, responsible for having saved the lives of some ten thousand Jewish children. In Lithuania, Jan Zwartendijk, the Dutch Consul, is said to have saved the lives of three to six thousand Jews.

In April 2008, Corrie and her father were honored by the Yad Vashem Museum:

The Israeli Ambassador to the Netherlands Harry Kney-Tal on Wednesday presented to family members a certificate posthumously honoring two Dutch Christians who saved nearly 800 Jews during the Holocaust. At a solemn ceremony in Harlem, Yad Vashem, Israel's Holocaust Martyrs' and Heroes' Remembrance Authority, honored Casper ten Boom and his daughter Elisabeth [Corrie] with the title of "Righteous Among the Nations" for their life saving work. A third family member, Cornelia, also helped rescue those fleeing Nazi persecution.[111]

The Jerusalem Prayer Team is, I believe, the most prophetic ministry for this time in history. There is an ongoing battle between darkness and light; it is unprecedented and unlike any battle in my lifetime. This is the hour for which God has called us to comfort the Jewish people, to pray for the peace of Jerusalem, and to stand in the gap for Israel. As we pray for and bless His people, God has promised we too would be blessed. This is God's promise for the Jerusalem Prayer Team.

At the first Jerusalem Prayer Summit in Dallas, Texas, in 2002, I invited a dear friend to pray for the Jewish people. Sister Deborah is a precious German nun. Her prayer moved me, and indeed, the entire congregation, to tears:

> I come as a German from a so-called Christian country. We, who say we love You, would love Your people in our midst that we would come to help them, but there was only suffering and death. You said, "Who touches them touches the apple of My eye." Lord, forgive what we have done to You, what we have done to Your people.

The God of all creation asked for someone to do His work. He could have created automatons and robots to do His bidding. He had legions of angels at His command. But He wanted His people to be willing to serve Him and to surrender to His calling.

Today, the God of Heaven wants you and me to freely, gladly, eagerly, and voluntarily commit to pray for and comfort the Jewish people just like Isaiah did. This will be no problem if we keep our eyes on the King of kings and Lord of lords. Once Isaiah caught a glimpse of the Holy God, he responded joyfully, "Here am I! Send me."

The Lord is calling us to awaken the mighty men and women! We must wake up the Esthers and Nehemiahs, the Moses' and Daniels. Will you respond today? Will you accept the call to comfort the Jewish people who risk their lives daily to preserve Jerusalem and their nation?

Great is the reward for obedience:

> *Have you not known?*
> *Have you not heard?*
> *The everlasting God, the Lord,*
> *The Creator of the ends of the earth,*
> *Neither faints nor is weary.*
> *His understanding is unsearchable.*

But those who wait on the Lord
Shall renew their strength;
They shall mount up with wings like eagles,
They shall run and not be weary,
They shall walk and not faint.

ISAIAH 40:28,31

By now you should know from God's Word and His heart that Christians should support Israel in any way they can. The reasons are many:

⟡ It is God's will for us to do so! It is impossible to believe the Bible and not be aware of God's love for all mankind and especially His Jewish people.

⟡ We are preparing for our Lord's return when we honor and support Israel.

⟡ God's promises are true, and He promises to bless those who bless Israel.

⟡ Anti-Semitism is contrary to God's loving nature and care for His people.

⟡ Comforting God's people brings us comfort.

⟡ God's gifts and calling to Israel have not been revoked.

⟡ God Almighty has preserved Israel.

⟡ God calls us to be intercessors for and watchmen over Israel.

⟡ Israel is precious to Him, and He wrote His name in Jerusalem.

If our Lord and Savior reached out in compassion to Israel and made prayer for her His highest priority, do we dare make it our lowest? There is a direct correlation between the power that Heaven promised for the Church at its birth in Jerusalem and the Church's obedience to be a witness in Jerusalem, Judea, Samaria, and the uttermost parts of the Earth. The Church cannot and must not ignore Christ's eternal mission for her and at the same time expect power from on high. We must comfort God's people.

AFTERWORD

Jerusalem seems to have always been a city under siege. It has been occupied at various times by the Babylonians, Alexander the Great, Egypt, Syria, Rome, Persia, the Byzantines, the Muslims, the Turks, and the British, just to name a few. It has been razed, burned, and its citizens carried captive to the four corners of the earth. The Jewish people have suffered at the hands of barbarians, been brutalized, battered, bartered like cattle, burned alive, and buried in mass graves.

Today is no different than it was in the day of King Nebuchadnezzar, who destroyed the Temple in Jerusalem and carried the Jewish people to serve him in Babylon. Now as then, politics seem to be the driving force, and no religious group is more political than Muslims. Historian Bernard Wasserstein wrote about the early Muslim attachment to Jerusalem:

> Surprisingly, the conquest of Jerusalem by the Crusaders was greeted at first by Muslim indifference rather than fervor for its capture. Even those Muslims who called for a holy war against the invading Franks refrained, with few exceptions, from stressing the sanctity of Jerusalem—which seems in this period to have been neither widely diffused nor deeply implanted in Muslim thought. A change of attitude emerges only in the mid-twelfth century—as so often in the history of Jerusalem, heightened religious fervor may be explained in large part by political necessity.[112]

Jerusalem has been a pawn in the hands of men such as the Ayatollah Khomeini, Yasser Arafat, Mahmoud Ahmadinejad, and the leaders of the nations that surround the city set in the Judean hills. It has even become a political tool in the chest of American presidents who try to use it to enhance the legacy of a term—or terms—in office. Each more than the last seems to want to be the one who wins the crown of securing peace in the Middle East. At the writing of this book, all have failed. Why? One after another left God out of the equation. Has His will, plan, and purpose for the City of David been a key factor in their plans? As the prophet Jeremiah counseled his listeners, so do these leaders need to hear,

> *For who hath stood in the counsel of the Lord, and hath perceived and heard his word? who hath marked his word, and heard it?*
>
> JEREMIAH 23:18 KJV

Few world leaders and politicians delve into God's Word to discover His guiding principles for the land He gave to Abraham, Isaac, and Jacob. They seek their own glory, not His.

Amid the strife, there are those who are still determined to entrap God's people in the Holy Land. Traps are set that are designed to cast them in yet another bad light—to cause yet more hatred and animosity towards the Jews. On May 31, 2010, Israel walked straight into such a trap—one set by a group of so-called activists determined to break Israeli attempts to halt the flow of arms and war materiel into the Gaza strip.

Having been warned in advance that the intent of the Free Gaza Movement flotilla was to shatter the Israeli blockade, the IDF prepared to board the ships and divert them to Ashdod for inspection. A member of the Free Gaza organization credited with launching the flotilla, Greta Berlin, clarified the intent of the group: "We're not trying to be a humanitarian mission."[113]

Apparently, Israeli intelligence was not informed that the ship carried seven hundred pro-Palestinian activists prepared to do whatever was necessary to reach their goal. American-born, pro-Palestinian activist Hawaida Arraf threw down the gauntlet with the assertion: "We fully intend to go to Gaza regardless of any intimidation or threats of violence against us. They are going to have to forcefully stop us."[114]

According to Israeli Deputy Foreign Minister Danny Ayalon, "The armada of hate and violence in support of the Hamas terror organization was a premeditated and outrageous provocation. The organizers are well known for their ties to Global Jihad, Al-Qaeda, and Hamas. They have a history of arms smuggling and deadly terror. On board the ship we found weapons that were prepared in advance and used against our forces."[115]

When confronted by the Israelis, five of the six ships' captains diverted to Ashdod; the sixth was decidedly on a mission of defiance. Obviously, the mistake made by the IDF was to assume that the voyagers on board the Mavi Marmara were a charitable group. Rather, it was loaded with pro-Palestinian terrorists with no specified humanitarian agenda and determined to create an international media incident.

The IDF deployed about a dozen soldiers with the intent of taking the bridge and diverting the flotilla to the Israeli port. Instead, the troops fell into the hands of an angry mob of rioters armed with clubs, knives, scissors, pepper spray, and sidearms after having disarmed several IDF soldiers.

The Israelis boarded with non-lethal paintball guns, the kind used by teens on paintball courses, and pistols they never thought they would have to unholster. A video shows the unsuspecting IDF paratroopers being assaulted as they reached the deck. One IDF soldier was thrown over a railing to a deck thirty feet below.

In a statement by Prime Minister Benjamin Netanyahu, he reiterated that this was "a clear case of self-defense because as our soldiers were inspecting these ships, they were attacked—they were almost lynched. They were attacked...and they had to defend themselves—they were going to be killed. Israel will not allow its soldiers to be lynched and neither would any other self-respecting country."[116]

Israel has maintained the blockade to halt the flow of weapons from Iran to Hamas, its armed and funded proxy in Gaza. In November 2009, the Israeli navy intercepted a huge cache of weapons headed from Iran to Hezbollah and Hamas onboard the Francop, a German container ship. The markings on the materiel discovered were clearly Iranian. The ship carried some three thousand missiles, including Katyusha rockets.

In 2008 Israeli President Shimon Peres held a "Facing Tomorrow' conference to which he invited some of the most noted thinkers in the world. One of the conclusions of the meeting was that wars of the twenty-first century would be fought first as a media war, secondly as an economic war, thirdly as a proxy war, and finally with boots on the ground. Israel has lost this media war and is well on the way to losing the economic war.

Israel ceded Gaza in hopes of achieving peace in the region; its hopes were dashed. Hamas continued to lob some twelve hundred missiles across the border at innocent Jewish civilians. Despite the ongoing provocation, Israel has allowed food and humanitarian supplies into Gaza through the Red Cross and UN.

This skirmish came amid plans for a meeting between Prime Minister Netanyahu and President Barack Obama. The aim of the summit was to keep Iran, not the Palestinian Authority, at the top of the agenda.

Iran found the perfect means to distract the liberal media—create a flag-waving, humanitarian crisis. The resulting propaganda-driven riots worldwide would certainly take attention from the IAEA announcement that Iran now possesses more than two tons of enriched uranium—enough for two nuclear warheads.

If you were sitting in the seat of power in what was ancient Persia, how would you react when confronted with new sanctions against your nuclear program? You would sponsor a David-versus-Goliath flotilla—a media extravaganza—carrying a Nobel Peace Prize winner, an American activist, and a Holocaust survivor. Central casting could not have done it better.

The question becomes: When is a humanitarian mission not a humanitarian mission? It fails the test when it is peopled with terrorists on a suicide mission.

The stated policy of President George W. Bush was that any state aiding, abetting, funding, or harboring terrorists was an enemy of the United States. President Obama seems to have wiped his feet on that policy. Under his administration, a terrorist organization can get away with anything by wrapping bombs in a humanitarian package and tying it up with "activist" bows.

For the past sixty-three years American administrations have stood by Israel as the most trusted and reliable ally in a region that is a boiling cauldron of hatred. It seems apparent that due to this president's lackadaisical attitude toward Israel, the tiny island of democracy will be abandoned to the hungry wolves seeking to devour it. The terrible result will almost certainly be another war that will engulf the region, one which will, perhaps, have global repercussions. If this outcome is not President Obama's objective, he needs to make immediate policy changes.

It seems that when anything happens in the region, Israel is faulted immediately and harshly. The finger of blame is permanently pointed at the Jewish state. One of the latest Israeli "threats to the peace process" involved municipal approval for sixteen hundred badly needed housing units in the Ramat Shlomo neighborhood, located—surprise!—in *northwest* Jerusalem. Yet the media reported it to be East Jerusalem.

It is a sign of the basic irrationality of the conflict that every point on the Jerusalem compass is referred to erroneously as "East Jerusalem." This loaded term is frequently used to designate anywhere that Arabs live in the city, despite the reality that more Jews than Arabs live in Jerusalem's geographically eastern neighborhoods.

Israel has been accused of fostering the inhumane conditions purportedly found in Gaza. This is a blatant misconception touted by a liberal media with an agenda. If Palestinians living in Gaza do without the basic necessities of life, the fault lies solely at the feet of Hamas, a terrorist organization more concerned with acquiring worldwide support than with taking care of the needs of its people.

Israel's first obligation, however, is to take care of its own population. It is this need that initially spurred the blockade. When Hamas seized control of the government in Gaza, it was with one purpose—to destroy Israel. Its leaders have stated unequivocally that it will not rest until Israel is no more. To achieve its stated aim, Hamas has lobbed thousands of Qassam rockets across the border, targeting innocent men, women, and children inside Israel. In order to halt the flow of war materiel into Gaza, Israel instituted what has heretofore been a peaceful blockade to search inbound vessels.

Obama and his administration have mouthed toothless platitudes regarding Iran, the power behind Hamas, Hezbollah, and even Syria. Israel has suffered the effects of the president's attempts to "engage" the Muslim world. However, rather than appear presidential, Mr. Obama's groveling has emboldened and empowered hostile regimes. The administration's lack of backbone toward these terrorists has only placed America and Israel in greater danger. President Mahmoud Ahmadinejad, speaking to a massive group intoning anti-Israel slogans, has already condemned Israel's raid on the flotilla as "barbaric," and has called for "the Zionist regime" to be broken in pieces.

Ahmadinejad understands clearly that America has become a toothless and clawless tiger, no longer able to stop his rogue state from using its enriched uranium to make nuclear weapons. God help us if his perception is true.

Hezbollah in Lebanon has presumably been the recipient of a gift from Syria—SCUD missiles that, when armed with nuclear, chemical, or biological weapons, would pose a lethal peril to Israel. Egypt, Israel's larger neighbor to the west, has recently conducted war games in the Sinai Peninsula. Is that nation practicing for another attack on Israel? And since we are asking questions, why has Egypt's President Hosni Mubarak not stopped Hamas from building the network of tunnels used to smuggle contraband into Gaza? By the way, Egypt has also had a blockade of Gaza in place since 2007. It has never backed down from using deadly force when necessary against those trying to run the blockade.

Does it seem that in the Middle East Israel is the bull's-eye in the target? Its long-time ally Turkey has in recent years slowly ended its ties with the Jewish state. At the same time, Turkish Prime Minister Recep Erdogan has openly courted Iran and welcomed the Islamization of his country. His recent move to join Brazil in an alliance with Iran in an attempt to forestall further sanctions against Ahmadinejad's regime is just one more link in the chain toward Muslim domination of Turkey. Is it a mere coincidence that Turkey supported the Free Gaza flotilla, even though it was backed by a Turkish terror organization, the IHH?

Fortunately, Israel still enjoys the backing of a large group of American congressmen and congresswomen, who remain very vocal with their support. Senator Joe Lieberman said, "We should be very clear about who is responsible for the unfortunate loss of life in the attempt to break the blockade in Gaza. Hamas and its allies are the responsible parties…Israel exercised her legitimate right of self defense."[117]

According to Senator John Kerry, "Israel has every right…to make certain that weapons are not being smuggled in after the thousands of rockets that have been fired on it from Gaza."[118]

Senator Harry Reid: "Israel has an obligation to protect its citizens and therefore has a clear right under international law to prevent weapons from getting in the hands of terrorists determined to target them."[119]

Newly elected Senator Scott Brown added, "Israel is at war. Each and every day thousands of its innocent men, women, and children face the threat of the lethal rocket attacks out of Gaza."[120]

Texas Representative Pete Sessions said, "This will likely not be the last time terrorist organizations—under the guise of humanitarian aid—seek to provoke Israel. As much of the world turns the other way, my support for Israel remains steadfast in its struggle for security."[121]

Texas Senator John Cornyn introduced Senate Resolution 548, which was then referred to the Senate Foreign Relations Committee. Its stated purpose was to: "Express the sense of the Senate that Israel has an undeniable right to self-defense, and to condemn the recent destabilizing actions by extremists aboard the ship Mavi Marmara."[122]

The Obama administration seems to have joined the ranks of the silent majority where Israel is concerned. Twice in the days leading up to the flotilla incident, the U.S. hiccupped when confronted with Israeli issues. The first was its refusal to block a UN thrust to force Israel to give up nuclear weapons. If Israel is forced to disarm, only her enemies will possess the nuclear weapons necessary to wreak havoc on the Jewish people. The second hiccup was when the U.S. failed to cast a vote against a UN Security Council document condemning Israel for the flotilla raid. Israel now faces the greatest existential danger since the Yom Kippur War in 1973. It must seem as if the United States has set Israel adrift at a time of great need.

In addition, rumors abound that the U.S. is trying to engage Hamas in talks. The deputy chairman of Hamas' political bureau has said, "Their [the U.S.] official policy states that there are no contacts with Hamas. However, they are engaging Hamas for objective reasons. There are several open channels [between the U.S. and Hamas]. Some are official and some are unofficial. All of those talking to us receive permission from the U.S. State Department and then the White House. The U.S. administration tells them to talk to Hamas but without causing a big fuss."[123] President Obama and Secretary of State Hillary Clinton are courting a viper whose bite is deadly.

When Jimmy Carter, a Liberal Left Democratic president, betrayed a Middle East ally, the Shah of Iran, the result was the growth of radical Islam. Obama now has a golden opportunity to stand up to Iran and to prevent a war in the Middle East. If he fails, he will have clothed himself in the same indecisiveness possessed by Carter, who allowed American hostages to be put through 444 days of hell.

The Obama administration must step up to the plate and give comprehensive and tangible evidence of its commitment to Israel before it fails "How Wars Begin 101." We must provide Israel the means to effectively defend itself. If we do not do so, America will find itself once again in the crosshairs of radical terrorists.

Even as I was putting the finishing touches on this book, President Barack Obama and Palestinian Authority President Mahmoud Abbas met at the White House for talks on Gaza. During the meeting Mr. Obama pledged $400 million in aid to Abbas, former CFO of the terror organization responsible for funding the Munich Massacre in 1972 during which eleven Israeli Olympic athletes and coaches were murdered.

Now the president has welcomed the PA leader, and with the usual aplomb of the Liberal Left, President Obama simply tosses money at the problem of Gaza. No stand is taken against the terrorist regime that holds the people in that region by the throat. Abbas goes home with a decidedly fatter bank account.

According to Mr. Obama, the money will be used for housing, schools, health, and infrastructure needs. In view of the fact that Hamas has control of Gaza and Abbas has no authority in the area, just how is he going to oversee the $400 million? Perhaps it will find its way into personal Swiss bank accounts, as did money funded to Yasser Arafat.

Given that terrorist organizations such as Hamas and Hezbollah have no problem using schools, synagogues, and even hospitals to hide their munitions and to launch their attacks against Israel, America could be aiding and abetting further terror attacks against Israel. Of course, Israel would be forced to retaliate. It's a lose/lose battle for the Jewish state.

The president set the tone for the meeting with Abbas by labeling the tense face-off in the Middle East "unsustainable." He also predicted that "real progress" would come with U.S. attempts to force the Israelis into more land-for-peace deals. I can find no mention in news from the White House about Egypt's blockade or why the building materials deemed necessary for Gaza's well-being have not been flooding into the area across the Egyptian border.

One can but wonder how tightly the thumbscrews will be applied to Prime Minister Netanyahu and the Israeli government in order to try to coerce them into reopening talks with Abbas and the PA. It seems that concessions are Israel's to make, but they are out of the question for the PA or Hamas in Gaza.

While Obama called again on Israel to stop building settlements in what he calls "disputed territories," he asked Abbas to make progress in the area of security. At this writing, Abbas has stated he would halt the peace negotiations if construction resumed when the 10-month limited moratorium confirmed in November ended on September 26, 2010. Netanyahu reiterated his plan to allow the freeze to expire. The question remains: How can Israel sit down at the bargaining table with people who refuse to acknowledge the Jewish state's existence?

Ever determined to force Israel to the bargaining table to give up precious land, Robert Serry, the UN Special Coordinator for the Middle East Peace Process has warned Israel that the UN might stand behind a Palestinian bid for a state if Israel refuses to halt settlement construction altogether. Standing in an olive grove in Palestine Serry warned, "If the freeze is not renewed, then yes, maybe this is going to happen."[124]

The threat to turn to the Security Council is nothing more than an attempt to force Israel to capitulate and stop construction. Israel has offered to extend that olive branch if the Palestinians would only recognize Israel as a Jewish state; this the Palestinians have repeatedly refused to do. Once again, the concessions are heavily loaded on the Israeli side of the scale while the Palestinian leaders seemed determined to uproot any hint—any tiny development of an agreement.

While Serry agreed that halting the settlements was a vital part of the negotiating process, he sidestepped Israel's recognition as a state by intoning the age-old excuse that "recognition of Israel as a Jewish state was an understood part of a two-state solution."[125]

Serry assured Palestinian Authority Prime Minister Salam Fayyad that he supported his two-year plan first proposed in August 2009, and assured the gathered media that;

> "All international players are now in agreement that the Palestinians are ready for statehood at any point in the near future. We are in the homestretch of your agenda to reach that point by August next year, and you have our full support."[126]

Apparently, Serry and Fayyad are seeking the full support of the United Nations Security Council despite the fact that Israel is the target of both Hezbollah and Hamas and is in the crosshairs of fanatical Muslim terrorists worldwide.

Mahmoud Abbas has remained adamant that all settlement construction "in Jerusalem and in the Palestinian territories" must be halted. The issue is that none of the territory in question "belongs" to the Palestinians. It is territory reclaimed by Israel after an unprovoked attack was launched by her Arab neighbors in 1967. Abbas has threatened Prime Minister Netanyahu that if Israel does not submit to the demands regarding a cessation of settlement construction, Abbas would ask the U.S. and the United Nations to recognize a Palestinian state based on the 1967 borders. He declared: "There must be a complete cessation of settlement construction if they want us to return to the negotiations."[127]

According to an October 2010 report published in the Arab newspaper *Asharq Al-Awsat,* the US may be negotiating the future borders of a Palestinian state with Israel. One reported option was that Israel would lease land in East Jerusalem from the Palestinian state for 40-99 years. A spokesperson from Netanyahu's office refused to confirm or deny the reports, and State Department sources told the paper that Israel and the US are discussing matters "as a part of the close relations between the two countries."[128]

On December 7, 2010, a senior U.S. official announced:

> "We reached the conclusion this is not the time to renew direct negotiation by renewing the moratorium [on settlement building.]"

While this capitulation would hamper the peace talks, it was not expected to totally derail the process. The U.S. was hopeful that indirect peace talks would resume in time.

It is also ironic and ludicrous that countries such as Iran and Saudi Arabia gather at the UN to chastise Israel about human rights. The Obama administration must rethink its policy toward Israel. Secretary of State Hillary Clinton must defend the rights of our closest democratic ally in the Middle East to keep its populace safe from terrorist attacks. The United States must not give credence to those who would deny Israel the right to self-defense.

At this writing Secretary of State Hillary Clinton is reportedly working feverishly on a letter that would detail specific understandings regarding another halt of building activity on the West Bank agreed to by Benjamin Netanyahu. The accords were reached during a meeting in New York City on November 11, 2010. A high-level U.S. official acknowledged, "It was always envisioned that there would be a letter detailing our understandings. We are nailing down the specifics."[129]

Netanyahu is hopeful that the anticipated document would be "designed according to these principles [of our discussions]...will be an excellent agreement for the State of Israel." Others feared the letter would be "so vague as to allow the U.S. to renege on any of its commitments."[130] Any agreement would likely contain wording that no other freezes would be forthcoming.

Secretary Clinton and the Obama administration were seeking ways to restart the peace talks between Israel and the Palestinians. There was no word on what, if any, issues the Palestinians would be asked to capitulate. The letter from Clinton was thought to simply contain language opposing "Palestinian efforts toward unilateral statehood at the UN, as well as a commitment to send twenty advanced F-35 fighters, when available, worth $3 billion to Israel." [131]

Gaza is governed by an organization whose charter denies Israel's very right to exist, and whose name is on the U.S. terrorist list because of its heinous activities. It is critically important that Israel maintain control over the entry points for any aid to Gaza. Should she relax her vigilance, Gaza would be flooded with war materiel and Israel would reap the whirlwind of Hamas' windfall.

Lebanon is controlled by Hezbollah, another group that wishes to see Israel decimated. The West Bank is home to the Palestinian Authority and Fatah. These are the men and organizations with which U.S. presidents want Israel to negotiate and ultimately divide the city of Jerusalem, David's capital and God's Holy City.

Lucifer boasted in Isaiah 14:13-14:

> 'I will ascend into heaven,
> I will exalt my throne above the stars of God;
> I will sit also upon the mount of the congregation
> On the farthest the sides of the north;
>   I will ascend above the heights of the clouds;
> I will be like the most High.'

The King of Kings and Lord of Lords will have the last word and the Enemy and his minions will be crushed. The prophet Zachariah foretold those events:

And it shall happen in that day that I will make Jerusalem
a very heavy stone for all peoples; all who would heave it away
will surely be cut in pieces, though all nations of the earth are
gathered against it.

ZACHARIAH 12:3

Then the Lord will go forth
And fight against those nations,
As He fights in the day of battle.
  And in that day his feet shall stand on the Mount of Olives,
Which lies before Jerusalem on the east.
And the Mount of Olives shall be split in two,
From east to west,
Making a very large valley;
Half of the mountain shall move toward the north
And half of it toward the south.

ZACHARIAH 14:3-4

Then the Lord my God will come, and all the holy ones with him.
The Lord will be king over the whole earth. On that day there
will be one Lord, and his name the only name.

ZACHARIAH 14:5,9 NIV

Then and only then will there be peace in Jerusalem.

APPENDIX A

SRES 548 IS
111th CONGRESS
2d Session
S. RES. 548

To express the sense of the Senate that Israel has an undeniable right to self-defense, and to condemn the recent destabilizing actions by extremists aboard the ship Mavi Marmara.

IN THE SENATE OF THE UNITED STATES

June 9, 2010

Mr. CORNYN submitted the following resolution; which was referred to the Committee on Foreign Relations

---

RESOLUTION

To express the sense of the Senate that Israel has an undeniable right to self-defense, and to condemn the recent destabilizing actions by extremists aboard the ship Mavi Marmara.

Whereas the State of Israel, since its founding in 1948, has been a strong and steadfast ally of the United States, standing alone in its commitment to democracy, individual liberty, and free-market principles in the Middle East, a region characterized by instability and violence;

Whereas the special bond between the United States and Israel, forged through common values and mutual interests, must never be broken;

Whereas Israel has an undeniable right to defend itself against any threat to its security, as does every nation;

Whereas Hamas is a terrorist group, formally designated as a Foreign Terrorist Organization by the Secretary of State, and similarly designated by the European Union;

Whereas Hamas is committed to the annihilation of Israel and opposes the peaceful resolution of the Israeli-Palestinian conflict;

Whereas Hamas took control of the Gaza Strip in 2007 through violent means and has maintained control ever since;

Whereas Hamas routinely violates the human rights of the residents of Gaza, including attempting to control and intimidate political rivals through extra-judicial killing, torture, severe beatings, maiming, and arbitrary detentions;

Whereas Hamas continues to hold prisoner Israeli Staff Sergeant Gilad Shalit, who was seized on Israeli soil and has been denied basic rights, including contact with the International Red Cross;

Whereas the military build-up of Hamas has been enabled by the smuggling of arms and other materiel into Gaza;

Whereas the Government of Iran has materially aided and supported Hamas by providing extensive funding, weapons, and training;

Whereas, since 2001, Hamas and other Palestinian terrorist organizations have fired more than 10,000 rockets and mortars from Gaza into Israel, killing at least 18 Israelis and wounding dozens more;

Whereas approximately 860,000 Israeli civilians, more than 12 percent of Israel's population, reside within range of rockets fired from Gaza and live in fear of attacks;

Whereas, in 2007, the Government of Israel, out of concern for the safety of its citizens, put in place a legitimate and justified blockade of Gaza, which has been effective in reducing the flow of weapons into Gaza and the firing of rockets from Gaza into southern Israel;

Whereas, at the same time, the Government of Egypt imposed a blockade of Gaza from its land border;

Whereas, according to Michael Oren, the Israeli Ambassador to the United States, 'If the sea lanes are open to Hamas in Gaza . . . they will acquire thousands of rockets that will threaten every single citizen in the state of Israel and also kill the peace process. . . . Hamas armed with thousands of rockets not only threatens 7,500,000 Israelis but it's the end of the peace process.';

Whereas the Israeli blockade has not hindered the transfer of approximately 1,000,000 tons of humanitarian supplies into Gaza over the last 18 months to aid its 1,500,000 residents;

Whereas, on May 28, 2010, the 'Free Gaza' flotilla, which included the Mavi Marmara and 5 other ships, departed from a port in Turkey and sailed towards Israel's defensive naval blockade of Gaza;

Whereas the sponsor of the flotilla was a Turkish organization, the Humanitarian Relief Foundation;

Whereas the Humanitarian Relief Foundation has aided al Qaeda in the past, 'basically helping al Qaeda when [Osama] bin Laden started to want to target U.S. soil,' according to statements by a former French counterterrorism official, in a June 2, 2010, Associated Press interview;

Whereas the Humanitarian Relief Foundation has a clear link to Hamas, according to a 2008 order of the Government of Israel, and the Humanitarian Relief Foundation is a member of the Union for Good, a United States-designated terrorist organization created by Hamas leaders in 2000 to help fund Hamas;

Whereas there were at least 5 active terrorist operatives among the passengers on the Mavi Marmara, with affiliations with terrorist groups such as al Qaeda and Hamas, according to the Israel Defense Forces;

Whereas the flotilla's primary aim was to break the Israeli blockade of Gaza, under the guise of delivering humanitarian aid to the residents of Gaza;

Whereas, on May 27, 2010, while the flotilla was moving towards Gaza, one of its organizers admitted, 'This mission is not about delivering humanitarian supplies, it's about breaking Israel's siege on 1,500,000 Palestinians,' according to news reports;

Whereas, based on interviews with Mavi Marmara passengers after the incident, the actual intention of passengers on the Mavi Marmara had been to achieve 'martyrdom' at the hands of the Israel Defense Forces;

Whereas Saleh Al-Azraq, a journalist who was aboard the ship, recounted that, 'The moment the ship set sail, the cries of 'Allahu Akbar' began . . . It made you feel as if you were going on an Islamic conquest or raid,' according to an interview recorded on Al-Hiwar TV on June 4, 2010;

Whereas Hussein Orush, a Humanitarian Relief Foundation official, read from the diary of a dead Mavi Marmara passenger: 'The last lines he wrote before the attack were: 'Only a short time left before martyrdom. This is the most important stage of my life. Nothing is more beautiful than martyrdom, except for one's love for one's mother. But I don't know what is sweeter--my mother or martyrdom.', and also stated, 'All the passengers on board the ship were ready for this outcome. Everybody wanted and was ready to become a martyr. . . . Our goal was to reach Gaza or to die trying. All the ship's passengers were ready for this. IHH was ready for this too.', according to an interview recorded on Al-Jazeera TV on June 5, 2010;

Whereas Ali Haider Banjinin, another dead Mavi Marmara passenger, told his family before departing on the flotilla, 'I am going to be a martyr, I dreamed about it,' according to news reports in Turkey;

Whereas Ali Ekber Yaratilmis, another dead Mavi Marmara passenger, 'always wanted to become a Martyr,' one of his friends told Al-Hayat Al-Jadida newspaper in an interview on June 3, 2010;

Whereas one female passenger on the deck of the Mavi Marmara stated, 'Right now we face one of two happy endings: either martyrdom or reaching Gaza,' according to Al Jazeera footage taken prior to the incident;

Whereas the Government of Israel had extended a reasonable offer to transfer the flotilla's humanitarian cargo to Gaza;

Whereas the Mavi Marmara and the other ships of the flotilla ignored repeated Israeli calls to turn around or be peacefully escorted to an Israeli port outside of Gaza;

Whereas, on May 31, 2010, the Israeli Navy intercepted the Mavi Marmara 75 miles west of Haifa, Israel, in an effort to maintain the integrity of the blockade and prevent potential smuggling of arms and other materiel into the hands of Hamas;

Whereas, upon the boarding of the Mavi Marmara by the Israeli Navy, the Mavi Marmara's passengers brutally and violently attacked the members of the Israeli Navy with knives, clubs, pipes, and other weapons, injuring several of them;

Whereas the members of the Israeli Navy, under attack and in grave danger, reacted in self-defense and used lethal force against their attackers on the Mavi Marmara, shooting and killing 9 of them;

Whereas the incident has fomented unwarranted international criticism of Israel and its blockade of Gaza;

Whereas, in the time since the attack, the United Nations has unjustly criticized the actions of the Government of Israel and called for an investigation of such actions; and

Whereas the actions of the United Nations are undermining Israel's inherent right to self-defense, compromising its sovereignty, and helping to legitimize Hamas: Now, therefore, be it

Resolved, That it is the sense of the Senate—
(1) that Israel has an inherent and undeniable right to defend itself against any threat to the safety of its citizens;

(2) to reaffirm that the United States stands with Israel in pursuit of shared security goals, including the security of Israel;

(3) to condemn the violent attack and provocation by extremists aboard the Mavi Marmara, who created a highly destabilizing incident in a region that cannot afford further instability;

(4) to condemn any future such attempts to break the Israeli blockade of Gaza for the purpose of creating or provoking violent confrontation or otherwise undermining the security of Israel;

(5) to condemn Hamas for its failure to recognize the right of Israel to exist, its human rights abuses against the residents of Gaza, and its continued rejection of a constructive path to peace for the Israeli and Palestinian people;

(6) to condemn the Government of Iran for its role, past and present, in directly supporting Hamas and undermining the security of Israel;

(7) to encourage the Government of Turkey to recognize the importance of continued strong relations with Israel and the necessity of closely scrutinizing organizations with potential ties to terrorist groups; and

(8) to express profound disappointment with the counterproductive actions of the United Nations regarding this incident.

ENDNOTES

1   *The New Yorker.* March 24, 2003.

2   Geostrategy-Direct.com, "Obama promises king Israel will withdraw from West Bank, Jerusalem." July 7, 2010. http://www.geostrategy-direct.com/geostrategy-direct/. Accessed July 2010.

3   *Jerusalem Post.* January 17, 1992.

4   Charles Krauthammer, "Terror—and Candor in Describing the Islamist Ideology Behind It." *The Washington Post.* July 2, 2010. http://www.washingtonpost.com/wp-dyn/content/article/2010/07/01/AR2010070104542.html. Accessed July 2010.

5   Melanie Lidman, "Police announce calm after riots end in east Jerusalem," *Jerusalem Post,* September 22, 2010, http://www.jpost.com/Israel/Article.aspx?id=188921. Accessed September 2010.

6   Associated Press, "New Round of Mideast Peace Talks Begin," *Las Vegas Sun*, September 9, 2010; http://www.google.com/search?sourceid=navclient&ie=UTF-8&rlz=1T4GGLL_enUS382US382&q=I+see+in+you+a+partner+for+peace. Accessed September 2010.

7   Transcription of telephone conversation with Ambassador Michael Oren from Mike Evans' personal files.

8   Barak: Arab parts of Jerusalem could become Palestinian capital," Haaretz.com, March 8, 2008; http://www.haaretz.com/news/barak-arab-parts-of-jerusalem-could-become-palestinian-capital-1.253169. Accessed September 2010.

9   "Barak: Israel ready to cede parts of Jerusalem in peace deal," Haaretz.com, September 1, 2010; http://www.haaretz.com/news/diplomacy-defense/barak-israel-ready-to-cede-parts-of-jerusalem-in-peace-deal-1.311450. Accessed September 2010.

10 Khaled Abu Toameh, "Abbas: No historic compromise on Jerusalem borders." *Jerusalem Post,* September 7, 2010; http://www.jpost.com/MiddleEast/Article.aspx?id=187417. Accessed September 2010.

11 *Jerusalem Post,* September 4, 2010; http://www.jpost.com/MiddleEast/Article.aspx?id=187041). Accessed September 2010.

12 Palestine Facts.org, "What Is the Significance of Jerusalem to Jews and Muslims?" http://www.palestine-facts.org/pf_early_palestine_jerusalem.php. Accessed June 2010.

13 David Weinberg, *Jerusalem Post,* "Woe Will Be a Divided Jerusalem." April 1, 2010. http://www.jpost.com/LandedPages/PrintArticle.aspx?id=172162. Accessed April 6, 2010.

14 San Remo Resolution, San Remo Conference. April 25, 1920. http://en.wikipedia.org/wiki/San_Remo_conference#Text_of_the_Resolution. Accessed May 2010.

15 *Ibid.*

16 In this document, the League of Nations recognized the "historical connection of the Jewish people with Palestine" and the "grounds for reconstituting their national home in that country." http://www.fordham.edu/halsall/mod/1922mandate.html. Accessed May 2010.

17 Charter of the United Nations, Chapter XII: International Trusteeship System, Article 80. http://www.un.org/en/documents/charter/chapter12.shtml. Accessed April 2010.

18 Fuel for Truth. http://www.fuelfortruth.org/thetruth/truth_10.asp. Accessed April 2010.

19 Mike D. Evans, quoted from *Save Jerusalem* (Euless, TX: Bedford Books, 1995), p. 94.

20   Personal interview with Prime Minister Menachem Begin.

21   Moshe Dayan. Address in the General Assembly. September 27, 1979. http://www.mfa.gov.il/MFA/For-eign%20Relations/Israels%20Foreign%20Relations%20since%201947/1979-1980/46%20Address%20in%20the%20General%20Assembly%20by%20Foreign%20Mini. Accessed April 2010.

22   Christopher Wise, *Derrida, Africa and the Middle East* (New York, NY: St. Martin's Press, 2009), p. 59.

23   Philip Misselwitz and Tim Rieniets, *City of Collision: Jerusalem and the Principles of Conflict Urbanism* (Germany: Die Deutsche Bibliothek, 2006), p. 49.

24   Teddy Kollek and Moshe Pearlman, *Sacred City of Mankind: A History of Forty Centuries* (Israel: Stei-matzky Group, 1987).

25   Maher Y. Abu-Munshar, *The Pact of Umar*. http://l.b5z.net/i/u/6053592/f/The_Pact_of_Umar_.pdf. Accessed April 2010.

26   Jordanian Nationality Law, *Official Gazette* No. 1171, Article 3 of Law No. 6 (February 1954), p. 105.

27   Richard Cohen, "Where Bigotry Gets a Hearing," *The Washington Post*, p. A21. October 30, 2001. Archives accessed May 2010.

28   Elie Kedourie, *Islam in the Modern World* (London: Mansell, 1980), pp. 69-72.

29   Suleiman Al-Khash in *Al-Thaura*, the Ba'ath party newspaper. May 3, 1968.

30   David K. Shipler, *Arab and Jew* (NY: Times Books, 1986), pp. 167- 170.

31   Mike Evans, *Save Jerusalem* (Euless, TX: Bedford Books, 1995), pp. 274-275.

32   Paul Charles Merkley, *The Politics of Christian Zionism 1891-1948* (London: Frank Cass Publishers, 1998), p. 191.

33   Philologos Bible Prophecy Research, "Armageddon," Submitted by: research-bpn@philologos.org. November 20, 1998. Undated: April 6, 2001. philologos.org/bpr/files/a0005.htm. Accessed April 2010.

34   Mike Evans, *Save Jerusalem*, p. 270.

35   Aleksandr Solzhenitsyn, "A World Split Apart," Harvard Class Day Afternoon Exercises. June 8, 1978. http://www.columbia.edu/cu/augustine/arch/solzhenitsyn/harvard1978.html. Accessed April 2010.

36   Dr. Harry A. Ironside, *Daniel: Ironside Expository Commentaries* (Grand Rapids, MI: Kregel Publications, Reprint 2005), p. 9.

37   Stephen Erlanger and Nicola Clark, "Europe to Ease Aviation Ban, Amid Criticism," *The New York Times*. April 19, 2010. http://www.nytimes.com/2010/04/20/world/europe/20ash.html. Accessed April 2010.

38   Arthur Joseph Toynbee and David Churchill Somervell, *A Study of History, Volume 1* (Oxford: Oxford University Press, 1946), p. 244.

39   Michael D. Evans, *Betrayed: The Conspiracy to Divide Jerusalem* (Bedford, TX: Bedford Books, 2008), p.104.

40   Personal interview with David Bar-Ilan, editor, *Jerusalem Post*, 1995.

41   Matthew Henry, *Blue Letter Bible, Matthew Henry's Commentary on the Whole Bible, Volume VI*. http://www.blueletterbible.org/commentaries/comm_view.cfm?AuthorID=4&contentID=1823&commInfo=5&topic=Hebrews. Accessed April 2010.

42 Amikam Elad, "Why did Abd al-Malik Build the Dome of the Rock?" *Bayt-al-Maqdis: 'Abd al-Malik's Jerusalem*, Julian Raby and Jeremy Johns, ed. (Oxford: Oxford University Press, 1992), vol. 1, p. 48.

43 Heribert Busse, "Jerusalem in the Story of Muhammad's Night Journey and Ascension," *Jerusalem Studies in Arabic and Islam* 14 (1991): 1-40. Quoted from Daniel Pipes, "The Muslim Claim to Jerusalem," *Middle East Quarterly*, Fall 2001. *www.meforum.org/490/the-muslim-claim-to-Jerusalem*.

44 Gil Ronen, "Video: Dr. Mordechai Kedar on Al-Jazeera, Eloquent and Unafraid." June 15, 2008. http://www.israelnationalnews.com/News/News.aspx/126500. Accessed April 2010.

45 Lela Gilbert, "Digging out the Truth," *Jerusalem Post*. February 25, 2010. http://www.jpost.com/Opinion/Op-EdContributors/Article.aspx?id=111160. Accessed May 2010.

46 "Alfred Dreyfus, an obscure captain in the French army, came from a Jewish family that had left its native Alsace for Paris when Germany annexed that province in 1871. In 1894 papers discovered in a wastebasket in the office of a German military attaché made it appear that a French military officer was providing secret information to the German government. Dreyfus came under suspicion, probably because he was a Jew and also because he had access to the type of information that had been supplied to the German agent. The army authorities declared that Dreyfus' handwriting was similar to that on the papers. Despite his protestations of innocence he was found guilty of treason in a secret military court-martial, during which he was denied the right to examine the evidence against him. The army stripped him of his rank in a humiliating ceremony and shipped him off to [life imprisonment on] Devil's Island, a penal colony located off the coast of South America. The political right, whose strength was steadily increasing, cited Dreyfus' alleged espionage as further evidence of the failures of the Republic. Édouard Drumont's right-wing newspaper *La Libre Parole* intensified its attacks on the Jews, portraying this incident as further evidence of Jewish treachery." (*Jewish Virtual Library*, Alfred Dreyfus and 'The Affair.' http://www.jewishvirtuallibrary.org/jsource/anti-semitism/Dreyfus.html. Accessed June 2010.

47 *The Cosmopolitan,* Volume 26, Schlict and Field 1900, p. 376. http://books.google.com/books?id=56 nNAAAAMAAJ&pg=PA376&lpg=PA376&dq=From+Jerusalem+a+light+has+arisen+upon+the+world+%E2%80%93+the+blessed+light+in+whose+splendor+our+German+people+have+become+great+and+glorious.&source=bl&ots=a9Q-Wo4nxL&sig=B3wxdZCd_b1Sr_aWCXeVFCgN7pU&hl=en&ei=U5Ub TJujHaPknQfq6fi0Cw&sa=X&oi=book_result&ct=result&resnum=4&ved=0CBsQ6AEwAw#. Accessed June 2010.

48 http://web.archive.org/web/20061018191000/http://www.pef.org.uk/Pages/WildZin.htm Accessed June 2010.

49 Yapp, M.E., *The Making of the Modern Near East* 1792-192. (Harlow, England: Longman, 1987), p. 290.

50 "Montagu Memorandum on the Anti-Semitism of the Jewish Government," August 23, 1917, *Jewish Virtual Library*, http://www.jewishvirtuallibrary.org/jsource/History/Montagumemo.html. Accessed June 2010.

51 Ben Halpern, *A Clash of Heroes—Brandeis, Weizmann, and American Zionism* (New York: Oxford University Press, 1987), p. 169.

52 Colonel C.G. Powles, *The History of the Canterbury Mounted Rifles, 1914-1919*, p. 195. *New Zealand Electronic Text Center*, http://www.nzetc.org/tm/scholarly/tei-WH1CMRi-t1-body-d14.html. Accessed June 2010.

53 Michael Makovsky, *Churchill's Promised Land: Zionism and Statecraft* (Yale University, 2007), p. 93.

54 Chuck Morse, *Jewish Magazine*, "The Nazi Connection to Islamic Terrorism. http://www.jewishmag.com/116mag/chuckmorse/chuckmorse.htm. Accessed June 2010.

55 Nabi Musa was a pilgrimage holiday that flooded Jerusalem with Muslims. It had been instituted by Salah a Din to counter the large number of Christian pilgrims who swelled the city at Easter. http://www.zionism-israel.com/dic/Nebi_musa.htm.

56   Walter Laqueur, *The History of Zionism* (London: L.P. Tauris & Co. Ltd, 2003), p. 557.

57   "Statement to the Knesset by Prime Minister Begin Following Historic Sadat Speech," http://www.jew-ishvirtuallibrary.org/jsource/History/begintoknessetsadat.html. Accessed May 2010.

58   *MidEast Web*, "President Harry S. Truman and U.S. Support for Israeli Statehood," http://www.mideast-web.org/us_supportforstate.htm. Accessed June 2010.

59   *Ibid.*

60   Larry Collins and Dominique Lapierre, *O Jerusalem!* (New York: Simon and Shuster, 1972), p. 411.

61   *Ibid.*

62   Personal Interview with Mordechai Gur, 1995.

63   *Ibid.*

64   Personal interview with Chief Rabbi Shlomo Goren, 1995.

65   *Ibid.*

66   Teddy Kollek, *Foreign Affairs*, Vol. 55, No. 4 (Council on Foreign Relations: July 1977), pp. 701.

67   *U.S. News and World Report,* November 7, 1994, p. 7.

68   "The Jarring Initiative and Response," February 8, 1971, Volumes 1-2: 1947-1974. http://www.mfa.gov.il/MFA/Foreign+Relations/Israels+Foreign+Relations+since+1947/1947-1974/28/The+Jarring+initiative+and+the+response-+8+Febr.htm. Accessed May 2010.

69   Abraham Rabinovich, *The Yom Kippur War* (New York: Schocken Books, 2004), p. 21.

70   "Jordan asked Nixon to attack Syria declassified papers show," November 28, 2007. http://www.cnn.com/2007/POLITICS/11/28/nixon.papers/. Accessed May 2010.

71   *Ibid.*

72   *Ibid.*

73   Simon Dunstan, Kevin Lyles, *The Yom Kippur War 1973: The Sinai* (Westminster, MD: Random House, 2003), p. 17.

74   Seymour M. Hersh, *The Samson Option: Israel's Nuclear Arsenal and American Foreign Policy* (New York: Vintage Books, 1991), p. 223.

75   Seymour M. Hersh, *The Price of Power: Kissinger in the Nixon White House* (New York: Summit Books, 1983), p. 234.

76   Norman Bentwich, *Hellemism* (Philadelphia: The Jewish Publication Society of America, 1919), p. 11

77   E. R. Bevan, Jerusalem under the High Priests (London: Edward Arnold, 1904), p. 43.

78   Personal interview with Menachem Begin, 1995.

79   William R. Johnston, updated March 2010. http://www.johnstonsarchive.net/terrorism/terrisrael-11.html. Accessed April 2010.

80   Anti-Defamation League, "Iran's President in His Own Words," March 12, 2010. http://www.adl.org/main_International_Affairs/ahmadinejad_words.html. Accessed May 2010.

81   "U.N. Delegates walk out during Iran president's speech," CNN, September 23, 2010; http://articles.cnn.com/2010-09-23/politics/un.ahmadinejad.walkouts_1_iranian-leader-iranian-president-mahmoud-ahmadinejad-attacks?_s=PM:POLITICS. Accessed September 2010.

82   "U.S. delegation walks out of U.N. General Assembly during Ahmadinejad's speech," Fox News, September 23m 2010; http://www.nypost.com/p/news/local/speech_delegation_walks_out_of_un_Hcdmd-0McoXGNeF4ydE8juN. Accessed September 2010.

83   "Iran, Hizbullah, Hamas and the Global Jihad: A New Conflict Paradigm for the West" 2007; Gen. (Ret.) Moshe Ya'alon, "The Second Lebanon War: From Territory to Ideology." Jerusalem Center for Public Affairs, p. 24. Accessed January 2008.

84   Jonathan Steele, "Lost in Translation," *Guardian,* June 14, 2006; http://commentisfree.guardian.co.uk/jonathan_steele/2006/06/post_155.html. Accessed March 2008.

85   "Israel can't do a 'damn thing' to stop Iran nuclear program," *Haaretz,* February 12, 2009. http://www.haaretz.com/news/ahmadinejad-israel-can-t-do-damn-thing-to-stop-iran-nuclear-program-1.2962. Accessed May 2010.

86   *Oxford English Dictionary; Webster's Third International Dictionary.*

87   Richard Cohen, "Where Bigotry Gets a Hearing," *The Washington Post,* p. A21. October 30, 2001. Archives accessed May 2010.

88   "The Middle East without Israel," *American Thinker,* September 17, 2005. Review of article by Joseph Joffe, http://www.americanthinker.com/blog/2005/09/the_middle_east_without_israel.html. Accessed May 2010.

89   Walid Shoebat quotes. http://www.shoebat.com/. Accessed May 2010.

90   Norman Golb, *The Jews in Medieval Normandy: A Social and Intellectual History* (Cambridge, United Kingdom: Cambridge University Press, 1998).

91   United States Holocaust Memorial Museum, *Holocaust Encyclopedia*, "Liberation of Nazi Camps." http://www.ushmm.org/wlc/en/article.php?ModuleId=10005131. Accessed May 2010.

92   Answers.com, definition, http://www.answers.com/topic/good-samaritan. Accessed May 2010.

93   Jimmy Carter, *Palestine Peace Not Apartheid* (New York: Simon & Schuster, Inc., 2006), pp. 147–150.

94   Yasser Arafat, 1929-2004, Passia.org. http://www.passia.org/Arafat/Arafat.pdf. Accessed May 2010.

95   Etgar Leftovits, "U.S. Congressmen Demand UNRWA Reform," *Jerusalem Post,* May 27, 2008. http://www.kibush.co.il/show_file.asp?num=27110. Accessed May 2010.

96   Lanny Davis, *The Hill,* September 9, 2009. http://thehill.com/opinion/columnists/lanny-davis/57983-time-for-transparency-and-accountability-for-unrwa. Accessed May 2010.

97   *Ibid.*

98   Jakub Grygiel, "The Power of Statelessness," *Policy Review,* April-May 2009. http://www.hoover.org/publications/policyreview/41708942.html. Accessed May 2010.

99   *Jerusalem Post,* August 19, 2002.

100 "International funding to Palestinians in peril Fears of corruption, killings of land sellers make donors hesitate," http://articles.baltimoresun.com/1997-06-06/news/1997157015_1_palestinian-authority-palestinian-leadership-support-for-palestinians. Accessed May 2010.

101 Roni Sofer, YNet News, "Netanyahu: If we leave Jerusalem, Iran and Hamas will take control," March 23, 2008. http://www.ynet.co.il/english/articles/0,7340,L-3522337,00.html. Accessed May 2010.

102 "The History of Ethiopian Jews," http://www.jewishvirtuallibrary.org/jsource/Judaism/ejhist.html. Accessed May 2010.

103 Simon Ponsonby, And the Lamb Wins (Colorado Springs: David C. Cook, 2008), p. 149.

104 Thomas L. Friedman, The New York Times (special edition), September 13, 1993. http://www.nytimes.com/learning/general/onthisday/big/0913.html. Accessed May 2010.

105 Mike Evans, The Final Move Beyond Iraq (Lake Mary, FL: Front Line, 2007), p. 219.

106 Personal interview with Benjamin Netanyahu, Likud Party Chairman, 1994.

107 Dr. Thomas Ice, "Globalism—Preparation for the Antichrist," Focus on Jerusalem. http://focusonjerusalem.com/Globalism.htm. Accessed June 2010.

108 Jeremy Rabkin, "A Dangerous Step Closer to an International Criminal Court," January 1, 2001. American Enterprise Institute for Public Policy Research. http://www.aei.org/issue/12313. Accessed June 2010.

109 Nora Bustany, "A Shift in the Debate on International Court," The Washington Post, November 7, 2006. http://www.washingtonpost.com/wp-dyn/content/article/2006/11/06/AR2006110601269.html. Accessed June 2010.

110 Bill Varner, "Obama's Envoy Voices Support for International Court," Bloomberg.com. http://www.bloomberg.com/apps/news?pid=20601103&sid=aYK_ULgi3Ix0. Accessed June 2010.

111 "Dutch Christian Family Who Saved Jewish Refugees from Nazism Honored," Catholic News Agency, April 18, 2008. http://www.catholicnewsagency.com/news/dutch_christian_family_who_saved_jewish_refugees_from_nazism_honored/. Accessed May 2010.

112 Bernard Wasserstein, Divided Jerusalem: The Struggle for the Holy City (London: Profile Books, 2001), p. 11.

113 "Israel Raid on Flotilla Sparks Crisis," Japan Today, June 1, 2010. http://www.japantoday.com/category/world/view/israeli-raid-on-flotilla-sparks-crisis. Accessed June 2010.

114 "Intention was to create conflict," Montreal Gazette, June 2, 2010. http://www.montrealgazette.com/intention+create+conflict/3100356/story.html?id=3100356.

115 Seizure of the Gaza Flotilla: Press conference with Deputy Foreign Minister Danny Ayalon.http://www.mfa.gov.il/MFA/Government/Speeches+by+Israeli+leaders/2010/Gaza_flotilla_Press_conference_DepFM_Ayalon_31-May-2010.htm. Accessed June 2010.

116 Statement by Israel's Prime Minister Benjamin Netanyahu. May 31, 2010. Ministry of Defense. http://houston.mfa.gov.il/mfm/web/main/Print.asp?DocumentID=146640. Accessed May 2010.

117 "Congress Shows Israel Support," Jerusalem Post, June 9, 2010. http://www.jpost.com/LandedPages/PrintArticle.aspx?id=177917. Accessed June 2010.

118 Ibid.
119 Ibid.

120 *Ibid.*

121 *Ibid.*

122 http://www.govtrack.us/congress/billtext.xpd?bill=sr111-548. Accessed June 2010.

123 Khaled Abu Toameh, "U.S. Administration Engaging with Hamas," May 31, 2010. http://www.jpost.com/MiddleEast/Article.aspx?id=176943. Accessed June 2010.

124 Tovah Lazaroff, "UN Backs Palestinian plans for statehood by August," *Jerusalem Post*, October 26, 2010, http://www.jpost.com/VideoArticles/Article.aspx?id=192836. Accessed October 2010.

125 *Ibid.*

126 *Ibid.*

127 Khaled Abu Toameh and Herb Keinon, "Abbas: PA will ask UN to recognize Palestinian state," *Jerusalem Post,* October 28, 2010, http://www.jpost.com/MiddleEast/Article.aspx?id=193159. Accessed October 2010.

128 "Israel may lease east Jerusalem from a Palestinian state," *Jerusalelm Post,* October 29, 2010; http://www.jpost.com/International/Article.aspx?id=193238. Accessed October 2010.

129 Tova Lazaroff and Associated Press, "U.S. Official says letter detailing freeze draft being drafted," *Jerusalem Post,* November 17, 2010.

130 *Ibid.*

131 *Ibid.*

ACKNOWLEDGEMENTS

My deepest gratitude goes to the men and women who have agreed to present and past interviews which have laid the foundation for this novel. These include: Israeli Prime Ministers Benjamin Netanyahu, Menachem Begin, Yitzhak Shamir, Ehud Olmert; Yitzhak Rabin, and Shimon Peres; Deputy Prime Minister, Lt. General Moshe Ya'alon, former Chief of Staff, IDF; President Mahmoud Ahmadinejad and more than a dozen Iranian diplomats; Her Majesty Farah Pahlavi, wife of the former Shah of Iran; a special thanks to Iran's last and most powerful ambassador to the U.S., Ambassador Ardeshir Zehedi; former President of the French Republic Valerie Giscard d'Estaing; President of Iraqi Kurdistan Massoud Barzani; editorial journalist Samuel Segev; journalist and terrorism expert Charles Villeneuve; Dr. Parviz Mina, Director, National Iranian Oil Company under the Shah; Dr. Abol-Majid Majidi, Minister of Planning and Budget under the Shah; Hubert Vedrine, adviser to President Francois Mitterrand and Secretary-General from 1991-1995; General Dani Yatom, head of Mossad, Israeli Intelligence Service; former Israeli Ambassador to Iran Uri Lubrani; former Israeli Ambassador to the U.S. Dore Gold; Marvin Kalb, award-winning reporter for CBS and NBC; Dr. Alan Dershowitz, professor, Harvard School of Law; Mr. James Woolsey, former director, CIA; Israeli Mossad agent Eliezer Zafrir; General David Ivri, Commander Israeli Air Force and Ambassador to U.S.; General Yitzhak Segev; Dr. Ahmed Tehrani; and Lt. General Shapur Azarbarzin. I especially want to thank Israeli, French, and U.S. intelligence operatives (whose names must remain anonymous.)

My sincere thanks goes to my executive assistant, Lanelle Shaw-Young without whose assistance this book would not have been possible. Thank you to Arlen Young for his proof-reading skills, and to editor Elizabeth Sherman whose insight and suggestions were invaluable. A book project of this magnitude demands a grueling schedule. For her patience, compassion, encouragement, and sacrifice, I am indebted to my beloved wife, Carolyn. This book is dedicated to my newborn grandson, Michael David Evans III, born just as this book was completed.